Literary Texts and the Roman Historian

Like other books in the series, *Literary Texts and the Roman Historian* focuses on the problems and methods involved in reconstructing the history of the ancient world. David Potter examines the different kinds of text from which Roman history is reconstructed by modern students, and he explores how ancient participants in the literary culture of the Roman empire constructed their own history. In contrast, he also discusses alternative forms of historical narrative, suggesting that those texts were produced to provide alternative paradigms to those offered in the traditional historical narratives. He also discusses the reception of classical visions of history in the late twentieth century and contextualizes the problems of the discipline in antiquity with current developments in the field.

Literary Texts and the Roman Historian provides an accessible and concise introduction to the complexities of Roman historiography which will be invaluable to students of all periods of history.

David S. Potter is Arthur F. Thurnau Professor of Greek and Latin at the University of Michigan. He is the author of *Prophecy and History in the Crisis of the Roman Empire* (1990) and *Prophets and Emperors: Human and Divine Authority from Augustus to Theodosius* (1993).

Approaching the Ancient World

Literary Texts and the Roman Historian

David S. Potter

Routledge
Taylor & Francis Group

LONDON AND NEW YORK

First published 1999
by Routledge
11 New Fetter Lane, London EC4P 4EE

Simultaneously published in the USA and Canada
by Routledge
29 West 35th Street, New York, NY 10001

Reprinted 2003

Typeset in Baskerville by Routledge
Printed and bound in Great Britain by T. J. International Ltd,
Padstow, Cornwall

British Library Cataloguing in Publication Data
A catalogue record for this book is available from the British
Library

Library of Congress Cataloging in Publication Data
A catalogue record for this book has been requested

ISBN 0–415–08895–X (hbk)
ISBN 0–415–08896–8 (pbk)

Parentibus Optimis
D.D.

Contents

Preface

I owe a great deal of thanks to many who have helped in the course of the composition of this book, though none greater than to my wife, Ellen, and our daughter Claire, for the way that they have dealt with a persistently distracted husband or father, and brightened every day.

To friends and students who have read this book, or been subjected to the formation of the opinions that have gone into it over the years, I owe a very great deal. So too it is a pleasure to thank Richard Stoneman for his invitation to write this book, and his extreme patience with a dilatory author. I would also like to thank Morgen Witzel for his copyediting, and Sarah Brown for seeing this book through the rest of the production process.

In particular I must thank Glen Bowersock, who read an early draft, and set me straight on a number of important issues. An extremely generous referee for Routledge contributed very helpful suggestions at a later stage. Brian Schmidt guided me on matters of Near Eastern history, and John Dillery contributed some extremely helpful advice throughout the process of composition. Maud Gleason read through the whole text with extraordinary care, correcting countless lapses of style and taste, improving virtually every page.

While I was finishing this book, my old friend George Forrest died. It was in his study, over countless afternoons, that I learned my way around the historiography of the classical world. If this book can help others in anything like the same way, it will have served its purpose.

The copy of Jacoby that I took with me to see George belongs to my father. My mother and father have encouraged me at every stage in my career, and it was at home in New York, in an apartment filled with books, that I first imagined what the study of history might be like. It thus seemed ever so appropriate that this book should be dedicated to them.

DSP
Ann Arbor
February 1998

Introduction

This book is about the use of literary sources to write ancient history. This said, from the outset there are two basic questions for which an answer must be offered: what is a literary source, and whose history?

I take a literary source to be any text that has come down to us through the manuscript tradition, although in practice I have tended to limit my discussion to texts that profess to offer a reconstruction or description of actual events. In discussing these texts, I have tended to concentrate on the process by which they were created, disseminated and read.

There are two answers to the question of whose history: theirs and ours. In the first instance, I am concerned with the way that full participants in the literary culture of the Roman empire constructed their own history. By full participants, I mean people who had received sufficient education to compose works of literature themselves, and members of their circles of acquaintance with whom they might share that culture. Much of this book is about the process by which people who were attached to the canons of classical historiography created narratives of their own times and past time. The canons of classical historiography did not provide the only model for constructing such a narrative. In *Prophets and Emperors: Human and Divine Authority from Augustus to Theodosius*,[1] I have dealt with some other forms of historical narrative, those purporting to be produced as a result of divine inspiration. While I have not repeated that material at any length, I will suggest that those texts were produced to provide alternative paradigms to the ones offered in the traditions that are the primary subject of this book.

A book such as this must also be concerned with the reception of classical visions of history in the late twentieth century. The canons of classical historiography have exercised an enormous influence over the way that history is studied in the western European tradition. I have therefore tried to contextualize the problems of historical writing in antiquity within current developments in the field of historiography. I hope in this way that the book will be of use to students who are coming to ancient history from other areas of historical study and, at the same time, that it will help students coming to the study of ancient history from the study of classical texts to see the subject in a broader context. I have attempted to illustrate various points with a number of specific examples, feeling that this is the best way to illustrate the range of behaviors in antiquity. If this book makes it easier for people coming to the subject, from whatever direction, to find their own way then it will have served its purpose.

The plan of the book

This book is divided into four sections that mirror, to some degree, the process that an aspiring Tacitus or Ammianus (for the sake of this volume let us call them Deutero-Tacitus and Pseudo-Ammianus) might follow in approaching the task of writing an historical work concerned with the Roman world. At a number of points, the modern problem mirrors that faced by a classical practitioner, although the contemporary response to that problem might be radically different – or not.

One major point of difference that must be faced from the start is that it was virtually inevitable that the ancient historical aspirant would be male, and of aristocratic status. Another is that the classical world did not have professional historians so much as aristocrats seeking alternatives to their public careers through literary production, and professional intellectuals who provided such people with instruction, amusement, information or an appreciative audience. Just as the real Tacitus wrote fiction and ethnography before he undertook a major historical work, or his friend the Younger Pliny considered taking the advice of a friend to write history, so might Deutero-Tacitus have wandered across various genres prior to settling upon history. Pseudo-Ammianus represents a creature of a different age, the former government servant – or soldier of decidedly unheroic proportions – looking to make a name for himself in retirement. Such men were aware that there were any number of things that they might write, and in coming to history such a person would have thought about how that form of literature differed from others.

Once he had decided upon writing history, Deutero-Tacitus or Pseudo-Ammianus would be faced with the mass of available literature. As educated people, they would have a broad mastery of the literature of their age. Trained in youth to be orators, they would have mastered the canons of rhetoric and the literary models upon which that education would be based. They would also be aware of the perils of publication, and the diverse channels through which their work might pour into the waiting hands of their public. Here the modern practitioner is very much at a disadvantage. The modern practitioner has limited access to the social world of ancient literary production and is often reduced to the study of sparse fragments to reconstruct the parameters of ancient thought. The modern practitioner does, however, have a vast array of approaches, derived from numerous other disciplines, that might help his or her account take a shape that might render any classical historian speechless with horror; unless, of course, they could be brought to agree with the notion that the point of the endeavor was to educate readers (or forward a career).

The modern practitioner and our imagined historians would join company more closely when it came to the next stage: the collection of material and composition of a draft. At this point, however, all three might fall into a desperate dispute as to how to evaluate this evidence. Should the document be privileged over the personal informant? How can one evaluate an informant? Are there cultural prejudices that might shape the choice of one sort of evidence or informant over another? How does the research plan and method of the historian compare with that of other researchers? Finally, how does one go about the physical process of gathering information, and how does one go about putting it into writing? Research methods do influence the final product. The ability to handle foreign languages could be an issue in antiquity as much as it is now; so could the technique of note taking and the movement from note to draft, from draft to finished product.

Once a draft had been composed, the classical historian had to be concerned with literary quality. This was the principal factor influencing the reception of the work by contemporaries. But how could one reconcile a desire for accuracy with the desire to be read? If he wanted to, an author could eschew the high style to simply place the product of his research before the public. If he was having a serious fight with someone, he might not choose to write narrative history at all, and turn instead to a form of representation that allowed extensive direct quotation of the sources. But if he did not make this choice he needed to be conscious – and his whole training might make him extremely conscious of this – that he was following in a tradition of representation that stretched back for centuries. He had, above all else, the great Thucydides to fall back on, and those who had commented on his work. Otherwise he might turn to Cicero, if he chose to write in Latin; or he could simply give up and produce a pastiche that imitated the canons of the discipline of whose results he had despaired. Whatever choice he made, the result could be another literary source for the modern historian.

Chapter 1

Definitions

At some point towards the end of the first decade of the second century
AD, Gaius Plinius Secundus (commonly known these days as the Younger
Pliny) wrote as follows to a friend:

> I heard a true story, but one that seemed like fiction, and one worthy
> of your broad, deep, and plainly poetical genius. I heard it at a
> dinner party when various extraordinary stories were being passed
> back and forth. I trust the person who told it, although what is truth
> to poets? Still, the person who told the story is one of whom you
> might think well if you were to write history.
>
> (9.33.1)

The story concerned a dolphin that had cavorted with children in a
North African harbor until the expense of putting up various dignitaries
who wanted to see it became such a burden that the locals decided to kill
it. Pliny had every reason to be interested in the story, but he need not
have waited until this dinner party to learn it; the same story appears,
with slightly different details, in a work that his uncle had completed
some thirty years earlier (*NH* 9.26). Who had the story right, Pliny's
dinner companion or his uncle? We cannot now know for certain. What
is perhaps more interesting is the conceptual framework within which
Pliny introduced the story. Reliability is defined in terms of a dichotomy
between poetry and *historia*, forms of narrative that are at the opposite
ends of the spectrum of narrative representation.

Pliny's framework is worth thinking about because it rests upon two
assumptions: that history will be "true" and that the expression of this
"truth" will be in the form of a narrative. In other words, the expression
of truth is a linguistic construct, a point that is at the heart of much
discussion of history, both ancient and modern, and a point that is

central to much of what will be discussed in this book. There is no point in suggesting that there can be only one way of describing history, either in antiquity or in the present age. As a linguistic discourse, history cannot simply be defined as a record of "things said, done and thought." Nor is it necessarily "the artificial extension of a society's memory."[1] It is certainly not, as one standard dictionary defines it, "a continuous methodical record of important or public events."[2] These definitions beg the question of what a record actually is (the use of the word "methodical" occludes the fact that "methods" are not necessarily consistent from one record to another). Indeed, it is arguable that the crucial feature of history is that it is a form of explanation based upon generally agreed principles for validating the statements used to sustain the argument that it presents even if general agreement about the principles of validation changes through time.[3] Another crucial feature of history is that the range of human activity defines the subject; there can be histories of just about any and every thing. A third point is that the historian has a central role in establishing the parameters of a given subject. To say this is not to decree that we have only the text; but it is to admit that historical narratives, however constructed, are ideologically implicated descriptions of a reality that is separate from whatever text the historian happens to create. There can be no universal definition of history or the historical process that does not allow for the ultimately subjective selection of both evidence and presentation.

The issue of subjectivity in the writing of history is a particularly difficult one, and will rear its head from time to time throughout the rest of this book. In the present context it may be worth examining the problem as adumbrated in some recent discussions of history in terms of linguistic theory, for those concerns will very shortly be raised in the context of classical definitions of what history was. The point at issue is the relationship between language and the reality that it either represents or constructs. On the most extreme view, the discourse of the past is a series of linguistic confections, and documents are as profoundly embedded in social constructions as the discourse that is based upon them.[4]

The linguistic approach to history is not simply the result of "postmodern" literary criticism. Clifford Geertz, for instance, suggested that cultures might be read as if they were texts, while emphasis on narratives as autonomous constructions and representations has a significant place in the evolution of "alternative" histories of various sorts (not least being the history of women and the oppressed for whom the chronology of the dominant class is of little relevance).[5] However, it remains the case that "postmodernism" is for many an important critical perspective from which to question the possibility that historiographic discourse can legitimately claim to represent an external reality, or referent, rather than the discourse about that reality.

But what is "postmodernism"? At first sight, the definition of a theoretical position that is in and of itself devoted to problemitizing definition as a culturally determined linguistic construct is a rather slippery business, and to do so is often to create a unity out of what is rather better described as a complex of approaches and concerns.[6] Postmodernism may be taken as a form of historical argument devoted to the view that the present has been so radically altered by new developments in the shape and availability of knowledge (chiefly the changes wrought by the evolution of electronic forms of communication) that the term "modern", appropriated to describe a previous style knowing and representing, is no longer a relevant term. Postmodernism may be a method of analysis that problemitizes the relationship between reality and perception, essentially a negative argument aimed at breaking down the intellectual structure of "modernism," or it may be a positive argument using the techniques of linguistic analysis to build a new discourse concerned with old problems.

In discussions of the relationship between historiography and postmodernism, there has been a tendency, particularly evident in writings of the late 1980s and early 1990s, to employ the forms of "negative" postmodernist argument to argue that the traditional claims of modern historical method to objective analysis are based on false premises. In this form it may be little more than a resurrection in new guise of longstanding debates within the historical profession about the possibility of objective representation.[7] Such a discussion has had an unfortunate tendency to deal in caricature rather than close analysis. In such cases, it might appear that the failure to arrive at a universally valid definition of history is an epiphenomenon of the essentially linguistic nature of the subject, as might also be the dependence of history in the European tradition on linear narrative as a form of exposition. When attention is turned from the modern to the ancient world, and it appears that classical definitions of *historia* varied between descriptions of method and result (the nature of the research and the resulting narrative), this too may be taken as a conscious or unconscious recognition of the instability of the subject. On the other hand, it may be stressed that classical definitions of history are bound by an external reality, the need to describe a linguistic (if not physical) reality that differed from other forms of discourse. In the same way, it can be suggested that even the most extreme modern exponents of a "textualizing" discourse of history (there is historiography rather than history) are constrained by the logical necessity to admit the existence of a reality that is being represented.[8] Such an admission is, of course, fatal to the extreme line, for if a text is describing something that is independent of itself, then there are external limits to the range of possible discourse. On the other hand, just as there are diverse forms of postmodern theory – not all of them insisting upon the demise of the external referent – so too there are different forms of history. A critique of one style of history, the history of ideas, for instance, does not necessarily apply to another with equal force, and the force of such attacks may be felt differently by different generations of readers. Thus the approach to the text that is advocated by some champions of New Historicism, treating it as an artifact that constructs its own ideological reality, should not be taken to imply that there is no history beyond the text, but rather that a text can construct a reality outside of itself.[9] In this sense, the New Historicism can be seen as offering a defense against a critique of intellectual history as having no significance beyond the individual text that was supported by some earlier postmodernists.

In recent years, the discussion has been somewhat more refined, aided by a more accurate presentation of what some of the primary thinkers of the poststructuralist school have had to say, and by newer movements in literary criticism, such as the New Historicism.[10] Jean-François Lyotard's discussion of the distinction between mythic and scientific forms of narrative, and the method by which the "truth" of the external "referent" of scientific discourse is validated, is not inherently a denial of the existence of reality.[11] Rather, it raises profound questions about institutional bias in determining what constitutes a valid referent, and that is not only a modern concern. I will suggest that techniques of validating fact in the ancient world were central to the discourse of historiography, and that there was by no means a unified approach to the subject.[12] This does not mean that there was no sense of the "fact" or reality, but rather that there was a very strong sense of the factually based discourse, just as there is in modern historiography; even if the terms by which statements were validated could be rather different. This point was emphasized in another context by Clifford Geertz (a social anthropologist) in his discussion of "common sense" as a cultural system. Here he suggested that the definition of a phenomenon as significant depends upon a series of cultural assumptions that need to be decoded on a case by case basis.[13] From a different perspective, the literary critic Jacques Derrida's concentration on the "textual" is not *a priori* a denial of the existence of reality, but rather suggests that the representation of that reality is knowable in ways that totality of the referent is not, and Roland Barthes's discussion of the linguistic features of historical narrative does not deny the existence of the initial referent.

The question of the validity of a narrative (its distance from the referent) has always been a feature of the western historiographic tradition. The issue raised by postmodernist critics as to the relevance of the narrative to society as a whole is answered in a wide variety of ways. Michel Foucault argued for a separation of small narratives, the story of those who were not primary actors on the grand narrative of the western tradition, from the "narrative myth" of western society.[14] While the classical world was not blessed with a theorist who could articulate the distinction between the subjects of narrative, it nonetheless remained the case that there were alternatives to the grand narratives of peoples and their leaders in the ancient world. Ultimately, the most powerful of these alternative narratives was that offered in the Christian gospels, and they in turn reshaped the world in which they were read.

In sum, history may be seen as the external reality that can never be perfectly represented in the textual discourse of historiography, just as historiography must be constrained by the existence of history. The form that historiographic discourse takes is conditioned by the interests of the authors whose concern is not merely the representation of reality, but also with the significance of that reality to others.

That historiography retains, at its core, the element of subjective judgment does not mean that history as a discipline sits as a house of cards, ascending ever higher upon a rickety table in an earthquake zone, ready to collapse into chaos at the slightest tremor. The inherent contradiction between the desire for accurate representation and the impossibility of absolute certainty with regard to explanation is the tension that lends history its abiding fascination.

Historia as inquiry, *historia* as story

The linguistic aspect of history is basic to one way of defining the genre in antiquity, a way that sees history as part of a linguistic process. Thus the Greek noun *historia* is derived from the verb *historeô*, whose basic meaning is "to inquire." The noun can mean "inquiry," whence the meaning "knowledge acquired through asking questions." Etymologically, it is connected with another noun, *histor* "witness," and it derives from the perfect form of the verb "to know," *oida*.[15] This complex of words is significant because it reflects a Greek notion that *historia* is connected with the process of knowing. It is significantly not knowledge itself. It is also significant that a practitioner of *historia* such as Herodotus uses the verb much very much less frequently to describe his endeavors than he uses other verbs for acquiring information, and when he does use it he appears to endow it with a special meaning: to determine which version of a story is preferable to others.[16]

If *historia* could only mean inquiry, and if it were the only word for what we call historical writing, then life would be relatively simple. But life is not that simple. Aulus Gellius, who made a collection of improving stories for his children on the basis of his readings and life experience in the mid-second century AD, wrote that "the *historia* about Papirius Praetextatus is written and told by Cato," (*NA* 1.23); or that "the *historia* about Quintus Caedicius the military tribune is derived from works of history (*annales*)" (*NA* 3.7). In other words, Aulus used *historia* simply to mean narrative, and he was certainly not alone in doing so.[17] The multiple meanings of the word lead to multiple words to designate what we call historiography.

In the last passage quoted from Aulus, he is distinguishing between a story and the vehicle for that story, works of history, which he refers to as *annales*. His vocabulary here is altogether ubiquitous, for some variation on the phrase, *annales nostri* (our annals) is a standard way of referring to Roman history. What is particularly interesting is the identification between the history of the state and the books that contained them. Even more striking is that the phrase is technically correct only for a specific form of Latin historiography that emerged in the later part of the second century BC. Indeed, it may first have been used in this way in a work that was not even in prose, the *Annales* of Quintus Ennius, a poetic account of Roman history that came to an end in 187 BC. The first prose author to entitle his work *annales* may have been Cassius Hemina, who wrote some time after 146 BC. But that did not stop people from referring to earlier books, with different titles, as *annales*, once the word had become established as a synonym for *historia*,[18] or from seeking to define the words in different ways. Perhaps the most interesting of these efforts appears in Aulus Gellius, who wrote that:

> some people say that *historia* differs from *annales* in that, while the narration of deeds is a feature of both, *historia* has the particular quality that the author was a participant in the events that he describes; Verrius Flaccus says that this is the opinion of some people in the fourth book of his work *On the Meaning of Words*. He

says that he has his doubts about this, but thinks that there may be some point to it in that the word *historia* in Greek signifies a knowledge of current events. We are accustomed to hear that *annales* are the same as histories, but that histories are not entirely the same as *annales*; for just as a human is necessarily an animal, an animal is not necessarily a human.

Some people say that histories are an exposition or explanation of events, or whatever other term is used; they are *annales* when the events of many years are set down with observance of chronological order.

(*NA* 5.18.1–6)

Leaving aside Verrius Flaccus's remarkable statement about what *historia* meant in Greek, the striking feature of Aulus's definitions is that they depend on outward form rather than method. A *historia*, or *annales*, for Aulus is a narrative of events, a definition that is certainly well within the range of his own usage of the words. It is also in keeping with definitions connected with other Greek words for works of history.

One Greek word for a writer of history was *suggrapheus*, and for a history was a *suggraphê*. As with *historia*, the complex of meanings associated with these terms is complex. The verb *suggraphô* means to write or note down, to describe, write or compose. It could be used to describe the writing of a contract or other agreement; if an architect used the word, it indicated his specifications; it could be used for painting, writing a speech or making a promise. A *suggrapheus* was not only a historian, he might also be a member of a commission appointed to write up something, a *suggraphê* might also be a contract, bond, or a mark on the eye. The important point here is that the word stresses the physical aspect of recording; it is not connected with terms for either narrative or investigation, even though its meaning might be extended to imply collation.

Suggraphê was not the only compound of *graphô* to be used in the context of history. Other words include *logographos* and *chronographos*, respectively a prose writer and a person who composed works of history according to a fixed chronological scheme. Here again, the point is that a definition appears to be offered in terms of the appearance of the final product, a work in prose. The two basic modes of definition of historical writing that were available thus proceed from very different points; one from a stress on process (inquiry), the other from a description of the finished product, a story in prose. The diversity of terms for a work of history reveals a tendency to conflate the method with the product.

However, they both establish historical writing as a distinct form of representation.[19]

Truth and history

Whatever word one used for the end product, the object of the inquiry is the true, *alêthês*, a word that is defined in opposition to *pseudês*, or the false. In the words of one late first century BC historian and critic of the discipline, "we wish *historia* to be the priestess of truth (*tês alêtheias*)" (Dion. Hal. *de Thuc.* 8). The distinction between the process, *historia*, and the object, *alethês*, is a crucial one in ancient thought. *Historia* is not, in and of itself, true. It is the historian's duty to inquire as closely as possible into the subject to determine what is true. Thus in the first half of the fifth century BC, the earliest Greek historian, Hecataeus, wrote that "I have written these things as it seems true (*alêthês*) to me," and Thucydides that, "I have made a point not to write the deeds of those who were active in the war by learning of them from anyone I happened to run into, or as it seemed to me that they happened; but rather, I was either present myself at them, or examined with a critical eye the accounts that I received from others as best as I could."[20] For Hecataeus, Thucydides and Herodotus, it was clear that a historian had to use innate good judgment and critical sense to do the job. There could be no hard and fast rules of procedure: one did the best that one could. The views of these Greek authors are relevant to the study of Roman history because Roman theories of historical representation were descended from them.[21] It is crucial to remember that the bulk of the literary evidence from the Roman empire is written in Greek rather than in Latin, and that Classical Greek historians provided the models and determined the range of discourse for writers in both Greek and Latin in the period covered by this book. The education of all people literate enough to write in Greek was based primarily on authors of the fifth and fourth centuries BC, while the basic material of Latin education consisted of authors who were themselves versed in Greek theory of earlier periods.

Good and bad history was evaluated in terms of its relationship to truth, "who does not know that the first law of history is that one should not dare to say anything false, then that he should fail to say something that is true" (Cic. *De orat.* 2.63). In addition to the distinction between truth and deliberate falsehood, there was a separate distinction made between true stories and *mythoi*, stories that contained elements of the fabulous. *Mythoi* were not necessarily lies, most people in antiquity believed that the gods took an interest in human affairs and that they could do astonishing things, but they were certainly not completely believable. Thus Dionysius of Halicarnassus notes, after telling the story of the she-wolf who suckled Romulus and Remus, that "others, who hold that nothing like *mythos* should be admitted to investigative writing (*historikê graphê*), asserting that the notion that the exposure of the infants by the servants was not according to instructions is unbelievable, and they disparage both the tameness of the she-wolf and the suckling of the children as being full of dramatic nonsense (*dramatikê atopia*)" (*Ant. Rom.* 84.1).[22] Dionysius's critical vocabulary is interesting as it is one level less severe than that of "truth" versus "lying," and it raises the issue of ancient notions of fiction: did the Greeks and Romans have a way of distinguishing between different types of fiction, and could they define them independently of the "true"/"false" dichotomy?[23] The answers to these questions appear to be "yes" and "no" respectively.

In the handbook on oratory that he wrote towards the end of the first century AD, Quintilian, the premier teacher of rhetoric at the capital, wrote that there were generally held to be three forms of narrative.

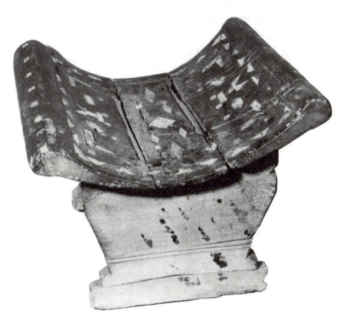

Figure 1 An inlaid reading stand, of wood, said to be from Medinet el Maadi, Egypt. The papyrus roll would be draped over one end.

Source: Kelsey Museum of Archaeology, University of Michigan

There were *fabula, argumentum* and *historia. Fabula*, the form of narrative used in tragedy and poetry, was distinct in both content and form from truth (*veritas*). Comedy made use of *argumentum*, which was false, but like the truth, while *historia* was the form of exposition used for things that happened (*Inst.* 2.4.2).[24] Quintilian was not being original here, for the theory of a tripartite distinction between types of narrative appears also in earlier rhetorical treatises, and in Sextus Empiricus's fascinating, if tortured, discussion of the analogy between grammar and history composed during the late second century AD. From Sextus, it appears that the theory was popularized by the work of Asclepiades of Myrleia, an intellectual of many interests who worked in the early first century BC.[25]

In Asclepiades's version of the theory, as represented by Sextus, the distinction is made between *historia* (narratives concerned with the true), narratives that have no connection with reality (which he refers to as *mythoi*) and narratives, *plasmata*, that represent reality in a fictional way (or are "as true"). In his view:

> *historia* is the exposition of certain true things that happened, such as that Alexander died in Babylon after being poisoned by plotters; *plasma* tells of things that did not happen, but are like things that did, such as comic plots or mimes; *mythos* is the exposition of events that never happened and are false, such as the tale that the species of venomous spiders and snakes were born alive from the blood of the Titans, or that Pegasus sprang from the head of the Gorgon whose throat had been cut.
>
> (*Adv. Gramm.* 263–4)

Asclepiades went on to say that within the category of true history there were three further subdivisions: history about the characters (*prosopa*) of gods, heroes and famous men; accounts of places and times; and accounts of deeds (*Adv. Gramm.* 1. 252–3). In the same discussion Sextus makes it clear that he is also accepting Asclepiades's assertion that *historia* was a sub-category of grammar, and that he, Sextus, thinks that grammar is not a technical discipline because it lacks a coherent "critical" method. A physician has reasons derived from a discipline to explain why something is healthy or unhealthy, the musician has reasons to know if a note is harmonious or not, but the grammarian makes a judgment on the basis of an epistemological and general observation about the truth of any particular statement (*Adv. Gramm.* 1.255). Since grammarians cannot have a consistent way of telling true from false, they have no method.

The inconsistency of Sextus's discourse derives from the nature of the task that he has set himself: the debunking of other fields of knowledge in the form of a rhetorical diatribe. Where Sextus is most interesting, and most original, is in raising the question of whether or not *historia* has a *technê*, or discipline. His answer is "no," which is inevitable in light of his overall rhetorical stance. On the other hand, it is significant that the points he expects historians to establish are concerned with what is "true" and what is not. If history had a method, this is what it would accomplish. Thus what may appear to be one of the most radical critiques of the discipline comes back around in the end to the same point as others.

The dichotomy between "true" and "false" in the evaluation of history may also be connected with the tendency to discuss the work of historians in language laden with moral overtones. The language reflects a tendency to attribute value to a statement because of a speaker's reputation rather than by invoking an external control of reliability. This was hardly a surprising development in a world where access to information was restricted, a function of the absence of information technology as well as class bias, since the well bred (and rich) man might be presumed to be a better witness than the ill bred and the poor unless there was a fundamental moral failure.[26] If a person did not investigate the truth accurately, the chances were that he was a self-conscious liar or a fool. Thus Plutarch attacked Herodotus as a man who told "lies" with an attractive style. The usual translation of the title of this work, *On the Malice of Herodotus* is moderately misleading. In Greek it is *Peri tês Herodotou Kakoêtheias*. *Kakoêtheia* is more than simple malice: it is bad moral character. The opening sentence of the work makes the importance of the moral criterion clear, as Plutarch writes "the style of Herodotus, my dear Alexander, thoroughly deceives many people as being true (*alêthês*), effortless and running easily over the subject; even more people have been deceived in this way with regard to his moral character (*êthos*)." It is Plutarch's view that Herodotus systematically distorted the history of the Persian wars by leaving out stories that reflected credit upon his subject (e.g. 866a–c), that he wrote with a serious prejudice against certain peoples (especially the Thebans) which led him to lie about them (864d; 865b), and that his desire to slander people led him into inconsistency (e.g. 861a; 861e; 863b). It is a basic sign of his *kakoêthes* that he will offer some preliminary praise so as to give his accusations additional force.[27] He is not a bad historian who had failed to do his research, he is a bad historian because he used his research with evil intent.

Centuries earlier, in one of the most pointed examples of professional historiographic abuse to have survived from the ancient world, Polybius assailed his historiographic foes for lying and a wide variety of other moral lapses that added up to their being unworthy to be considered historians. Timaeus, regarded in Polybius's own time as the authority on the Western Mediterranean is a "lover of quarrels, a liar and head-strong" (12.25.6).[28] He goes on to say that when "one or two lies are discovered in a history, and this occurs through deliberate choice, it is clear that nothing said by this historian is safe or reliable" (12.25 a 2). Timaeus is guilty of distorting things said by speakers, a sin in Polybius's view because, "it is the first task of investigation (*historia*) to know the words that were spoken in truth (*kat' alêtheian*), and second to know the reason that something that was done or said worked or failed" (12.25b 1). Similarly Arrian, writing in the second century AD explained his selection of sources for his account of Alexander the Great's conquests on the grounds that "it seemed to me that Ptolemy and Aristoboulos were more reliable in their narrative, Aristoboulos because he had served with Alexander, Ptolemy because he also served with him, and because it would be more disgraceful for him, as a king, to lie (*pseusasthai*) than it would be for another" (*An Praef.* 2). The moral distinction is fundamental.

A lesser problem was a person who, although not morally bankrupt, was sufficiently close to it that he wrote out of partisanship. When Tacitus says, at the very beginning of his *Annals*, that he will write without "anger or partisanship" (*sine ira et studio*), he is not saying that he is writing without passion, but rather that he does not have specific axes to grind with individuals because "I have distance from their affairs."[29] Statements of this sort are commonplaces, not simply because no historian would try to attract an audience by saying that "I intend to lie through my teeth," but rather because the need to assert independence was a standard feature of the critical discourse.[30] In a world of monarchs and dictators, as the Mediterranean world was, this is no small claim and it seems that this feature of historiography became more pronounced after Alexander the Great. It may be seen in Hellenistic literature when Timaeus attacked Callisthenes for his history of Alexander on the grounds that he was no more than a flatterer, and thus deserved to be tortured to death; and when Polybius said that this was even more true of Timaeus (Pol. 12.23.3). Lucian, whose *How to Write History* offers an astute critique of the sorts of historical writing spawned by imperial campaigns in the second century AD, observes this problem most succinctly when he says that the best praise that an historian can hope to have was that "he was a free man, full of frankness, with neither flattery or servitude anywhere, but truth in everything" (*Hist.* 61). The notion that contemporary history was dangerous because powerful people could take offense is a commonplace amongst Roman historians.[31] It does not appear in Greek historians of the fifth or fourth centuries BC.

A high moral standard, devotion to the truth, was thus the most important feature of historical exegesis. Another important feature was style. Historians had a duty not to be boring. If they were, their work could not be instructive. It was the historian's duty to select evidence not only in terms of what was "true," but also in terms of what would make a readable story. Efforts to say everything were not appreciated. Thus Tacitus wrote that:

> when Nero (for the second time) and Lucius Piso were consuls, little worthy of record took place, unless it is pleasing to someone to fill volumes praising the foundations and timbers with which Caesar built the amphitheater on the campus Martius, even though it is in accord with the dignity of the Roman people to record famous events in *Annales*, and events such as these in the daily record of the city.
>
> (Ann 13.31.1)

This is an important issue, for not all records of events could qualify as the result of proper *historia*. Some things were written down so that others could use them later, but these records were not history. The point is often made, but so too is the point that genres could be confused; what presented itself as a mere record, might in fact be a finished work. Thus Cicero, in his praise of Caesar's account of the conquest of Gaul, wrote:

> I have read a number of those *commentarii* that he wrote about his own deeds. They must be strongly commended, I think, for they are spare, straightforward and delightful, although the dress of every ornament of oratory has been omitted. But, while he wished to have material prepared for others, whence those who wanted to write *historia* might take something, he did a favor only for idiots who would want to burn them with curling irons: he deterred sane men from writing; for there is nothing more pleasing in history than pure and outstanding brevity.
>
> (*Brutus* 262)

After truth, style was a crucial component of "full" historical writing. Style could often compromise truth and this too is a feature of classical thinking about the record of the past. There is perhaps no issue with either ancient or modern historiography that has attracted more attention than this one, but for present purposes it is only significant to see that the terms of the discourse are consistent: the necessity that the process would result in a well-written product that was judged in terms of a standard described as "truth."

Some rules

The ancient meaning of *historia* as inquiry remains today a viable definition for historical study: an inquiry about the past. The classical belief was that people could learn from this inquiry, and pedagogy, it may be hoped, is also a purpose of modern endeavor. In this regard, the statement that history is the artificial extension of a society's memory is important. History must remain an inquiry into the past that enhances the present by making the varieties of human experience more comprehensible. It does so by using a narrative mode of discourse based on inquiry into an external reality. The shape that the narrative takes is determined by the historian, whose personal opinions and moral judgements will infuse the text with meaning. The question is the tool that the historian uses to shape the narrative, for questions will shape not only the body of evidence that will be used, they will also shape the answers that the historian obtains. The tests of a good question are that it is possible to answer it in empirical terms, that it is sufficiently flexible to allow for refinement, that it can be broken down into constituent parts, that the assumptions that lie behind the question are clear, and that it is phrased in such a way that it does not contain an inherent answer to itself.[32]

Within this broader context, it is worth pausing briefly to reflect on what the constituent elements of viable historical questions might be. Questions define the sort of evidence that will be used in answering them, but they should not, in and of themselves, dictate the answer. In this regard every question worth discussing actually contains a hierarchy of questions about the texts that are used to study it:

1   What is the evidence that is available to answer this question?
2   Do I understand the transmission of the evidence: is the manuscript tradition sound, am I quoting a text in its original context or another, *et cetera*?
3   Do I understand the language of the evidence accurately?
4   What are the circumstances under which the evidence was composed?

5   Are there problems with the evidence that limit the ways that it
     should be used (errors of fact, authorial bias etc.)?

Classical historians are often faced with the further problem that the
evidence they use comes from very different kinds of texts, spread over a
vast period of time. The modern American historian would shudder to
find a colleague writing about the 1960s with anecdotes drawn from the
1760s, but modern historians of Rome will very often use examples that
were recorded hundreds of years apart. When they do this, they need to
know when this is valid procedure, and when this is not. There are
points when it is simply not possible to learn more by asking more questions, or even different questions. Even good questions may not allow for
definitive answers.

The shortage of evidence means that historians cannot be satisfied
with a single type of evidence, or a single series of questions. The literary
evidence for Roman history that is the subject of this book is rarely
going to be sufficient to offer a thoroughly satisfactory answer to major
questions. But it is a starting point, and it does raise issues that are peculiar to ancient history and can thus be discussed in their own right.
These issues stem from the very different sorts of literature that have
survived, and they are the subject of the next chapter.

Chapter 2

Texts

Sorting things out

The last chapter was particularly concerned with the definition of history in the Roman world. The point of general importance is that history falls at one end of a notional spectrum of mimesis, or representation. The definition of history reflects assumptions about forms of representation at other points on the spectrum: that there were fictions that imitated life, and that there were narratives that were essentially fantastic. One basic method of determining where a work lay on the spectrum was to analyse the nature of representation: contrasting narrative prose with poetry, and categorizing history as being a specific form of narrative. An issue connected with this mode of generalizing about history is that the dividing line between different points on the spectrum is very often obscure. For example accounts of gods and heroes could be treated as either *historia* or *mythos* depending upon the mode of representation that an author selected.

The main point of this section of the book is that while ancient distinctions may yield important clues as to classical expectations of a text, they are not invariably useful to a modern scholar who is attempting to make sense out of the Roman world. A work of fiction may tell us more about the experience of ancient slavery than any other kind of text.[1] Furthermore, so little of what was once written in antiquity has survived that the context for what we have must often be provided out of fragmentary information about texts that have been lost. The emphasis of this chapter will be on providing context for what we have, and the issues will be threefold. One issue is the importance of process: whatever the text, there were specific ways in which it became known to readers. The second is the methods for providing context. There is no point in asserting that context can only be provided from within a fragmented body of material; relevant questions must be constructed both from within and without the surviving corpus. Within this corpus there is perhaps no form of evidence more characteristic of the modern study of the classical world than the fragment, a quotation from or a description of an otherwise lost work. The study of fragments has its own peculiar rules and the great collections of fragments have helped shape important areas of classical studies.

A final process that needs to be discussed is that of categorizing evidence. In doing so, it is plain that the study of literary sources is but one part of the study of Roman history. There are certain kinds of studies for which evidence derived from the manuscript tradition will be of only limited value. The documentary record offered by inscriptions, papyri and coins allows for a range of studies that cannot be readily executed on the basis of literary sources alone. Basic studies of the structure of, for instance, the ancient economy, demography, wages, prices, trade and food supply depend on statistical analyses that are simply not possible on the basis of literary evidence. There are very few (if any) studies for which the evidence will be completely satisfactory.

The problem in the handling of literary evidence is simplified somewhat through a basic sorting process that every historian, implicitly or explicitly, engages in whenever confronted by a new task and/or text. This sorting process consists of two basic questions: what sort of text is this, and what should one expect to get out of it? In this regard it is not particularly helpful to think of texts solely in terms of the multifarious genres of ancient literature. Texts that are ostensibly part of the same genre may not provide the same kind of evidence: a letter from Marcus Cicero to his friend Atticus that was never meant for publication can tell us quite different things than a letter in a collection that was specifically designed for a broader audience. The preliminary sorting exercise that every historian must employ when confronted by a piece of evidence is a crude exercise based on the function of the text in antiquity. As a first step it is necessarily simplistic, the categories of evidence will obviously overlap somewhat, and all works assigned to a certain category cannot be expected to provide evidence that is of equal quality. When it comes to the sorting of evidence, the answers that a historian seeks must forward the investigation: it does not help the historian very much to conclude that an epic poem is an epic poem and should be treated as such.[2] The historian needs a way to categorize this information: will the text help reconstruct a specific incident in the past, or will it help explore general attitudes towards some issue, or is it an independent effort to produce an account of a period of history? A text may fit into one or more of these categories: Silius Italicus's *Punica* does, after all, offer a reconstruction of the Second Punic War. A letter of Cicero may fit one category for the historian of political violence in the 50s BC, and another for the historian of social attitudes. But this does not free the historian from the preliminary responsibility to define categories of evidence in terms of the task at hand.

Two basic categories of evidence are "first-hand" and "second-hand." Both of these categories are problematic when it comes to Roman history because of the physical process by which we have the literary texts that have survived. This physical process includes the intervention of editors or copyists at numerous different stages – we have no video-taped interviews – and literary canons which dictated the improvement of first-hand records (almost all of which are now lost). Despite these problems, there is still a difference between what comes down from a participant in events and from one who was not; and not all "second-hand" texts are of the same sort.

A more useful way of thinking about these texts may be as "participant," "illustrative" and "narrative." Participant evidence is provided by texts purporting to report or influence a specific event, or closely linked series of events, by a person who was involved either as an actor or witness. Illustrative texts are primarily concerned with ideas and habits, not intended to influence specific contemporary events. An illustrative text tends to be a work that is written for the education and/or amusement of the reading public. This is the broadest category: an illustrative text can be virtually any text that survives from antiquity, though for practical purposes it can be restricted to texts that can neither be used as eyewitness accounts or narratives without straining credulity. By narrative, I mean a work purporting to give a chronological account of the author's own times and/or the author's reconstruction of events occurring prior to his time (all known narrative historians of the Roman world being men). A "narrative" is distinguished from a "illustrative" and "participant" text in that it is a systematic effort to represent a series of events on the basis of a critical examination of reports from other sources for an audience that has independent access to the same or comparable sources. The author of such a narrative may be writing in the hope of modifying attitudes or conduct in the future, just as might be the author of a text in my other two categories. At no point should it be assumed that one variety of text is a priori more objective in intent than another. It is entirely possible to construct an "objective" discourse for a subjective purpose.

Participant evidence

A historian of the modern world is used to dealing with autographs (extant documents in the hand of the original author), volumes of state papers that are transcriptions of texts written at a specific moment in time, or eyewitness accounts. The ancient historian is rarely so lucky.

The papyrologist and epigraphist work with and edit texts that modern historians would recognize as "documentary" in that their composition corresponds closely to the specific point in time with which their contents are concerned. However, for many periods of ancient history these texts either have not survived, or survive from regions or levels of society that are not the direct concern of the historian. Very few texts in the manuscript tradition represent exactly what was said at a specific moment: we know that ancient shorthand would not permit this, and that even ostensible verbatim records in direct speech are compositions based on notes.[3] The canons of rhetorical performance ordinarily precluded the use of written speeches in court or in public, and we have very few texts that were written to be read out from a script. We do have some collections of private letters, the most famous of which are those from Cicero to his friend Atticus, that appear to be preserved in the form in which they were actually sent and were not edited for public consumption by the author.[4] In other cases the hand of an editor may be an issue. Cicero himself once remarked that there were letters for the personal enjoyment of the author, and others for more general audiences.[5] He allowed the compilation of a book of seventy such letters "for the general public," which he explicitly says that he had revised.[6] Other letters, such as those of the emperor Julian, appear to have been preserved by their recipients, and further letters, including several descriptions of Christian martyrdoms, appear to have been preserved as they were written for doctrinal reasons.[7] Marcus Aurelius's *Meditations* seem to descend from an autograph that the emperor never intended to publish, and some letters of the emperor Augustus have come down to us from a collection that may have been made after his death. At least some of the letters in the version of the collection that Suetonius knew were in Augustus's own hand .[8] The correspondence between Pliny and Trajan, unlike other parts of Pliny's correspondence, also seem to have been preserved as written.[9] Texts such as these should satisfy the modern historian's definition of documentary evidence. However, there is much else in the extant corpus that does not, and any document torn from its original context can be a dangerous thing. Without further evidence we can only assume that Pliny is telling Trajan the truth, that the other documentation that once existed for his governorship would confirm the same patterns of conduct.

Context, or lack of it, may alter the value and meaning of participant evidence for the modern scholar. There may be no area where this is more true than in the realm of the occasional poetry, lyric or elegiac that has survived from the Roman world. Catullus's rejection of Caesar in poem 93:

> I have no interest in pleasing you, Caesar,
> or even in knowing who you are

is every bit as much a document of the political discourse of the late Republic as it is an example of Catullus's verbal facility. But we do not know if it or other attacks on Caesar in the extant corpus aside from the poem about his relations with Mamurra, were amongst those that Suetonius said that Caesar felt to have damaged his reputation.[10] We do know that Quintilian regarded poem 93 as the sort of thing that one did not write about a powerful person, but that critical statement may be more important as evidence for habits in the late first century AD rather than the 50s BC (*Inst.* 11.1.38). On quite a different note, the poems in Martial's *On Spectacles*, commemorating events connected with the opening of the Colosseum in AD 79 are of great value as illustrations both of the sort of thing that one might see in general, and as record of specific events on that occasion that would otherwise be lost to us.[11] Genuinely autobiographical lines in Statius or Ovid (as opposed to those constructed to suit a poetic persona) enable us to recreate careers in a milieu where evidence is otherwise scanty, and a poem such as Statius's consolation to Claudius Etruscus is on a par with evidence for careers offered by letters of Pliny.[12]

With occasional poetry, the problem is often not so much the status of the document as a participant statement, but rather with finding a context within which the participation took place. Thus a poem of the Greek poet Apollonides concerning the first appearance of an eagle at Rhodes is of considerable interest precisely because it situates itself at a specific moment, "when Nero held the island of the sun, and in his house I stayed, [the bird was] tame to the hand of the ruler, not fleeing the Zeus to be."[13] The appearance of the eagle is reported by Suetonius in the context of Tiberius's recall from self-imposed exile on Rhodes in AD 2, and the use of the name Nero, which Tiberius gave up after his adoption in AD 4, places it in close temporal connection with the bird's appearance. The statement that Tiberius was then a "Zeus to be" suggests rather more confidence in the outcome of the transactions than circumstances (and other sources) might allow with Gaius Caesar, the ostensible heir apparent, still being alive. A poem by Bassus, who composed in Greek while Tiberius was on the throne (AD 14–37) is placed in the mouth of the God Hades, who is ordering the gates of his realm to be closed so that Germanicus, recently deceased (in AD 19) cannot enter, his proper home being in the stars. The context here is provided by Tacitus and inscriptions preserving a substantial portion of the posthumous honors voted on that occasion, but the poem's assertion of Germanicus's divinity looks rather like a reading of the honors which stopped short of actual deification. The reference that he makes to the stars may be an allusion to Germanicus's translation of Aratus's poetic treatment the heavens in the *Phaenomena*, and thus also a reference to the placement of his portrait with those of men of great genius in the portico of the temple of Apollo on the Palatine.[14] Three poems by another contemporary Greek poet, Crinagoras, have no such obvious context. These are one that appears to celebrate Germanicus in life, one that can be read as a reference to a disaster in Germany (Rome will be safe so long it retains faith in Caesar even though the Germans are drinking the whole Rhine), and one that celebrates the accomplishments of Tiberius (referred to as Nero) in both east and west.[15] Specific events appear to lie behind all three, but we lack the information to be sure just which ones they might be. At best the poems stand as reflections of Augustan ideology.

With poems that connected to a specific moment in time when they were composed and recited, there is no reason to think that their contents were altered for later consumption. However, it is often the case that we only know of them through the work of later compilers, in the case of the Greek texts mentioned above, through in the *Garland of Philip*, assembled under Caligula (AD 37–41), and then excerpted into the *Greek Anthology* or that of Planudius many centuries later. We cannot know for certain, much as we might like to, how Catullus arranged his poems, or what got left out. The same is true of other poets. A Horace, Propertius, Ovid or Statius who edited books of their own verse that have come down through the manuscript tradition were presumably selective (in Ovid's case this is a certainty with regard to his *Amores*). With such samples, we cannot be certain how representative of a total output they might be. The extreme specificity of some poems may cause confusion for the interpretation of others. Although we can be sure that Bassus was writing about something that happened, can we conclude that it is likewise safe to generalize about, for instance, Augustus's imperial designs on the basis of general remarks in Horace? Here the answer is probably no, and with all such participant evidence, the effort to contextualize it fully may not be rewarded with great success. Furthermore, with forms of literature that respond to each other every bit as much as they respond to "real life" situations, the tension between text as self-contained artifact, reinventing itself with each new reading, and the relevance of the circumstances of original composition is particularly severe.[16]

In the case of short occasional poetry, concern about significant later reworking need not always be great. The same cannot be said of other relics of specific moments in time. What do we have when we look at a speech that has come down through the manuscript tradition? What is the relationship between this text and the speech actually given? When Cicero delivered his first Catilinarian oration in 63 BC, his intention was to drive the conspirator Catiline from Rome, but his later publication of the speech, along with a number of others that he had delivered in his year as consul, was intended to enhance his reputation as a statesman in the eyes of both his contemporaries and later generations.[17] Another speech, against Curio and Clodius, that he had fabricated on the basis of a debate in the Senate, was released against his will while he was in exile in 57 BC (to his considerable embarrassment).[18] He himself said that most orations were written down after they were delivered rather than before (*Brut.* 91), and it is clear that he regularly rewrote sections of his own speeches for the subsequent delectation of others. Thus in 61 BC he wrote to his friend Atticus that he had added a topographical description of the area around Puteoli and Misenum to one speech, and that he had made some other additions to a speech concerning Metellus (Cic. *Att.* 1.13.5). All the *Verrine* orations after the first were never delivered, nor was the second *Philippic*, and the speech in defense of Milo that has survived in the manuscript tradition is the one that he sent Milo after his conviction.[19] Milo said that if Cicero had actually given this speech, Milo would not be enjoying the fine food of Marseilles (his place of exile).[20] A version of the speech that he actually gave was preserved in the records of the trial, and these court *commentarii* were regarded by Quintilian as the most faithful record of what was actually said, as well as Cicero's source in preparing the "official" version of his orations.[21] We know, on the basis of papyrus records of trials, that even these would not be true "stenographic" records, and are told by Suetonius that court recorders had trouble keeping up with a fast speaker like Julius Caesar.[22]

In the generation of Quintilian, the Younger Pliny wrote that a good speech in a court was one thing, a good oration was another (Plin. *Ep.* 1.20.9). In his day it seems to have been the practice to write out the speech before, rather than after, delivery, and then to produce another version for publication once the speech had been delivered. Thus he wrote to a friend who asked for a copy of a speech that he had delivered in court that "I am sending you the speech that you have often asked for, and I have often promised, but not all of it, for part is still being worked over" (Plin. *Ep.* 2.5.1). In the case of the panegyric that he delivered in AD 100 to thank the emperor Trajan for the consulship, he expanded it so much that it took him three sessions to read it out to his friends (Plin. *Ep.* 3.13). It is likely that we now have no speech from the Roman world in the form in which it was delivered. The point of the publication of these speeches was not to preserve an accurate record of the event; it was to enhance the image of the author, a point that Cicero also makes quite plain, and to provide models for other students of rhetoric.

Were published speeches "free compositions," and what did it mean to "publish" something anyway? The answer to the first question seems to be yes and no. Cicero used the record of what he had said as the model for "published" versions, and it appears that even when he said something that later proved embarrassing, he could not cut it out. In the first speech against Catiline, he announced that "I have learned every-thing" about a treasonous meeting. The remark seems to have been regarded as stupid by his critics, who evidently told "Cicero jokes" in which the line featured. Cicero was not amused: but he still knows every-thing in the first *Catilinarian*.[23] He also appears to have felt some constraint in changing a speech once he had offered a written version to the public. In a letter of 45 BC, he said that he could not add anything about the wife and stepdaughter of a person who had appeared in his speech for Ligurius because it was already widely circulated.[24] The texts of the prose panegyrics that have survived in Latin from the fourth century seem likewise to have frozen at some point relatively close to the time at which they were delivered: the text of the panegyric delivered on the occasion of Constantine's marriage in 307 that exalts Constantine's father-in-law, Maximian, over Constantine cannot have been rewritten extensively much after the event.[25] The situation that it describes ceased to be relevant little over a year later, and we have some reason to think that the texts of such speeches were requested by other prospective panegyrists fairly quickly. Thus we find that a speech in praise of the emperor Julian that was delivered in Constantinople on 1 January 363 had reached Antioch sometime after the beginning of March (and not much later than that) in the same year.[26] The letters of the orator

Libanius, which enable us to watch this happening, also reveal the orator delivering a speech before the emperor, and then asking him for suggestions on how to improve it for publication.[27] Julian's responses allow us to see the emperor's appreciation for an effort to "set the record straight" in accordance to his wishes.[28] In these cases, as with Cicero, we cannot know just exactly what was said, but we can know that the extant speeches offer a record of what participants thought should have been said (even if it was not) in close temporal relationship to the actual delivery of the original speech. The ability to engage in the sort of "reception criticism" is invaluable, even if it is extremely unusual. Despite the scarcity of direct evidence, the similarity in practice between the middle of the first century BC, the early second century AD and the early and late fourth century AD, from Rome to Gaul to Antioch, is striking.

Speeches cannot be classified as "documents" in the modern sense, but they can be classified as "eyewitness" or participant narratives. What they have to tell us demands the respect accorded to any eyewitness. This respect must always be cautious. Ancient historians, as well as modern ones, realize that eyewitness accounts are liable to deep corruption, even as they show a marked preference for eyewitness accounts over documentary sources. People remember details selectively, and may invent contexts for what they have seen. Oral history in the modern sense involves the recording of memories of events, and does not (or should not) pretend to anything more. Memories can change under questioning, be checked against other records or other memories, and are manifestly subject to an individual's perspective. The individual soldier must, if honest, give a very different account of a battle than the general. Caesar can tell his readers why he placed his troops where he did before a battle, and we may think that he knew what he was talking about. The author of the *Spanish War* in the Caesarian corpus cannot tell us that.

The Caesarian corpus should also serve to illustrate the fact that ancient generic distinctions are not necessarily a good guide to the kind of information that a text can convey. *Commentarii* such as those written by Caesar were meant to provide the information that other authors could use in writing a real history. But Caesar, like Sulla before him, wrote with an eye to a broader public, and it is notorious that he appears to have used literary accounts in his description of places that he himself had seen. We can no more assume that Caesar described a barbarian custom from personal observation simply because he wrote about it, than we can assume that he provides accurate numbers for the Gauls whom he defeated.[29] So too, in a full-blown "history" such as that written by Ammianus Marcellinus, the reader is tossed to and fro between first hand accounts of things that Ammianus had seen himself and passages drawn from other people's writings. There are few passages in ancient literature as evocative as Ammianus's account of the terror that he and his colleagues felt when they were sent to assassinate the general Silvanus at Cologne in 355, or his flight from a Persian patrol to the city of Amida and subsequent escape from that city on the night that it fell to the Persians in 359.[30] But Ammianus's account of the customs of the Gauls depends on literary works (including Caesar's), and his narrative of Julian's campaign against Persia in 363 is ultimately based upon an account written by some one close to Julian as well as his own recollections.[31]

Publication and literary fashion

What do I mean by publication? Publication in antiquity cannot readily be compared with publication in the post-Guttenberg age. The printing press allows for the massive dissemination of written works on a scale that was unimaginable for most of human history. In the classical world, publication meant that an author had lost control of his text. He (almost always he) could lose this control in a variety of ways. Cicero remarked in his letter to Atticus of 45 BC that the text of his speech for Ligurius was too widespread for him to introduce further changes; Horace observed that an author lost control of a work after it left his study.[32] The younger Pliny drew a strict distinction between work that was still in progress that he would send to friends for comment, and work that was "published." Tacitus seems to have had the same idea, for he sent a work to Pliny for correction before he gave it to the world at large.[33] Recitation of a work did not mean that a work was to be regarded as finished. Vergil received a substantial reward from the passage concerning Marcellus in Book 6 of the *Aeneid* several years before he asked that the whole work be burnt as unfinished, and Propertius clearly distinguishes between Vergilian poems that were "public" in the 20s and the *Aeneid* when he refers to them.[34]

In general terms, publication appears to have involved three stages. The first was *ekdosis*, when a text that was considered finished and was handed on by the author. "Handed on" does not mean that it was placed in general circulation. Plato's finished works, *ekdoseis*, were given to his followers rather than to the world at large, and anyone who wanted to consult them had to pay a fee to their owners.[35] A work that was given to the world at large was a *diadosis*, and a text that passed from one generation to another was a *paradosis*.[36] The crucial point here is that which separated the *ekdosis*, or completion, from the *diadosis*, or distribution. The movement from one phase to another was not always under the author's direct control.

"I think that it is a good idea to explain first the reason for the mutilation [of my works], and then to make a list of the works that I have written" (Galen, *De libr. propr. proemium*). Perhaps the most coherent discussion of the issues connected with publication comes from the pen of the great second century AD doctor, Galen.[37] Towards the end of his life, he decided to produce a list of his works that he regarded as authentic. Taken with other remarks spread throughout his extensive corpus, we can see that Galen was troubled by the prospect of some future scholar attempting the sort of exegesis that he had engaged in on the works of the Hippocratic corpus, and discovering that what passed for the work of Galen was not what Galen might have wished.

The first cause that Galen gives for the chaos that he perceived to be afflicting his legacy was that, when friends or students asked him for his works, he did not give them copies that were suited for publication (*ekdosis*), but rather "notes" (*hypomnemata*) (Galen, *De libr. propr.* 9). When some of these friends died, their companions took the works that the deceased had received from Galen and published them under his name. Elsewhere, Galen says that he gave his notes (*hypomnemata*) on Chrysippus to a gentleman of Pergamon. Years later these surfaced as a "work of Galen," since copies had been distributed by servants to those who had asked (Galen, *De libr. propr.* 43). Galen may not have been pleased with the response, since he goes out of his way to say that he had produced them when he was a "kid." In another case, "notes" that he had given to friends had been stolen by servants and then published. In some of this, he appears to be constructing a history of his publishing career to parallel that which he had reconstructed for Hippocrates, whose unfinished *hypomnemata* needed to be distinguished from his completed *syggramata* (Galen, *In Hipp. art. comment.* 3.32).

Lectures were another source of texts. Galen himself dictated his works to scribes trained in shorthand; others sent such scribes to his lectures. In one case, he claims that dictations taken down by the stenographers of a friend were circulated as his own (Galen, *De libr. propr.* 14). We may think whatever we want about his professed surprise that this should have happened (one doubts that he could have been so innocent), but for now it is worth noting pirated copies of books were a feature in a world where oral presentation was a central feature of cultured life, just as the sale of video tapes taken in theaters or pirated recordings of music is a feature of ours. Galen's problem was not a new one. He knew perfectly well that some philosophers had drawn distinctions between *exoterika*, or works that were for general consumption, and *esoterika*, which were for their students only (presumably a different distinction than that between *ekdosis* and *diadosis* as he implies that *esoterika* may not be fully polished). He ridicules the notion that one can make such a distinction when he does not appeal to it as an explanation for sub-standard work on his own part.

Then there were technical problems in the preparation of a manuscript. Galen tells us that he would at times write twice on some matter, with one version as a part of a continuous text and another in the margin. "The first person" to copy the book would then copy out both treatments, and, since Galen would not check carefully what had happened, the work would be "published" with material in it that Galen had not intended to include. At another level, when Galen had given copies of unfinished works to friends, and lost others, so he says, in the fire that destroyed the Temple of Peace at Rome, he was able to recover copies from his acquaintances (Galen, *De libr. propr.* 41).

Figure 2 The library of Celsus at Ephesus. Libraries such as this one, founded in honor of the consul of AD 92 and his son, consul of 110, not only housed collections of books but also celebrated the dominant culture represented by those books. Readers were not ordinarily allowed to borrow books, but rather consulted them in a central reading room.

Photograph: David Potter

Galen's problem with unauthorized publication arises from senseless acts of generosity on his part (or so he would have us believe). Actual publication (*ekdosis*) was likewise an act of generosity, a gift judged finished. The first official recipients of a work were people known to the author, and they were often the very people who arranged for the further distribution of his work, just as the unauthorized distributors of Galen's works had access to them through friends who had received or transcribed them.[38] One of the marvels of Galen's career was that his works were widely disseminated during his lifetime. Authors were not supposed to be much concerned with such things (note that Galen's discourse suggests that wide dissemination is the foe of accurate transmission), and certainly could not expect to get rich from it. Some perspective on Galen's dilemma is offered earlier in the second century by the orator Regulus, who had a thousand copies of a eulogy for his deceased son created. It was a sign of grief (Pliny thought it was in bad taste) and, presumably, virtually everyone who met Regulus had a copy pressed upon him.[39] The bad taste might be compounded by the fact that Regulus's activity was imitating the style of the death announcements of members of the imperial house. Cicero's friend Atticus was famous for providing good copyists to assist the literary endeavors of his friends, which was taken as a sign of his benevolence rather than desire for commercial profit (which in any event was unlikely to be forthcoming). A situation similar to that of Atticus may be detected in fourth-century Antioch, where Libanius maintained a copyist to make sure that his friends received his latest works; but as it appears that he only maintained one copyist at a time, he also appears to have asked that recipients see to the further circulation of his work themselves. In an interesting parallel to Pliny's remarks on Regulus, Libanius also expresses some embarrassment when Strategius Musonianus, Praetorian Prefect of the East from 354–8, employed ten copyists to distribute versions of the panegyric that Libanius delivered in his honor.[40] The dispatch of a new work of literature was an act between friends, not intended for use by the recipient for self aggrandizement. This may be the reason why Galen suggests that his *hypomnemata* only entered general circulation after their original owners had died.

Galen was not the only person to produce new versions of works after losing control of an earlier version: Tertullian appears to have given two somewhat different versions of his *Apology* to the public with the result that two versions of the speech that cannot be reconciled exist in the manuscript tradition.[41] Ovid explicitly says that he produced a new edition of the *Amores*, minus two books, and Martial seems only to have given a selection of his vast output to the public: people who had their own copies of an epigram were presumably free to do with it as they pleased even if it was not included in the final collection.[42] Texts that were placed in public libraries appear to have had the status of "official" texts, but all texts were not treated in this way. The *Oracle of the Potter*, a prophetic text that was originally composed in the Ptolemaic period, never seems to have been deposited in a library, and now exists in three third-century copies. Two of these copies differ so much from each other that they must be read separately.[43] Early Ptolemaic papyri have shown that our common text of Homer came into existence by the later second century as a product of the book trade even though scholars attributed this development to Aristarchus, possibly out of a desire to find a point when the text of the Homeric poems became fixed, though other manuscripts with other readings could be consulted.[44] In some cases, we know that there was concern that better readings were not included in readily available texts; scholars in the second century AD were concerned with the possibility that texts "from Vergil's house" contained readings that were not in the library text.[45]

Study of Greek literary papyri have revealed several remarkable facts about the circulation of literature in the Roman empire. The first is that very little "formal" literature was broadly circulated, confirming the impression that Galen's circulation was unusual. We have more oracular texts on papyrus than we do works of imperial history known from the manuscript tradition (there is only one, dubious, fragment of Appian). The vast bulk of the literature that has survived on papyrus stems from the fifth to third centuries BC.[46] Many of these texts are copied on the back of documents: the most extensive copy of the famous fourth century *Hellenica Oxyrhynchia* is written on the back of a land register of the Arsinoite nome that was composed in the reign of Commodus. The emerging study of papyri in their original archaeological context is now giving us a clearer picture of just who the people were who were responsible for having these copies made.[47] A house in Karanis that was inhabited by a local tax collector has revealed that his library included some grammatical texts, one of the so-called *Acta Alexandrinorum* (texts purporting to record exchanges between Egyptian notables and Roman officials) and Menander's *Epitreopontes*. The latter was written by a professional copyist on the back of a late first century AD document. Indeed, it seems to have been common practice for officials to give their longer public documents to copyists who would provide them with texts of the works of literature that they desired. A much less common phenomenon was the use of a roll that was "dedicated" to one literary work for another. Nonetheless, we do have texts such as a remarkable fragment of Xenophon's *Cyropaedia* that may have been copied in the first century AD with a Christian exegetical work copied on the back of it in the fifth century.[48] This is a book that had clearly remained in circulation for many centuries before a Christian owner decided to give it to some one to copy the Christian material on to it.

There is far less information about the circulation of Latin literature. However, the evidence of an antiquarian author such as Aulus Gellius or Macrobius confirms the impression that may be gleaned from the habit of allusion in late antique authors. This impression is that Romans of the imperial period tended to the creation of a classical Latin literature that included works written between the late third century BC and the time of Augustus. Both Ammianus and Augustine reveal an education based on Vergil and Cicero, as well as other authors of this period and earlier. Ammianus's observation that the Roman aristocracy of his time read Juvenal and Marius Maximus appears to be a suggestion that they were people of poor taste for reading such "unclassical" tripe, while "real intellectuals" such as himself contemplated the improving *sententiae* of Cicero.[49] Some of this may go back to rhetoricians of the late first century AD like Quintilian, who suggested that this was appropriate for the training of rhetoricians; and it appears to have become a topos that anything written after the "decline of freedom" was not as good as that written before the accession of Tiberius.[50]

The feeling of inferiority, or discourse of inferiority, did not silence literature, and it most certainly did not, in the unfortunate rhetoric that appears in the work of some modern critics, "kill" genres "stone dead." What the imperial "discourse of inferiority" is a sign of, however, is a much more complicated issue. This is the differential speed at which works of literature could have an influence. What may be true of the speed with which Livy or Cicero became classics could not be true of any work in the second century AD; literary and cultural fashions were in constant flux. It could take centuries for a work to become a "classic," and this may have had some influence on attitudes: if you could not hope for the recognition of Livy while you were alive, perhaps you were not all that good. It does not seem to have been until the fourth century that Tacitus attained "classic" status; he does not seem to have been so highly regarded in the second century. He is praised as one of the four great Latin historians in the *Historia Augusta*.[51] Cassius Dio, writing his history of Rome almost two centuries earlier, never seems to have read him. This is not a question of Latinity. It is a question of taste and, possibly, of the doctrine that an historian of the past should consult the earliest available account.[52] The practice of referring to the earliest historian to write about an event, while ostensibly sound, denied the possibility that an author like Tacitus might have improved upon these writers either through his own researches, or by exercising greater care in dealing with material that was already known.

The nature of ancient education is inextricably linked with the issue of the circulation of literature. Our Egyptian book owners reflect the literary tastes of their schoolrooms, which have been shown to be highly class-conscious. Primary education was fairly common in antiquity. Schoolmasters who taught the alphabet to children in their early years may have been ubiquitous, but literary education for adolescents was expensive.[53] Good teachers were attracted to major cities, and a person who wanted a first-class education had to be ready to travel.[54] This cost a great deal of money. Cicero seems to have dedicated the income from two tenements to the maintenance of his son in Athens. Romans of the upper class regularly spent some years abroad learning the craft of rhetoric from famous teachers in the Greek world if their fathers could afford it.[55] If they could not, a career in public life was still possible, but problematic. Aulus Hirtius, consul of 43 BC through the favor of Julius Caesar, is a significant prose author. He wrote the final book of Caesar's *Commentaries* on the war in Gaul, and may be the author of some of the civil war histories; but he is also found taking elocution lessons from Cicero in 46 BC.[56] He may be typical of a class of Roman aristocrat who had exhausted parental resources, or found alternative careers before completing the full course of study needed to flourish in the world of letters as it was defined in his lifetime. In thinking about education and literature, we need always to be aware that we are not dealing with a monolithic cultural and educational establishment. There are many layers of accomplishment even within the governing class, with layers ranging from the Roman officers scribbling bits of Vergil on Masada, to Tacitus. The multiplicity of layers may, indeed it must, reflect differential reception of new books. It also had an impact in the form that a text could take.

Texts

The ideal that there was a "perfect" text of some work certainly seems to have existed in the Late Republic and empire.[57] The development of this ideal is, in and of itself, an interesting issue since it is plainly not a necessary concomitant to the existence of a sophisticated literature. In the Greek world, the earliest evidence that we have to suggest that a person was concerned with concocting the "correct text" of a literary work ("correct texts" of laws and works of religious significance are another matter entirely) is the story that the Athenian tyrant Hipparchus commissioned an edition of the poetry of Homer.[58] If this tale is true, it is important to realize that written versions of the text of Homer had been circulating for nearly two centuries before the effort was undertaken, and what is essentially our text of Homer was being standardized through the book trade at roughly the period of Hipparchus's alleged activity. It may also be interesting that it may have been at roughly the same time, and for quite different reasons that the priestly rulers of Judaea decided to create the "true text" of their own sacred works, an editorial enterprise that is now the basis of the Hebrew Bible. The emergence of the text of Homer and of the Hebrew Bible appear to be isolated phenomena stemming from specific needs of the moment. The true birth of the scholarly tradition of textual analysis and exegesis lay several hundred years in the future.

In the generation after Alexander the Great, developments in Greek poetry led to an interest in the systematic study of texts.[59] The roots of this movement may lie in the Aristotelian school of philosophy with its stress on classification, but the prior efforts of Aristotle and his associates are not, in and of themselves, a sufficient explanation for the new study of language that is associated with the rise of "learned" poetry and the editing of texts within royal libraries. The creation of the library of Alexandria provided a new forum for intellectual activity; the demise of the Persian empire led to a new fascination with the history of Greeks in the pre-Persian era; the massive political shifts that accompanied the emergence of supra-regional Greek states created a new desire to preserve the memory of the past. Perhaps most important of all was the increasing sense that ethnicity could be transmitted culturally rather than biologically. If one knew the right sort of Greek, read the right books and exercised in the nude, then one could become a Greek.

The first textual critic to emerge in an environment of scholarly discourse that could institutionalize his methods appears to have been Zenodotus of Ephesus, the first chief librarian at Alexandria.[60] The primary object of his labor was Homer: the irony of the fact that he was attempting to create the "true text" of an oral poet never dawned on him. Likewise, the notion that authors are incapable of mistakes appears to have become an unacknowledged principle of the endeavor to improve the text that one has in front of one. If there were errors in a text, they were introduced by others and had to be removed. The process of textual criticism, as Zenodotus and his successors envisioned it, involved the careful study of diverse texts, the history of their language, and the production of a new text that was both free from accretion and was properly organized. Zenodotus's pioneering effort failed to convince on many points of detail, but the solidification of "technical" methods for the study of the texts that he set in motion was critical. It is likely that the "fixing" of the Homeric vulgate was indeed influenced by another librarian of Alexandria, Aristarchus.

At roughly the same time that Zenodotus was at work on the text of Homer, the earliest works of Latin literature came into being. However, the idea that they should be passed along in versions that were as true to an autograph as possible was not born with them.[61] Suetonius preserves a story about the way that the notion of "grammatical science" arrived at Rome in the mid-second century. Implicit in the story are some basic assumptions about the way that Latin literature came into being, the task of the grammarian, and the circulation of books:

> The first person who brought the study of grammar to the city, in my opinion, was Crates of Mallos, a coeval of Aristarchus, who was sent to Rome by king Attalus between the second and third Punic wars at about the time of Ennius's death. When he broke his leg, falling into a sewer-hole in the region of the Palatine, he gave numerous lectures during the whole time of the embassy and his recovery, held frequent discussions, and left an example for our people to follow. Still, they imitated him only to the extent that they carefully reviewed poems that were as yet little known to the public, being the work either of dead friends or of some others of whom they approved, and made them known to others through reading and commenting upon them: thus C. Octavius Lampadio divided the *Bellum Punicum* of Naevius into seven books (it had previously been set forth in a single volume with continuous writing), as Q. Vargunteius later did with the *Annales* of Ennius (*De gramm.* 2).[62]

As we have already seen, there is an assumption here that authors naturally lose control of their texts, and that grammarians reorganize them for their readers; with authors whose work had been around for a while, this could also mean that the grammarian had to remove mistakes added by copyists. Galen, who fancied himself an excellent judge of what Hippocrates wrote, claimed that he did not know how many people had commented upon the master's works, but he did know that they had altered the text. His answer was thus to search out the oldest commentaries and work from them (*In Hipp. Epid.* VI *comment.* proemium). Good writers of commentaries preserved what was written, while solving difficulties through some small addition or subtraction (*De diff. resp.* 3.2). As there could be errors introduced into his work by scribes who had incorporated his marginalia by mistake, Hippocrates's scribes could have done the same thing. These errors were retained because earlier scribes were not so quick as modern ones to change an old reading, or make good an omission (VII 892.7–16 Kuhn).

Changes made in the course of transmission are inevitable, especially in an age where books were, for the most part, created through private initiative. If a person wanted a copy of something, it would be unusual to be able to go to a bookseller and pull it off a shelf. Booksellers themselves might not always be interested in parting with the copies of the books that they had, unless the manuscript could command a high price as a result of the special quality of its production, or could be connected with a famous individual (or could be claimed to be such; the second century AD seems to have been a great age of antiquarian forgery, as readers of Latin decided that their "classic" literature was Augustan or earlier).[63] The more typical process was to write to a friend who had a copy and ask for the desired book to be reproduced, or to have a library text copied. Under such circumstances, people were not always as careful as they might be, or less restrained than they might be about changing things. Quintilian complains that people who copied old books changed archaic spellings, and of people who rewrote the first line of Livy's preface because they did not like the fact that it began with an hexameter.[64]

Authors could not only lose control of their texts, they could also lose control of their identities. Implicit in the process of discovering what had been added to a text is another process: the determination of true authorship. The point of Zenodotus's work on the text of Homer was to remove things not written by Homer. As the practice of claiming authority for one's own productions by passing them off as the work of a respected person in the past was extremely common in the Greco-Roman world, grammarians also became the arbiters of what was really by a person, and what was not. The story with which Galen opens his work on his own books is especially revealing in this regard. One day, so he tells us, he visited a bookshop in Rome where a prospective buyer was examining a book that was allegedly by Galen himself. The buyer insisted that a *philologos* be summoned to authenticate the volume. The *philologos* duly arrived and pronounced it a fake, on the grounds that Galen could not have written something that showed such poor knowledge of Greek. It was Galen's hope that *philologoi* such as this one would continue to care for his legacy, as he had cared for that of Hippocrates.[65]

The problem of public documents

A second variety of "eyewitness" evidence is the record of a public document or other act of state, either preserved in its entirety or summarized
by a second author, or edited for inclusion in another work. Suetonius
and Aulus Gellius, for example, preserve letters written by Augustus to
various family members. Once it has been determined that they were
not quoting forgeries, these sections of their work should be treated as
eyewitness accounts, though the absence of the full corpus of Augustus's
letters means that we cannot know how the texts we have fit into the
broader context of his written legacy, and we cannot know if he edited
his letters or if they were edited by a successor, or simply collected
according to no general principles of organization.

More serious problems may arise in cases such as Eusebius's quotation
of letters by the emperor Constantine. While it is no longer reasonable to
think that Eusebius forged these texts himself, the use of these texts is
complicated by the fact that we lack a context for them in Constantine's
overall production.[66] The severity of this problem may be seen in the fact
that, while the documents quoted by Eusebius should leave no doubt as to
the emperor's religious inclinations, a city in Italy could still write to him
in the last year of his life asking if it could erect a temple in his honor.
Constantine's response, which is without parallel elsewhere, can only be
interpreted in light of evolving Christian doctrine concerning the involve-
ment of Church members in civic cult. It is also notable that when he
writes to this city, he makes no reference to his Christianity, while when he
writes to an avowedly Christian community he refers to its inhabitants as
"partisans of our sect," where the Latin word for sect (*secta*) is one that is
used of any philosophic group.[67] Furthermore, we also need to be aware
that Constantine's role in drafting these texts is itself problematic.
Although all imperial legislation was issued as a first-hand communication from the emperor, the texts that have come down to us all emanate
from the office of the quaestor of the sacred palace. This may explain
why the closest parallel to Constantine's statement in a letter to the
Church of Alexandria that issues connected with the divinity of Christ
ought never to be discussed appears in Diocletian's edict against the
Manichaeans.[68] Do we therefore have Constantine, and insight into his
view of intellectual problems connected with his faith, here? Or do we
have the stock language of the chancery?

The question of how to handle legal texts from the Roman world is a
subject for another book in this series. For present purposes, it is enough
to observe that we need always to be aware of the hand of the compilers

of the Codes and other works that preserve these verbatim records. People did not collect documents for a single purpose. The authors of the Codes were interested in specific points of law, and simply quoted sections of texts that were relevant to their concerns.[69] We may use their efforts for purposes which were never intended, but we must always do so with care. The same is true of any other second-hand citation of a document. In some cases it is possible to reconstruct the circumstances under which a certain text was written, but in many cases we cannot, and what is more, we cannot always know what impact the statement had.

The same caveats must attend records of other sorts of communication. We hear of a great number of public acts through the work of narrative historians who appear to have read the texts that they are discussing, but the more that we know about individual documents, the more conscious we must be of selective reporting. Tacitus's account of the funeral honors for Germanicus displays some verbal parallels with the three partial versions of the text that have survived on bronze tablets from Italy and Spain.[70] It also omits any mention of major portions of these documents. Thus Tacitus tells us nothing about the extensive changes made in the procedures governing voting in the *comitia centuriata*, and reveals nothing of the several steps that went into the composition of such a decree: a letter to the emperor inviting him to select from the honors proposed in the senate, the letter from the emperor indicating his selection, the passage of the senate's decree and the final vote on the matter by the Roman people. He could take knowledge of this process for granted amongst his immediate audience. More significant is his handling of the subsequent trial of Piso, an event that has recently been illuminated by the discovery of multiple copies of the final disposition of the case in the Senate.[71] There are numerous points of contact between the official version of Piso's deeds, preserved on the inscription, and the narrative in Tacitus's *Annales*. But there also appears to be a tendency to explain away some of Piso's misdeeds. While Tacitus is by no means an apologist for Piso, he mitigates the force of the charges by adopting the suggestion that Piso was acting on secret orders from Tiberius, and mentioning the tradition that he was duped at the trial by Sejanus (*Ann.* 3.15.1). As Werner Eck has suggested, the rehabilitation of Piso's family under the later Julio-Claudians may have drawn attention to "facts" that were needed to supplement the official version. They may not have been true facts – they almost certainly were not – but Tacitus felt that they were at least as important as some things that could be found in documents.[72]

Illustrative evidence

Depending upon the question that one asks, all evidence, even factually inaccurate evidence, from antiquity is "illustrative" in that it may matter more to the historian that a person in antiquity could say whatever is in a text than that this person actually saw it happen. A legal text such as Diocletian's edict on the Manichaeans contains material that reflects on the development of attitudes towards Persia and "eastern wisdom" in general as well as on a specific problem.[73] Constantine's edict restricting "abduction marriage" is similarly informative both about an otherwise unattested act of government and the broader subject of social customs in the countryside.[74] Augustine's *Confessions* can be read as a guide to the social history of the later fourth century as readily as they can be seen as either an autobiography or work of philosophy. The work of any narrative historian is informed by the social and political realities of the author's class and situation. But to stress the homogeneity of "textualization" is to risk insensitivity to the different ways in which ideologies are expressed. The vast bulk of surviving literature is of a very different nature than that which was discussed in the previous section in that it is not "event oriented," and it differs from the historical narratives that will be the subject of the next chapter, for those texts are composed according to their own generic rules, and play a different role in the reconstruction of ancient history. Narrative histories, however composed, offer a chronological context for other texts, both in antiquity and now.

The point at issue in this chapter is the problem of contextualizing texts, either factual or fictional, that are not directly connected with a specific event. Such texts may include technical manuals, or philosophic dialogues as well as some occasional poetry and a variety of forms of oratory; novels and epic. The questions connected with the use of such evidence are often related to broad social structures and institutions. In this context, the explanation for Caesar's crossing of the Rubicon is less interesting than the connection between his action and the structure of politics in his generation, or what perceptions of his act in later generations can tell us about the way that the past was imagined and reconstructed. The outcome of Clodia's complaint against Caelius Rufus may be less important as a point of Roman law or political history than for what the event can tell us about the power of aristocratic women in her generation, or Cicero's depiction of appropriate gender roles.

Among the difficulties that historians, ancient and modern, encounter in using evidence of this sort include the multiplicity of possible interpretations and irrelevant or inaccurate citation, the latter problem often stemming from the "dumping" of note cards into a single paragraph without rechecking the original context. It is crucial to keep the perspective of the author in view. If a person is trying to describe Roman dining practice and chooses to quote passages from Petronius's *Satyricon*, this person had better be very clear that it is a satire. There are few ways to irritate a reader more rapidly than by asserting, for instance, that Roman newly-weds celebrated their wedding night with the anal penetration of bride by groom on the basis of a line in Plautus, or that a Christian text of the second century AD necessarily reflects the attitudes of gentile society.[75] Ignatius of Antioch appears to have thought that being torn apart in the arena was a tremendously exciting prospect, but the average polytheist may have thought that he was a lunatic (Ig. *Ep. ad Rom.* 5.3).

The most serious difficulty with all of our literary evidence from the Roman world is that it derives from a very restricted class. It is almost exclusively male, and almost exclusively rich. As we have already seen, literature circulated very slowly in the Roman world, the Latin literary canon dated from a very different period from the Greek, and the diffusion of literature was anything but uniform. If a scholar wants to reconstruct the attitudes of a peasant, this scholar is going to get into trouble very quickly with literary texts. These texts may impose attitudes upon peasants and other members of the lower classes that were antithetical to them; and, while there are ways to test for the dissemination of upper class attitudes throughout society, primarily through the study of inscriptions and papyri, even the most careful testing may still yield a very incomplete picture.[76] There are also cases where attitudes that were distinctively non-classical could begin to spread upwards throughout society. The rise of Christianity was easily the most important historical phenomenon in the history of the first four centuries AD: the transformation of the eschatological predictions of a Jewish Rabbi into a Mediterranean religion was without parallel and is not readily explicable in terms of the "trickle down" models of social organization that are often fundamental to the study of Roman institutions. The study of Judaism in the empire must also serve to remind us that there were significant communities that did not easily share in the culture of the urbanized elite.

The problem of perspective in dealing with the bulk of our texts becomes more complex as questions broaden. The historian who is interested in the religion of the upper classes at Rome will turn with glee to a work such as Cicero's *Concerning Divination* or Lucretius's *Concerning the Nature of Things*. This historian should also be concerned with the meaning of the dialogue as a form of literature, the relationship between Lucretius and Epicurus, and evidence for abuse of the religious conventions of the age by Cicero's colleagues.[77] If this same historian then turns to the broader question of the way that the inhabitants of the city of Rome saw their relationship to the gods in the lifetime of Cicero, these works will not be nearly so helpful, and may occlude distinctions that need to be drawn between aristocratic and sub-aristocratic culture. The problem will grow all the more severe if the subject becomes religion at Rome from Sulla to Nero. Here the question of profound shifts in attitude may become important, and if that is so, the value of the *Concerning Divination* as evidence changes. The age of Augustus followed on from that of Julius Caesar and Cicero, which suggests that the value of proper observation of the state religion was enhanced rather than destroyed by the events of the 50s BC, and that even members of Cicero's own class may have become less comfortable with the easy skepticism evident in his dialogue: the civil wars could be taken as proof of how the gods felt about the way things were going.[78] And it was the Roman people, the humble inhabitants of the city rather than the exalted members, that first decided that the murdered Julius Caesar was actually a god. So too the Roman people turned to Sibylline verses after a great fire destroyed Rome in AD 64 to express their feelings about Nero, who many blamed for the disaster, just as centuries before many had turned to the *carmina Marciana*, oracular verses bearing on the disasters that Rome was suffering at the hands of Hannibal.[79]

Another basic problem with "descriptive texts" that confronts the historian who is concerned with "what happened" rather than what people thought about what happened, is that when they refer to events in the public sphere, it is often very hard to decide just what value to assign to their information. In these cases we are dealing with perceptual problems identical to those raised by "eyewitness" texts. Did the author know what he was talking about, and why would this author choose to describe the event in the way that he did? A passage from Cicero's *Republic*, discussing the tribunate of Tiberius Gracchus in 133 BC, is a case in point. Some scholars have pressed the remark that the result of Gracchus's legislation was that "our allies and the Latins are roused against us, treaties have been broken, seditious triumvirs are plotting some new villainy daily" to provide evidence for the contents of Gracchus's agrarian bill (in this case to prove that Italians were included along with Roman citizens in the land distributions).[80] Others would simply regard this as an exaggerated remark that is appropriate in context to the speaker. Although we know that Cicero took care to get the correct characters in his dialogues, it is anything but likely that the absolute historical accuracy of each point was a matter of urgent concern to Cicero in this context.

Drama and other forms of poetry are different sorts of descriptive texts, and here too immense care needs to be taken in the evaluation of any work or part of a work. How, for instance, should the role of a slave such as Chabrias in Plautus's *Casina* be viewed? Should the dominant role that he plays in the humiliation of his master, Lysidamus, be seen as a reflection of the freedom that was possible for a slave? Or should more attention be paid to the horrible punishments with which the overseer Olympias threatens him? Should the negative portrayal of tyranny in Seneca's *Thyestes* be read as a veiled commentary on Neronian tyranny, or as a sign of interest in the subject, even in Nero's court? To what extent can a remark such as that attributed to the fictional Maternus in Tacitus's *Dialogue Concerning Oratory* be used to decide the issue? When Maternus observes that if he had left anything out of his *Cato* (which is said to have offended those in power at the time), it could be found in the *Thyestes* that he was even then writing, he gives the plain impression that such mythological dramas could contain scarcely veiled discussions of the contemporary political situation (Tac. *Dial.* 3.3). But is this relevant to Seneca? In my view, the answer must be no: we cannot use a fictional piece of literature to analyse the intent of an author whose works cannot be firmly dated. Since we cannot know more than this, all we can say is that despotism was an acceptable subject for literary discourse under the Julio-Claudians; and we cannot know why Maternus's play could have been found offensive, because it never existed. We are in much better shape with a speech that was actually delivered by the orator Libanius, containing sections that were critical of the (deceased) Caesar Gallus. It had to be delivered before different audiences, so that only Libanius's closest friends could hear what he really had to say, and the full version was never circulated. The disgraced ruler still had too many friends amongst the living (Lib. *Ep.* 283 [Foerster]).

Maternus's remark, and Libanius's actual experience, only serve to remind us that, under some circumstances, just about any form of litera-ture could be regarded as treasonous. So too a passage in Suetonius's *Caligula* serves to remind us that one person's treason is another person's classic. The Senate ordered that the historical works of Cremutius Cordus be burned by the aediles after he committed suicide to forestall conviction on the charge that he had expressed treasonous sentiments in them.[81] Given the way that books circulated in antiquity, this sort of action was purely symbolic, and may have involved no more than the incineration of copies to be found in libraries. It was Caligula who decreed that copies could be circulated again, and no one at the time believed that the books really had much to do with Cordus's fate. He was notorious for making rude remarks about Aelius Sejanus, the powerful praetorian prefect of Tiberius.[82] The restoration of his work was as symbolic as its removal: Caligula was making a point about his uncle.

The cases of Maternus and Cremutius Cordus are linked with one of the greatest problems connected with the use of literature to reconstruct the mentality and imagination of an age. This is the selection of the appropriate paradigm. Well before modernism, or postmodernism, relativism or objectivity, the use of internal and external paradigms for the study of history had been an issue. An internal paradigm assumes solutions from within the existing data set (e.g. ancient texts); an external paradigm introduces questions and methods from other disciplines in the hope that these may illuminate otherwise intractable issues. One reason that Gibbon's *Decline and Fall of the Roman Empire* had the impact that it did in 1776, and is still read today, is that Gibbon was able to fuse the internalist traditions of *érudits* like Le Nain de Tillemont with the *philosophe* tradition of Montesquieu and Voltaire. A major point of his autobiography is to show how the total life experience of the historian contributed to the history. On the other hand, the great contribution of August Böckh was to systematize knowledge of antiquity, to gather the evidence so that it would be possible to answer basic questions about the structure of the Athenian economy or the Athenian year.

In the course of the nineteenth and twentieth centuries, as technical historiography confronted the natural sciences and, later, the emergent social sciences, the dialogue has taken on many new forms. Prior to the emergence of the social sciences, one of the most significant new tools of analysis was offered by Marxism. By calling attention to the economic underpinnings of social structures and ideologies, Marxist historians opened up many novel forms of inquiry. Internalists might deplore this as a form of intrusive "presentism" far removed from the explicit concerns of the texts. There are cases where this criticism may well be justified, but there are others where it is not. As an intellectual position from which to initiate debates, Marxism has proven extremely fruitful, creating a place for the discussion of working classes and popular culture that had not been possible before.[83] Nor has all of this work been notably doctrinaire in its approach. Richard Cobb's brilliant analysis of Parisian police archives is "Marxist" essentially in that it is a study of the lower classes, just as *The Great Fear of 1789: Rural Panic in Revolutionary France* by Cobb's teacher, Georges Lefebvre, can be read without the aid of a copy of *Das Kapital* to hand.[84] E.P. Thompson, the author of an extraordinary study of the English working class, went so far as to distinguish between the Marxism of Marx (what he referred to as the Marxism of closure) and a tradition derivative from Marx, of open investigation and critique.[85] Indeed, Thompson's fellow traveler, Eric Hobsbawm, has suggested that the real influence of Marxist thought upon the writing of history is evident in what he would term Marxian, or "vulgar-Marxism." This "vulgar-Marxism" embraces seven main elements (although experience suggests that one does not have to indulge all seven in order to join the club). These elements are:

1   the economic interpretation of history, a belief that the economic factor is the fundamental one;
2   a model of base and superstructure, ordinarily viewed as a simple relation of dominance;
3   class interest and class struggle, albeit often defined without great precision;
4   historical laws and historical inevitability, in some ways the most controversial (dubious) tenet, but one that reflects Marx's own insistence on a systematic and necessary development;
5   specific subjects derived from Marx's own interests (e.g. a history of capitalism);
6   specific subjects of investigation derived from the interests of movements associated with Marx's interests (e.g. histories of peasants, rioters, bandits);
7   a strong view of the limitations of historiography that undermines notions of strict historical objectivity.[86]

Marxism has had a rather less positive image in the United States than in Europe. Prior to the Second World War, charges of Marxism, which could be equated with the evil of "present-mindedness" were leveled against relativists like Charles Beard. After the war, it became something of a catchword to designate forms of historical writing that violated the then dominant "objectivist" orthodoxy.[87] It continued to be problematic even after Thompson's *History of the English Working Class* made it respectable to write from an openly Marxian perspective, rapidly being confused with broader categories of social history, and then confused with virtually any sort of thinking that avowedly conservative historians or politicians did and do not like.[88] On the other side of the coin, Marxist historians have complained that new forms of social history, written without an overt interest in politics, have served to further the agenda of those conservative elements precisely because they are not interested in politics.[89]

Another form of history, emphasizing social structures rather than political events, the history of collectives rather than individuals, and drawing strength from studies outside the discipline of history rather than from within, began to make itself felt with particular force in the English speaking world at about the same time as the Marxian studies of Thompson and Hobsbawm began to have a broad impact. The school of thought was associated with a journal founded by Lucien Febvre and Marc Bloch in 1929, *Annales d'histoire économique et sociale*. The journal became the organ of a new school of thought, and in the 1950s and 1960s its presiding genius was Fernand Braudel.

Although it is fair to say that the work of Braudel, both as an historian in his own right and as an organizer of intellectual activity, elevated the Annales school to international prominence, the story begins much earlier.[90] It is perhaps best to pick up the thread with the arrival of Marc Bloch and Lucien Febvre in Strasbourg, newly recovered from Germany after the First World War, in 1920. Both were premodern historians, though both defined their subjects with extraordinary breadth, and sought to break down what they regarded as artificial barriers between disciplines. They were interested in the study of "modes of feeling and thought," and the interplay between physical geography and human society. It was Febvre who took the young Braudel under his wing, and encouraged a study that went well beyond any of his own in Braudel's *La Méditerranée et le monde méditerranéan à l'époque de Philippe II* (*The Mediterranean and the Mediterranean World in the Age of Philip II*).

The great strength of Braudel's approach in *The Mediterranean and the Mediterranean World in the Age of Philip II*, and his subsequent three volume work, *Civilisation matérielle et capitalisme* (rendered in English as *Civilization and Commerce*), lay in his ability to describe phenomena that moved at different speeds. In *The Mediterranean and the Mediterranean World in the Age of Philip II*, Braudel opens with the slow pace of geographic change, the *longue durée*, and then moves to more deliberate processes of social structures, before turning to the history of events, *l'histoire événementielle*. In *Civilization and Commerce*, the three speeds of history are "material civilization," "economic life" and "capitalist mechanisms." The different time frames interact with each other through *conjonctures*, a word that Braudel used to designate the connection between diverse, but simultaneous movements.[91]

The greatest importance of Braudel's work lay beyond the books, splendid though they are. Braudel tended to treat statistics as a form of decoration rather than as crucial data, and he had little interest in the history of culture.[92] But neither he nor his associate, Ernest Labrousse, stood in the way of others who had interests and skills that they lacked, so long as the latter subscribed to the essential program of the *Annales* school; to write a new form of history through the integration of disciplines, turning the paths marked out by his predecessors into highways.[93] While not a Marxist, he allowed that studies influenced by Marxism had value; while not an anthropologist, he allowed that anthropology had a place in history. Thus, in recent years a combination of the Annalists with followers of Marxist traditions has opened the way to broad new alliances between history and the social sciences. Foucault followed upon the heels of Braudel; Geertz and Sahlins impinged upon the historiographic consciousness in the wake of Hobsbawm and Thompson to reinforce trends and tendencies that had long been features of the profession.[94]

The importation of methods from other disciplines, and the refinement of those methods, is a critical feature of historiography. So too is the dialogue between internalist and externalist modes of thought, even though the level of debate has often attained the level of the downright vitriolic. It has even become conventional in some corners of the North American historical profession to write of the collapse of methodological consensus within the discipline as the "end of history."[95] Such rhetoric is not notably productive, and obscures the main point, which is that methods must be evaluated by the results they produce. As Lawrence Stone has observed, the influence of the social sciences has had a number of valuable effects on anglophone historiography (in this case it is fair to say that the influence extended to both sides of the Atlantic). The first of these was to force historians to be more precise about their assumptions, and the second was to force them to be more explicit about their terminology. Having actually to define "feudalism," or a "slave system," "middle class" or "aristocracy," historians were led to greater precision in all areas. Further contributions were to help define problems and research strategies, and, where relevant, to introduce quantification in place of adjectives. Finally, Stone would suggest that the social sciences offered a new series of hypotheses against which to test the evidence of the past.[96] If a paradigm drawn, for instance, from symbolic anthropology serves to illuminate the role of ritual as a unifying factor in a society, then it is helpful.[97] If the evidence can be found, the data set created, that will enable statistical study of the Roman population, and for this to be placed in the context of the study of other populations, that is a step forward.[98] So is the analysis of Livy's use of source material in Book 6.[99] Just as G.E.M. de Ste. Croix has shown that the study of society through the relationship between the dominant means and mode of production can illuminate issues that are not obviously economic,[100] the countless philological studies of Louis Robert have brought life to ancient texts that would not have been possible by other means. Marxist analysis will not explain the workings of a Greek festival in anything like the way that Robert's study of an inscription from the Letoon near Xanthus has done, or enable one to understand the impact of the oracular snake of Abonuteichos in the second century AD in the way that Robert did through the study of coins, inscriptions and images.[101]

It is always worth looking at the way that paradigms are selected, and in this case it may be particularly useful to review (albeit more briefly than may be desirable), paradigms that have influenced the study of two rather different literatures of the Roman empire: the Latin literature of the Augustan age, and the Greek literature of the second century AD. In one case the issue is the impact of tyranny upon literature, the other is that of colonial regimes upon conquered peoples. Are these the correct paradigms to use? They are forceful because they are "relevant," but do they do justice to the experience of the diverse inhabitants of the Greco-Roman world? And how can we know?

There can be no question, as many scholars have seen, that Vergil's picture of Rome's history in the *Aeneid* is anything but rosy. Aeneas is a complicated figure; he is not always the epitome of human virtue, and the new society that he is to found in Italy will emerge after a bloody war. But does this mean, as some would have it, that Vergil "subverts" his own work, or that his message is in some sense "anti-Augustan" in spirit? The critical issue is complicated by the tendency of modern scholarly discourse to bifurcate into rival camps whereby the "only logical conclusion" that can be drawn from point A is point B, when point B is dictated by "critical stance" rather than text. In a splendid analysis of Vergilian criticism, Ralph Johnson showed how two schools of thought, "optimists" and "pessimists", developed in the years after the Second World War. In this analysis, he makes clear the tendency of scholars who were capable of a brilliantly nuanced study of a text as one pole of their analysis to rely on controversial secondary literature for the other.[102] Subsequent scholars have tended to apply the conclusions of this school to other Latin authors, both Augustan and post-Augustan, as if the circumstances of one generation should automatically be true of another. Is this the best way to proceed?

If Vergil questions the value of heroism, does this necessarily mean that he is questioning the achievement of Augustus? If some people saw Augustus as a bloodthirsty tyrant, does this mean that their view was a majority view or that Vergil necessarily shared it? Similarly, if the tone of the preface to Livy's history is pessimistic, should this be read as "subverting" passages where he explicitly praises Augustus? If Velleius Paterculus presents the history of the first century BC as a series of dreadful civil wars from which Augustus finally saved the Roman people, does his less than positive picture of pre-Augustan Roman history "subvert" the image of Rome as having been built by the great men commemorated in Augustus's forum? These views are possible, and there are times when work on Latin literature appears destined to prove that every surviving text from the Julio-Claudian and Flavian period is in some sense "opposition" literature because it does not strictly toe "the imperial line." Different questions might yield different answers. Livy, Vergil and Velleius need not then be seen as closet Solzhenitsyns, producing Aesopian versions of the Roman experience destined to fool all contemporary readers as to their real meaning.

Complex literary forms do not readily lend themselves to criticism based on simple polarities. Students need to read them as part of ongoing discussions, as participating in a discourse. It is far more interesting to be able to reconstruct the image of Roman history that existed in the minds of educated people at the time of Augustus's establishment of the principate than it is to simply assume that Augustus was evil and that every author we choose to admire is morally obligated to see things this way. From a methodological point of view, it is obviously preferable if a critical feature of an analytical tool is not based upon an unprovable assumption.

Indeed the questions about Rome's past that emerge in authors whom we know to have been widely read in Roman society may help explain the peculiar form that the Augustan regime took, with its stress on restoration, renovation and, above all, peace. Romans appear, on the whole, to have held a linear view of historical progression. Such views are very dangerous in that the line is rarely, if ever, flat. It has a very unpleasant tendency to head either up or down. In the age of Augustus, very few people questioned the notion that the virtues that had enabled the Roman people to conquer the Mediterranean world had dissipated. People could, and did, debate crucial turning points: the return of Manlius Vulso's army from the east in 187 BC, the destruction of Corinth and Carthage in 146 BC, the murder of Tiberius Sempronius Gracchus in 133 BC, or Sulla's return from the east in 82 BC.[103] Some, like Sallust, could even have it more than one way: pointing to Sulla when it was rhetorically useful in his monograph on Catiline, and to the fall of Carthage (with the Gracchi thrown in for good measure) in his *Jugurtha*. In other words the prevailing historical paradigm at Rome was precisely the opposite of the "Whig" paradigm of progress towards a higher good that dominated Anglo-American historiography for so long.[104]

Augustus sought to provide another turning point that would send the line heading upwards. Not everyone saw it his way, and people continued to debate the point at which the monarchy could be said to have begun. Cassius Dio quite explicitly states that the monarchy began in 31 BC.[105] The vehemence with which he states this view suggests controversy. So do other texts. Standard "popular" accounts of imperial history such as those that appear in two Sibylline oracles, suggest that the monarchy began with Caesar.[106] So too, by implication, does Suetonius when he chose Julius rather than Augustus as the first of his twelve Caesars. Tacitus seems to have decided that the death of Augustus marked a major turning point in the history of power, and then to have repented of this opinion which appears to have been influenced by his view of the connection between literature and politics.[107] Even before this, he had written that the Republic had been destroyed by Marius and Sulla (Tac. *Hist.* 2.38). Velleius Paterculus sees Augustus as the culmination of a process by which individuals dominated the Roman scene, suggesting that he too thought that the age of Marius and Sulla was critical. While Sulla was abominable, Augustus was good.

Issues change from generation to generation, or even faster than that. Paul Zanker's brilliant study of the image of Augustus stands as a crucial reminder that the monarch was constantly changing the way that he appeared to the public.[108] Did popular perception also change? Certainly we can see that the images of Augustus influenced choices in household design; public monuments could influence the images on dinner ware. Do changing tastes reflect changing perceptions? We cannot assume that people never changed their views. Was Ovid always dubious about Augustus? After his exile he alludes to a poem and a mistake that led to his misfortune. He clearly did not aim to get himself exiled, and after his exile, he retained close connections with associates of Germanicus.[109] The fate of his poetry suggests that he did not continue to be regarded as inherently "anti-imperial" or subversive. Are we therefore entitled to read the disappointment (to use no harsher term) with the Augustan regime that is obvious in *Tristia* 2 as paradigmatic of his attitude towards the regime throughout?[110] What is more, are these complicated issues of one person's personal psychological state more important than the evidence that Ovid's exile poetry can provide for the communication of imperial ideology between Rome and the fringes of empire? In the latter case we are on much firmer ground than the former, for whatever one thinks of his tone, the fact of his information is indisputable.[111] The same is true of Lucan. Did everyone who went to Nero's parties think that he was a monster? Or did they adopt this view once they stopped getting invitations? Or can we know? Is his *Civil War* better read as a veiled assault upon the whole concept of monarchy, or a trenchant discourse on the horrors of civil war, and testimony to the fact that *bellum civile* remained the political nightmare of Roman society? Aside from his participation in the plot against Nero in AD 65, the most blatant insult that he offered Nero was to recite a line of the emperor's poetry while defecating in a public toilet (Nero Fr. 5 Courtney). It is more useful to write about the poem that we have than the personality that we have lost.[112]

In more general terms, it does appear that monarchy and civil war were topics that attracted a great deal more interest after Actium than before. Discussion of either was not inherently "oppositional" in that both civil war and the unique position occupied by Augustus were authorized as subjects of discourse by Augustus himself, and by his successors. An "authorized discourse" is an idealized form of communication that requires dialogue if it is to be effective.[113] If one is to discuss monarchy, then it is entirely likely that one will discuss tyranny as well. Such discussion may in fact be welcome, for its very existence may be taken as proof that the ruler is not, in fact, a tyrant himself. One of the most vicious satires directed at a Roman monarch, Seneca's *Apocolocyntosis*, although self-evidently an attack on the deified predecessor of the reigning emperor (Nero), is part of a program of ideological distancing from Claudius indulged by Nero's court. One of the great sins of Gnaeus Calpurnius Piso, who committed suicide as his defense on charges of treason was failing in AD 20, was that he had dared to incite a civil war, a form of conduct that had been ended for ever by Augustus and Tiberius (so we are told by an official source).[114] Discussion of civil war, and of its evils, lies at the heart of the Julio-Claudian monarchy. Julius Caesar himself had to remain an ambiguous figure, excluded from representations of dynastic groups, in part because what he did in crossing the Rubicon was wrong, even if the end result was for the good.

The issue of "opposition" has been raised in a rather different way in connection with Latin lyric and elegy on the subject of love, perhaps most significantly in a recent book by Elaine Fantham.[115] The point at issue here is once again the compromise between an "authorized discourse," in this case the public presentation of the Augustan princi-pate, and the forms of negative response that are defined by its very existence. The point being that if Augustus had advertised free love as the centerpiece of his public presentation, the natural response might well have been an appeal to "traditional values." Having set the terms of the discussion by defining permissible terms of dissent, the dominant partner in the discourse may then censor those forms of alternative discourse that lie outside the area of compromise that it has described. It might be one thing, therefore, for a poet to suggest that he was staying home in the arms of a lover while a friend went off to serve the state, entirely another to suggest that this was true of Augustus.

The ideology of public service and family duty that Augustus absorbed into his own self-presentation had defined its own opposite in the later years of the Republic (if not earlier). The Roman who went off to war and the government of provinces, remaining chaste as he did so, featured prominently in, for instance, Marcus Porcius Cato's presenta-tion of himself. It was rather less obviously a feature of Julius Caesar's. The young Caesar had adopted a mode of dress and cultivated a style of life that involved rumor as well as, almost certainly, the reality of affairs with many women.[116] The style of Cato marked him as a man of the establishment, then intimately connected with the victory of Sulla; that of Caesar marked him as the establishment's foe. When Catullus wrote of himself as the distraught lover, overcome with grief at the failure of his great love, or devoted to that passion, he was participating in the same discourse, albeit in a very different way.[117]

The inner and outer man were intimately connected in classical thought, and the process by which the ideal man was constructed was a very difficult one, involving years of training.[118] His opposite was the effeminate, likewise an idealized construct. One could play the game of masculinity in various ways, either striving to construct oneself as the ideal man, or implying aspects of the effeminate to lend tension to one's own performance of masculinity. Thus, as Maud Gleason has shown, the sophist Favorinus, who flourished in the first half of the second century AD, made use of his physical peculiarities (he was born without testicles) to create a particular style, to create new space for himself, in the world of competitive rhetoric.[119] Caesar may have allowed the suggestion that there was more to him than the staid aristocrat precisely because it made him all the more interesting, and his challenges to orthodoxy all the more significant. The skill that it took to make this work was very great indeed, for the standard discourse of Latin invective derives much of its force from the assumption that the effort of a man to show himself to be a proper person in public life could be undermined by the demonstration that he failed to live up to that image in private.[120] Although Cicero might attack the younger Cato precisely because the strength of his inflexible image made him inhuman, his usual tactic appears to have been to paint his foes as being failures in the game of true masculinity. Real men did not, like Cicero's Verres, dress up in purple cloaks and carouse on beaches. Real men did not, like Antony, drink so much at a party the night before that they vomited in the forum, and they certainly did not act like elegiac lovers with their wives; an inversion of the proper relationship in that it implied an excessive interest in carnality, especially as too much sex was bad for real men.[121] Augustus even appears to have gone so far as to claim that he abstained completely from sex when he was nineteen because it was bad for his voice and strength (*FGrH* 90 Fr. 129).

In the world of male achievement a successful insult was damaging.[122] Q. Caecilius Metellus Celer was outraged when he heard that Cicero had got a laugh in the Senate at his expense; Caesar said that the poem that Catullus had written about him and his associate Mamurra permanently damaged his reputation, and got truly angry when people suggested that he had been the passive partner of King Nicomedes of Bithynia.[123] What is at issue then in the discourse of Latin love poetry is not the reality of dissipation, but the creation of a *persona* who pursues an alternative to the public career; in a sense, it is a sort of invective directed against oneself. The form of the *propemptikon*, whereby the poet bids farewell to a friend who is traveling off on a tour of duty while he remains at home in the arms of a lover, may thus be read as the rejection of the public ethos.[124] The *paraclausithyron*, where the poet addresses the door of the house from which his lover has excluded him, is a confession of acts that would disgrace the public man. The man who gives himself over to the world of emotion is rejecting the man who puts service to the state before all other things; in Catullus 72, the love affair that he has is juxtaposed to the ideal married condition that the poetic *persona* envisioned. Elsewhere, the image of the poet as the master of the arts of love, master of all the tricks of the trade, self-consciously offers a connection between the poet and a procuress.[125]

The failed lover is a ruined man, the master of love is a mistress of prostitutes. Hardly the masculine Roman ideal. But does Latin love poetry, *a priori*, question the validity of the Augustan regime, an ideology laden with the image of the ideal male and his family, so much as it questions the parameters of the idealized discourse of public life? The form of this question is dictated by the dominant discourse. Such a rejection of the male ideal was not new with the emergence of the monarchy, and there were other, rather more obvious ways of rejecting the structures of aristocratic life. One could, for instance, become a gladiator, or act upon the stage, forms of rejection that are well attested, and, unlike the writing of love poetry, sanctioned as it was by tradition, were outlawed.[126]

The discourse of legitimacy that Augustus inherited shaped his presentation of himself. Recent studies of Augustan art have shown a much deeper pattern of reference to earlier traditions of self representation than had previously been recognized.[127] So too the discourse of rejection was well founded, both in conduct and literary form, well before the battle of Actium. The second book of Ovid's *Tristia* is perhaps most striking precisely because of the way that Ovid drives home the point that the rules that he is said to have broken were violated by others every day because they were not the real rules.[128] The discourse of the public man drew its strength from the dialogue with the discourse of its opposite.

"We pray for good emperors, put up with whomever we get."[129] The fact of the monarchy separates the generation of Cicero, where it was regarded as a possibility, from that of his son. But concern with this issue was not uniform throughout the empire, and the victory of Augustus did not transform social attitudes in an instant. The fact of the monarchy does not, for instance, occupy any place other than the coincidental in the Christian literature of the first century AD, or in that of any author who resided outside of the immediate ambit of the emperor. In turning to the literature of the Greek world, issues of cultural identity, negotiating local and provincial power structures, are far more important than the moral degeneration or improvement of Rome. And in all cases it was possible to think about things that had nothing to do with politics. As we have already seen, the evidence of book-owning and readership offered by the papyrological record suggest that most people who read books in the Roman world read old books.

It is possible to offer social critique that is not directly concerned with the fact of the monarchy. It is plain that the image of the poet as lover is at odds with the image of the ideal Roman devoted to public service. It may also be the case that the discourse of the Greek subject is more concerned with the discourse of other Greeks.

The Greek literature of the Roman empire, a far more extensive corpus than the Latin, must therefore be read in light of habits of reading and education that were forming even as Rome began to rise to dominance over the eastern Mediterranean in the second century BC. The single most important cultural movement in this era is the invention of a common Hellenic culture for the diverse peoples who fell under the sway of Alexander the Great and his successors, and the consequent cultural necessity for non-Greek peoples to adopt Greek forms to explain themselves in terms that were comprehensible to their new masters. Perhaps the most famous example of this process is the translation of Hebrew Scriptures into the Greek during the third century BC, but it was scarcely the only one. It was also an unusual one, as the straightforward translation of an indigenous text was rare. More common was the adaptation of Greek forms to tell traditional stories, and the search for a place in the Greek scheme of history for one's own people. The cultural archaism that this spawned is often, erroneously, taken to be a phenomenon of Roman rule and, sometimes as a reflection of the political inferiority of the "culturally superior" Greeks.[130]

The attribution of the cultural archaism of Hellenistic and Roman Greek literature to Roman domination may obscure more than it explains.[131] While it is obvious that different people felt differently about Rome – the view of a Jew in Palestine might be very different from that of a Jew in Sardis – is it possible to construct a single, overarching paradigm that accommodates all reactions? It is particularly curious in that the most commonly observed feature of "political" ethnography is the description of subject peoples in such a way that they are made to conform with the cultural ideals of the politically dominant society.[132] Precisely the opposite trend is evident in the Greek literature of the Roman world, where arguments are made in some detail, and accepted by the Romans themselves, that the Romans were really Greek. The most significant illustration of this tendency is Dionysius of Halicarnassus's *Roman Antiquities*, a work of the Augustan period. Nor was the situation static; indeed, it was so fluid that an attempt to distinguish a dichotomy between Greek and Latin culture in terms of subject and ruler fails to explain much of anything. In the fourth century AD, the most important Latin books were translations of Christian texts, while at the same time, Greek authors will refer to themselves as *Rhomaioi*.

The Greek literature in the Roman world is perhaps best studied outside of the context of imperial power and subject, and perhaps better studied in the context of the political significance of education. Common trends and aims in education created a politically dominant class in the cities of the Roman world that was remarkably homogenous in terms of its values and aspirations in either Greek or Latin. Education was a tool in the hands of its possessors that enabled them to exercise control over their environment and each other.[133] Men of letters could become extraordinarily powerful precisely because it was embarrassing for the leaders of Roman society not to be seen to appreciate them. At the same time, power could also accrue to eccentrics of limited or no education if they could convince people that their lifestyle was such that they were in direct contact with the divine. Power had many dimensions and pathways that the Roman state had to respect if it was to control them.

It is within the context of competing intellectuals that the satires of Lucian find a home next to the orations of Dio Chrysostom and Aelius Aristides.[134] Philostratus's hyper-competitive sophists may readily evoke the response of Pausanias: the past should be studied rather than invented.[135] A man named Celsus might write a fictional dialogue called *On True Doctrine* to evoke the extraordinary response of a Christian sophist named Origen, whose skill at invective was matched by his interest in textual criticism and philosophic deconstruction of the relationship between his God and that of God's son.[136] Centuries earlier, Polybius sought to establish himself as the pre-eminent authority on the western Mediterranean through his skill (not always as great as he claimed) at disentangling the truth from disparate accounts and vehement invective against his rivals. He watched the Roman conqueror of Carthage shed tears over the city that he was burning, and saw himself as thoroughly Achaean.[137] In the fourth century AD, the rhetorician Libanius trained polytheist and Christian alike in the oratorical skills needed to defend civic dignity against the encroachment of imperial officials. He also felt that he had to defend the culture that he had inherited against a new intellectual system that was gaining strength throughout his lifetime. Struggles changed, but the venue remained astonishingly constant: control of culture, the ability to define it and exploit it opened avenues of power between the rise of supra-regional states that followed upon the death of Alexander the Great and the collapse of the classical city state in the sixth century AD – venues that were unthinkable in the generation of Pericles.

The world of literature and high culture was not the only one in which people contended with one another. It would be wrong to think that all power flowed naturally to the well-educated. This is another of the problems with our evidence. When Herodes Atticus, arguably the richest inhabitant of old Greece in the later second century AD, launched into an intemperate invective before the emperor Marcus Aurelius, a praetorian prefect who appears to have had little sympathy with his lifestyle offered to plunge a sword into him (Phil. *V. Soph.* 561). The pinnacle of Augustine's rhetorical career appears to have been the opportunity to deliver a panegyric to an emperor (*Conf.* 6.9). Neither could hope to achieve the power held by members of the military establishment, whose accomplishments were infrequently of a literary variety. Many others may simply not have cared to try: recent work on demonic possession in antiquity has suggested that the poor could attract attention to their demands by foaming at the mouth.[138]

Anecdotes

It is very difficult indeed to measure Greco-Roman social attitudes. What did people really think about the emperor, or their husbands? No public opinion polls survive from antiquity, and there was no one who could take one. The best that can be hoped for is an impression. This tends often to result in accounts that consist of stories that the ancient author hopes are illustrative of more general trends. It is thus possible to produce an enormous amount of material that attracts contemptuous dismissal from some historians on the grounds that it is "anecdotal."[139]

Anecdotes are short stories that circulate about people and events even though the connection of their authors to those events is not clear. Indeed, it is not unusual for the same story to be told about more than one person, a phenomenon known as a "floating anecdote," an unfortunate phrase that implies that the story could control the way it was used. This is plainly absurd, and the condemnation of such stories as useless is often a mistake. Thus a story related by the third century AD historian Cassius Dio, about an old woman who approached the emperor Hadrian and demanded that he attend to her complaint, should not simply be dismissed as fantasy because it is very similar to stories told about the Macedonian kings Philip II and Demetrius the Besieger. A society's fictions can be an important guide to its attitudes; in this case, even though we are not required to believe that this story, or the others, may recount an actual event, it is still very valuable evidence for ancient attitudes towards monarchy. The monarch was supposed to answer his mail and to be attentive to the welfare of the lowly.[140] From the perspective of the subject it did not matter if the emperor did this himself, or a secretary did it: the important point is that it shows us that people might think of the emperor as representing a side of government that helped rather than exploited them.

It is significant as well that much of the literature that survives from the ancient world is essentially anecdotal by nature. People learned their behaviors by hearing stories about others. The vast Rabbinic literature of the Roman empire consists of the study of Jewish law through stories about what famous teachers had to say about it.[141] It also offers stories whose imagery reflects the way that people perceived the institutions around them. Modern studies of sub-literate and semi-literate societies can offer suggestions about the way that others in antiquity may have learned through listening as well.

From a methodological point of view, the use of stories as evidence for social mentality is not separated by any great space from the attempt to reconstruct social ambiance through simile and image. There is no description of a chariot race in the ancient world that conveys the emotions of a spectator nearly so vividly as Vergil's description of the boat race in Book Five of the *Aeneid*. There is no account of the conduct of fans on an ordinary day at the circus as compelling as Ovid's account of trying to encounter a potential lover in the stands.[142] There may be no more powerful image of the way that a Roman magistrate appeared before provincials than the Rabbinic text that describes Yahweh as if he were the magistrate cut off from the crowd behind his curtain deciding a case.[143] All these texts are anecdotal and impressionistic: but to exclude them from the study of the empire would be to lose a great deal.

Narrative

Seven original narrative histories have survived from the beginning of the third century BC to the later half of the fourth century AD. Two each are by Caesar and Josephus, one is by Eusebius, one is by Arrian and the last is by Herodian. Between them, they cover the history of the Jews from Abraham to the fall of Masada, a decade of Caesar's military activity, the Christian church from the crucifixion to Constantine, Alexander the Great's conquest of Persia, and the history of the Roman empire from 180–238 AD. The diversity evident in this collection is testimony first and foremost to the diversity of cultural experience in the Roman world: the most obvious thing, aside from completeness, that these books have in common is that none of them is a history of Rome written in Latin. The existence of four short histories written in the late fourth century for the education of imperial bureaucrats (whose total length is less than two hundred pages in modern critical editions) does nothing much to improve the situation. It is sobering to realize that the great works which form the basis of our knowledge of Rome's rise to empire, the histories of Livy and Polybius, are not preserved in their entirety, nor are both of Tacitus's histories of the first century AD, and much of Dio's history of Rome is known from later summaries.

The failure of major narrative histories to survive intact is a very serious problem, and the historian of the Roman world must consequently become familiar with the particular problems posed by "fragments." On a generous estimate, the texts that we have from the classical Greek and Roman world amount to something slightly more than 2.5 percent of what there once was, and it is impossible to write about this 2.5 percent without attempting to take account of the rest.[144] In doing so, it is worth noting that strong objections have been raised to this exercise precisely on the grounds that it requires a concentration on fragments, and a concentration on fragments obscures the study of the authors from whom the fragments are drawn.[145] This is true, but what is done is done, and it does no good to throw out the old because it does not conform with the new, and there is no need for there to be a conflict. The study of Plutarch's *Greek Questions* is not precluded by the study of fragments, the two operations are both features of an effort to understand the past.

The study of ancient history is littered with fragments of all sorts: incomplete papyri, broken inscriptions, shattered statuary, unprovenanced artifacts, incomplete texts and so forth. A fragment of an otherwise lost historian can be something known only from a single papyrus or inscription. The famous Parian Marble (where the text can be read) giving a chronology of Greek history from the earliest times to the period of Alexander's successors is an example of a fragmentary history on stone. The rather less famous *Chronicum Romanum* (inscribed on a stone found at Rome) is another, giving, as it is currently preserved, sections of Roman history in the 80s BC and a history of archaic Greece in the sixth century.[146] The second century AD *Chronicle* of Phlegon of Tralles (if the identification is correct) stems from quotations in various later texts and a papyrus found at Oxyrhynchus.[147] Fragments that are preserved in the manuscript tradition are quotations or summaries of authors whose work we do not now possess. There is no simple way to describe such relics. They might be allegedly verbatim quotations, or the statement that information on a topic can be found in the works of an author. A fragment might be presented as a summary of the work of an author, or follow upon the statement that "the following account is based upon the work of…." In most cases the question of where to draw the line between quotation, summary, and free composition is deeply problematic, and the handling of fragments by even the best of editors can be uneven. There is every reason to think that the bulk of Diodorus Siculus's *Universal History* for the fourth century down to 341 BC is based on the *Universal History* of Ephorus, and some reason to think that his account of the Successors to Alexander the Great is based on the work of Hieronymus of Cardia.[148] No one has yet printed several books of Diodorus as fragments of either historian, but what is very nearly a whole book of Diodorus has been printed as a fragment of Ctesias of Cnidus (*FGrH* 688 Fr. 1).

How close does a summary have to be before it counts as a fragment? If we have no original to test the fragment against, how certain can anyone be about the technique employed by one author in quoting another? The study of Tacitus offers many cautionary examples, among which the most obvious may be the speech that he places in the mouth of Claudius on the subject of the entrance of Gauls to the Roman senate. His account is arguably a "fragment" of Claudian oratory, and may be used to analyse another fragment, the section of the very same speech surviving on a bronze tablet from Lyons. But while Tacitus has caught the gist of the Claudian statement, he seems to have changed the form rather radically.[149] Livy offers a good deal of evidence for the contents of laws passed in the fourth century BC, a fundamental feature of our understanding of the "conflict of the orders," but how well does he do it? Different approaches to the question emerge from Rotondi's *Leges publicae populi Romani* and M.H. Crawford's *Roman Statutes*.[150] The nature of quotation is a fundamental issue in *Quellenforschung*, the study of an author's sources, of which the process of identifying fragments is a feature.

The definition of a fragment is inherently slippery, and the use of fragments by ancient historians is further complicated by the nature of the extant collections. Collections of fragments are a useful device in that they offer a context for quotations. Without them, one would be forced to review the contents of all classical literature to know what an author had to say about something, and who else was writing at the same time in related genres, a task made only slightly less daunting by readily searchable databases. But for all their convenience, computer databases cannot by themselves tell us what constitutes a fragment or a quotation, or offer a ready guide to other texts that might be relevant. Neither fragment collections, nor computer databases, can ever be more than a starting point. The original context of a quotation always needs to be examined, no matter how good the collection might be, and it is arguable that really good collections create problems in and of themselves.[151] As Ronald Syme remarked in reviewing T.R.S. Broughton's splendid *Magistrates of the Roman Republic*, "its precise and ready answers may encourage young and old to neglect the reading of Latin authors."[152]

Collections of fragments can influence the way that a subject is studied, and for the purposes of the present chapter it may well be useful to examine the nature and impact of collections of fragments upon the study of historiography. There are three that attempt to completeness in this regard. Two are essentially works of the nineteenth century. These are Müller's *Fragmenta historicorum graecorum* compiled from 1841 to 1872 and H. Peter's *Historicorum romanorum reliquiae*, which, although completed just before the author's death on 16 February 1914, reflects the thinking of his youth in the previous century.[153] Müller's work offers fragments of historians from the earliest period of Greek historiography to the sixth century AD in chronological order. For the fourth to sixth centuries AD it has still not been replaced, although there have been significant modern editions of five of the historians from this period.[154] Peter's work, which contains extensive discussions of the fragments that he collected, remains the only work dedicated to historians who were Roman citizens and wrote about their city in either Greek or Latin, and is organized chronologically. The third collection, now in the process of completion by a new board of editors, is Felix Jacoby's *Die Fragmente der griechischen Historiker*.[155]

Jacoby and ancient historiography

Jacoby's collection is organized in terms of genres of historical writing, with authors organized by date within each section. It is this organization, as well as the critical notes with which he equipped most of the authors he treats, that makes Jacoby's work just as fundamental to the student of the Roman world as it is to the student of Greek history. A substantial proportion of the authors whose works he collects are in fact writers of the imperial period, and the organization of the collection has implications for study of the discipline of classical historiography as a whole.

The centrality of Jacoby's work makes it necessary to examine his principles, and his final doubts about the project. The first point is that, in 1909, Jacoby believed that it was possible to draw clear links between different genres of the writing that he studied.[156] While his stemmatic approach, borrowed from textual criticism, is arguably open to serious question, his fundamental perception of the multiplicity of texts that fit the classical understanding of *historia* is unassailable.[157]

Given the breadth of his vision, it is perhaps a bit odd that Jacoby originally defined his position with a series of negative arguments. The first was that history did not derive, as Wilamowitz thought, from priestly chronicles; the second was that it defined itself in opposition to epic. His first historian was Hecataeus, the author of two seminal works, the *Genealogies* and *Description of the World*.[158] The *Description of the World* had prose predecessors of a sort (Euthymenes of Marseilles and Scylax of Caryanda), but these lacked the interest in ethnography that emerges in the very first lines of his history.[159] The *Genealogies* certainly had verse predecessors, but these lacked an interest in linking the past with the present that Hecataeus established as a field of historiographic endeavor, for it was this work that drew the boundaries for "historical space" that his successors accepted, and infused historical writing with the necessary element of criticism.[160] The fact of the *Genealogies* both prevented Herodotus from writing simply about the land of the east and west – it had already been done – and provided the model for writing about the reasons why they fought each other.

With the *Genealogies*, Hecataeus laid the foundation for three of the four types of historical writing that emerged in the fifth century BC: genealogy (mythography), ethnography and contemporary history.[161] The fourth variety, horography or local history, emerged from the practice of public record keeping in the states of Greece.[162] The descendants of the *Genealogies* include Hellenicus, Ephorus's idea of universal history and the whole notion of "tragic historiography."[163]

There are a couple of problems here. The first is that we know so little about either Scylax or Euthymenes that it is impossible to speak with anything like Jacoby's confidence about what they did, or did not, say. Second, in an important passage of his essay on Thucydides, Dionysius of Halicarnassus gives a list of historians whom he says lived either before or during the Peloponnesian war. The list probably derives from Theophrastus and is likely to have been used to illustrate a theory of the development of historiography in terms of prose style; hence the suggestion that Herodotus raised the art to a new level, and Thucydides did so again.[164] Jacoby rejected this list as inaccurate on the grounds that it depended upon "peripatetic theory" and thus placed local chroniclers alongside of genealogists at much too early a period.[165] Jacoby's argument for rejecting early dates for local chroniclers is no better than Theophrastus's argument in favor of it, or rather worse, since Theophrastus may actually have read the texts that he is discussing. Moreover, as recent work has shown that Herodotus was writing well into the 420s BC, and that there is good reason to think (independently of Dionysius) that a number of the historians whom Theophrastus mentions were writing either at exactly the same time as Herodotus, or even earlier, the stemmatic view that Jacoby espoused cannot be maintained.[166]

Jacoby's other stemma descending from the *Description of the World* includes Herodotus, Thucydides and specialized works on Greek history.[167] The reason for this is that Jacoby thought the ethnographic tradition gave rise to works on individual nations such as Xanthus of Lydia's *Lydian History*, and that these in turn gave rise to works that were concerned with the deeds of a people, and, more particularly, the deeds of a people at a particular moment in time.[168] Thus we can see the transformation of Herodotus from a writer of ethnography to the writer of the history of a war, and then the possibility of a work such as that of Thucydides. With Thucydides, we see a new kind of history: the tale of a single event. His successors are therefore the authors of "monographs" such as histories of the Sacred War in the fourth century, or individual moments of Hellenistic history, and, finally, Sallust in Latin. The development of the monograph is a parallel development to the growth of the form of literature that is best known to modern readers through Xenophon's *Hellenica*, or a book about the deeds of the Greeks over a part of their history: more than a war but less than a complete account. In this category we find works such as histories of the events during the lifetime of an individual such as Theopompus's *Philippica* or histories of Alexander the Great, or histories of an era such as that of Alexander's Successors. Biography is the final genre to emerge, again before the end of the fourth century BC, but later than the others.

The role of genealogy in creating a framework for the past was not lost upon Jacoby. He saw Hecataeus's *Genealogies* at the root of a strand of historical writing in its own right. This strand included universal history, and rhetorically improved "tragic historiography." The point here is that the *Genealogies* took in the whole Greek world rather than parts of it, and they were concerned with the time at which people lived. It was Ephorus in the fourth century BC who first attempted to write such a thing, and it was with Ephorus that the influence of another field began to be felt. This was the rhetorical school of Isocrates, and thus we begin the descent towards the "tragic" history that is attacked by Polybius. Well before Ephorus, and indeed before Thucydides, we have the development of the other family that emerged from the *Genealogies*. This is chronography. It begins to take shape with Hippias of Elis's work in the second half of the fifth century BC, and it concerns itself with the comparative chronology of the states of the Greek world. The comparative aspect distinguishes chronography from the chronologically arranged histories of individual states that constitute horography.[169]

Horography is the poor cousin of all other forms of historical writing.

It is local in orientation, lacks literary quality, and cannot possibly be descended from Hecataeus, for it is older.[170] A dim-witted elder sibling to other forms of history, even it did not lack for children in the form of the antiquarian literature of the Hellenistic world and the epideictic demonstrations of sophists about individual states that extend into the Roman empire.[171]

Where does it all end? As a practical matter, Jacoby decided that different genres could be cut off at different points. Most historiographic genres could end with the foundation of Constantinople, but this was not the case with all of them. Chronology had to be extended down to the decades before the Arab conquest, and he was well aware that the classical forms of historiography extended beyond the limits that he imposed upon them. But this was not the least of his problems. The initial plan of the work was ten volumes to be organized as follows in accordance with his theory:

I   testimonia and Hecataeus
II   genealogy
III   ethnography
IV   Greek contemporary history
V   chronography
VI   horography
VII   biography and literary history
VIII   geographical literature
IX   works whose contents is unclear.

He then changed his mind. His subsequent plan, and the one that survives into his great collection is:

I   genealogy and mythography
II   universal and contemporary history
III   ethnography and horography
IV   antiquarian history and biography
V   geography
VI   authors whose topic cannot be determined and theory of historical
       writing

Jacoby defined an approach to the entire subject of ancient historiography, and the fact of his collection (parts I–III are completed in multiple parts, amounting to many volumes) means that, to a greater or lesser degree, his approach is prescriptive. It is also complex. If one wants to contemplate the work of the third century AD historian Dexippus, one goes to the section on historians of individual periods and reads him in the context of other historians of similar ilk (*FGrH* 100). One does not read his work in other possible contexts, which is to say with writers of chronography and the history of imperial wars. Nor is this the only problem. In order to find any author, a person may either guess where Jacoby thought he belonged, or keep a copy of Volume IIIc numbers 709–856 with its index of authors to hand. One also needs a fair degree of personal dexterity, since the ancient text of an author will be in one volume, the notes on that author in a second volume, and the notes to the notes in a third. In addition, Jacoby varies in his practice of determining what constitutes a fragment between exact quotations identified as such by another author, passages that are contiguous to one containing an identified fragment and thus felt to descend from the author of the specifically identified text, and passages that Jacoby has decided may be from the author in question. Sometimes these are given in different typefaces, sometimes they are not, and sometimes relevant information is not printed (it being humanly impossible to make the correct decision on every possible occasion).

Problems in points of detail and definition still operate within the framework that Jacoby established. By the end of his life, faced with the immensely difficult task of categorizing the information that he had left to the last three volumes, Jacoby appears to have had concerns about the validity of his generic divisions.[172] Failure of the generic divisions to explain historiography through their evolution from each other calls into question a theory that depends upon the notion that human history could be written in the same way that one prepares the stemma of manuscripts in editing a text, tracing what we have back to the "perfect original." Such a theory is connected with the historiographic technique of "source criticism" that aims to reconstruct the text that an extant author was reading in order to explain his thought, and will be dealt with more fully in the next chapter. For now, to anticipate the conclusions of that chapter, it is fair to say that within limits, it is a technique that can serve to illuminate the way that a person's mind worked, but it is not sufficient to explain it. So too, Jacoby's approach, while important in drawing attention to the fact that historical writing was evolutionary rather than static, is too restrictive as an explanation. Although an expert on dealing with the problem that what we have from antiquity is but a very tiny proportion of what existed, Jacoby still felt that what we have can offer the sole explanation for itself. This is a critical error.

Biography and horography

The most obvious problems with Jacoby's scheme lies in the treatment of biography and horography. He saw both genres as inferior descendents of narrative. Such an explanation fails to explain either genre.

Jacoby's treatment of biography has long since been the object of considerable difficulty. As Momigliano has shown, the roots of this genre are far earlier than Jacoby allowed, and far different. Momigliano saw the roots of biography in the habit of collecting stories about people – anecdotes, sayings and so forth – and in rhetoric, speeches offering a defense of oneself and, it might be added, speeches attacking someone else. Aristocrats, traditionally fascinated with themselves and their families, turned to constructing genealogies that reached back to the distant past. The great figures of literature remained a perpetual fascination, leading to the invention of stories about them that, while they have little if any grounding in reality, still represent an early stage of scholarship in that they tend to be informed by texts – in these cases, the surviving poetry and inferences drawn about the social world of the poet from the same source.[173] Hence the blindness of Homer. Political biography may stem from slightly different sources, memoir literature such as the work of Ion of Chios and Stesimbrotus of Thasos being early examples. In a world that lacked well-developed chronological systems, stories about people were the one way of structuring the past. Political biography, however, rapidly evolved beyond the form, often short, of the life of a poet. The authors of the lives of great men (always men, it seems) found themselves increasingly drawn to the methods of narrative historians, creating a quite independent genre in its own right.[174] In the Roman world, biographies could become a substitute for narrative history as the history of the empire came to be viewed in terms of the lives of the emperors.

Biography could become a substitute for narrative history, but it still had its own rules. In terms of form, perhaps the most important point is that it allowed for direct quotation of documents in a way that the generic rules for narrative history did not. It is not altogether clear why this should be so, but it may be that the tradition of the eyewitness memorialist influenced later practitioners in such a way that they too wished to include first-hand statements about their subject. Moreover, as we shall see, there were various forms of historical writing that stood as alternatives to full-blown narrative which also allowed for direct quotation at some length.

Jacoby includes the first writers of Roman history amongst the horographers on the grounds that they were concerned with the history of a single state, and that their work was organized according to the city's annual chronological scheme (a point that is open to some question in the case of the earliest Roman historians). Perhaps more important than the actual form that these lost histories took, as far as Jacoby was concerned, was the fact that Roman descriptions of their earliest historiography are virtually identical with his view of what horography was like:

> *historia* was nothing but the assemblage of annual accounts, for which reason, and for the sake of preserving public memory, from the beginning of Roman history until the pontificate of P. Mucius Scaevola, the *pontifex maximus* entrusted all the events of an individual year down to writing, and he recorded them on a white tablet, and he put the tablet up in front of his house, so that the people would have the ability to know what had happened, and these tablets are known, even now, as the *annales maximi*. There are many who have followed this monotonous style of writing, people who leave only the remains of times, people, places and deeds without ornament.
>
> (Cic. *De orat.* 2.52–3).

Cicero goes on to mention "Pherecydes, Hellanicus and Acusilaus and many others were like this amongst the Greeks, and thus, amongst us, were Cato, Pictor and Piso."[175] The authors that he selected include two characters whom Jacoby describes as mythographers of early fifth century date (Acusilaus and Pherecydes) and an author whose considerable corpus ranged from mythography to horography. Hellenicus's most famous work is the history of Attica in two books that was completed near the end of the fifth century and attracted Thucydides's ire for its failures to record things accurately. In other words, Cicero's view of the development of historical writing is radically different from that of Jacoby in that he sees distinctions in terms of style between historians rather than between the types of history that they wrote. He does not see a distinction between "local history" and works that are organized chronographically.

Cicero's account of early Roman history is quite similar to that offered two generations later by Dionysius of Halicarnassus. He observes that there was "not a single ancient historian or chronicler of the Romans, each of them wrote by drawing from the ancient accounts preserved on the sacred tablets" (Dion. Hal. *Ant. Rom.* 1.73.1). The authors of whom Dionysius approved are the Greek and Latin annalists, saying that he gathered the material that he had not obtained from oral sources from, "the works that Porcius Cato, Fabius Maximus, Valerius Antias, Licinius Macer, the Aelii, Gellii, Calpurnii, and the crowd of other notable men who are respected by the Romans themselves, that are like Greek chronographies" (Dion. Hal. *Ant Rom.* 1.7.3). The really important distinction that Dionysius saw amongst Greek historians was between those who pieced together the past from local traditions, confining themselves to the history of a single location or race, and those who combined the history of many nations or wrote about a single topic (Dion Hal. *De Thuc.* 5–6). In other words, he saw three basic sorts of writing: local histories, general histories covering a variety of nations, and event-oriented histories.

The second basic distinction that Dionysius, and many others, drew was between histories that treated events that were contemporary with the historian and those that were about the distant past. The choice of form did not, however, preclude the mixing of contemporary history with past history. Dionysius himself said that he was deterred from writing about Roman history after the outbreak of the first Punic War because the earliest annalists had personal knowledge of those events. A century and a half earlier, Polybius, whose modesty was insufficient to preclude his attempting any sort of intellectual activity, had likewise drawn a clear distinction between his ability to write about events before his own time and those for which he had personal information (3.2). In the Latin tradition, the clearest statement of the difference between the two sorts of writing appears in Aulus Gellius's discussion of the difference between *historia* and *annales*, where he allows that *historia* is livelier than *annales*, which may be no more than a bare reckoning of events; an interesting distinction that he does not maintain elsewhere in his work (*Noct. Att.* 5.18.1–5), and is not representative of ordinary Latin usage.

Chronographic local narrative was a far more flexible form than Jacoby allowed, and the divergences in form cannot be explained on his model. To see in Tacitus the intellectual descendent of the first person to record the events of a city in a temple chronicle, helps neither to explain Tacitus nor our theoretical original horographer. To see Polybius as an intellectual child of Hecataeus would probably make him roll over in his grave. Polybius thought of himself very much as a creature of his time, at war with other authors who thought that they could explain their times better than he could, and with predecessors whom he regarded as charlatans. We can trace the influence of these authors in his thought, but we cannot understand him through them any more than we can explain Hecataeus solely in terms of a reaction to epic.

Hecataeus fits into a context of new "professionals" in Ionia who used prose to describe and analyse the world around them. His intellectual compatriots were early Ionian philosophers and the founders of the Hippocratic school of medicine. The crucial feature of these endeavors was the use of prose – possibly as a rhetorical foil to traditional forms of description in verse – and the stress upon the interpretation of observed phenomena.[176] In doing so they set themselves apart from earlier users of prose in the Greek world to record events and matters of practical importance such as treaties, laws and property ownership. They also distinguished themselves from the traditions of historical writing in the Near East, where prose chronicles and other types of prose record of the past had a very long tradition prior to the Greeks. The evolution of historical writing cannot simply be explained as a process that is internal to the genre, one author taking over a form from predecessors and using it as it suited him. Each author must be seen in the broader context of the generation in which that author wrote. General theories of historiographic development may be eloquent, but if they are detached from other forms of intellectual history, they are bound to be deceptive. The broad distinctions between the three sorts of history that were recognized in antiquity are sufficient to describe the basic forms of ancient narrative history, though we shall also see that it is less satisfactory for explaining other sorts of systematic cultural recording. These are works such as Varro's account of Roman institutions, or Aulus Gellius's *Attic Nights*. For these arise from very different roots, and the notion that the history of culture is not "history" in a true sense, may remain as one of the least lamented casualties of the broader definition of the subject that is primarily owed, in the present generation, to the *Annales* school of historical writing.[177]

Reconstructing fragmentary authors

Fragments are a fact of life for the ancient historian. As a practical, technical point, it is necessary for historians who use them to be aware of the sources from which they are drawn. Some of the issues connected with the use of fragments have already been discussed in general terms, and it is now time to turn to some specific problems inherent in dealing with authors whose works, though fragmentary, are not included in the collections created by Jacoby and Peter.

In some cases, consciousness of the state of an author's preservation is easy to come by. There are the parts that we have, and those that we do not. Velleius Paterculus survived the Middle Ages in a single manuscript, and that is now lost, so we are dependent upon early printed editions and a late transcription for our entire knowledge of what he had to say.[178] Tacitus's historical works descend in two manuscripts, one for books 1–6, another for 11–16 and the surviving portions of the history.[179] He provides some clues through cross-references as to what he had to say in some of the sections that we do not have, but not all.[180] Since he wrote the *Histories* before he wrote the *Annals*, we cannot know what his final judgment on the fall of Nero was, or if he really ever did talk about it, since the text that we have suggests that he may never have finished the *Annals*. If this is the case then we cannot really know what Jerome was talking about when he said that Tacitus wrote about the lives of the Caesars from Tiberius to Domitian in thirty books.[181] With Livy, we have summaries of all but two of the 142 books that he wrote to go with the thirty-five books from this total that have come down to us. Comparison of the summaries with the extant books reveals that they are not great guides as to the content of the books that are lost, but it also shows us that the scope of Livy's coverage expanded enormously as he reached the first century AD, and that what we have (especially the earliest books) is not really representative of his fully developed style.

The case of Livy is unusual in that we have three self-confessed epitomes of his work, and what is effectively a fourth in Paulus Orosius's *Histories Against the Pagans*, composed some time after AD 417.[182] The differences between these summaries are illuminating both for what they can tell us about the way that Livy was used, and what it was that he said. They may also remind us that the ancient equivalent of "Cliff Notes" are a very poor substitute for the real thing.

Orosius, who was interested in demonstrating the truth of Augustine's assertion that life had been far worse before the adoption of Christianity, wrote seven books giving the history of the world from the creation down to his own time. Book 1, which is based primarily on Justin's epitome of Pompeius Trogus's history and Herodotus, treats Near Eastern history. Book 2 combines material from Justin, Herodotus and Livy, carrying the history of the world down to the sack of Rome by the Gauls. Book 3 continues to combine information from Justin and Livy, down to the wars of the Successors of Alexander the Great in the late fourth century BC. Books 4–6 are essentially a summary of the rest of Livy, from the war with Pyrrhus to the time of Augustus. Book 7 treats imperial history, based on Suetonius, Tacitus, Eutropius and Latin continuations of the Chronicle of Eusebius by Jerome and Rufinus. In the sections of his history where he summarizes Livy, Orosius retains some of the furniture of annalistic writing (such as consular dates) and, in places, reflects Livy's adaptation of his sources. This is perhaps most interesting in the tale of the first war between Rome and Carthage (264–41 BC), where what Orosius has to say may be compared with what Polybius says that Rome's first historian, Fabius Pictor, said (Oros. 4. 7–11).

The author of the Oxyrhynchus summary of Livy is a very different sort of reader. He breaks down his book-by-book entries by consular year, turning Livy's narrative into a sort of chronicle of Roman history. Julius Obsequens, who composed a list of 505 prodigies from Livy (now preserved only after 190, and with what look like substantial ommissions) had a completely different interest. His book, where prodigies are placed by consular year, may resemble the books of the augurs or haruspices, which would likewise have contained chronological lists of portents than anything else we have from antiquity. It might be a sort of "bluffer's guide" to the divine. Finally we have the author of the *Periochae*, or *Summaries*, which report what Livy had to say, book by book, in a relatively literary style, not always with consular dates.[183]

The difference between the Oxyrhynchus summaries and the *Periochae* may perhaps be seen most clearly in the treatment of the end of Book 53 and the beginning of Book 54. The Oxyrhynchus summaries reveal that Livy did not end Book 53 with the end of the consular year (141 BC), but rather delayed discussion of the defeat of the consul Pompeius, to the beginning of Book 54, a variation of style that may have emphasized the importance of the war. The author of the *Periochae* simply says that Pompeius made a treaty with the Numantines that was repudiated by the people. By combining the two summaries we can get a better idea of what Livy was doing, while being reminded at the same time of just how problematic the use of these summaries can be.

The different summaries of Livy are but the tip of an interpretative iceberg, whereby the contents of partially preserved histories may be reconstructed through a combination of books in a manuscript tradition, summaries and extensive quotations in other places. If one is to understand the text of an author such as Polybius or Cassius Dio in modern editions it is necessary, above all, to be familiar with the collections that preserve much of their writings. These are the surviving Constantinian Excerpta, so called because they were compiled under the direction of the tenth-century emperor Constantine VII Porphyrogenitus as part of his *Encyclopedia of History and Statescraft*.[184] In the introduction to the volume devoted to virtues and vices, it is explained that Constantine decided that the mass of history was disorganized and very long, and thus in need of reorganization into anthologies so that it could be put to better use. The person in charge of overseeing this process was a character named Theodosius the Small, and he cast his net very widely indeed. The historians whose works were chosen for excerption were Herodotus, Thucydides, Xenophon, Polybius, Dionysius of Halicarnassus, Nicolaus of Damascus, Josephus (the *Antiquities of the Jews* only), Appian, Arrian (only the *Anabasis of Alexander*), Cassius Dio, Herodian, Eusebius, Dexippus, Eunapius, Petrus Patricius, the Anonymous Continuator of Dio, Zosimus, Priscus, Malchus, Malalas, John of Antioch, Procopius, Agathias, Menander Protector, Theophylact, Theophanes, Nicephoras Patriarches and George the Monk: an impressive collection, possibly supplemented by Iamblichus's *Babyloniaca*, a novel. Even more impressive is the fact that the manuscripts that the excerptors were using appear to have been complete. This enables us to see that a great deal of Greek imperial historiography survived the transfer from roll to codex, a transition that is generally viewed as the stage at which a great deal of Latin literature disappeared.

The work of the excerptors was mind-numbingly mechanical. They read through all the texts in front of them and extracted the passages that were relevant to the subject of the book that they were composing. Some dealt with bureaucratic subjects such as embassies, accessions and depositions of rulers, administration and colonial policy; others dealt with points of literary interest such as speeches, letters, *sententiae* (wise sayings) and curiosities. Of this great labor, that once extended to some seventy one volumes, only four books survive. These are the *Excerpts Concerning Embassies*, *Excerpts Concerning Virtues and Vices*, *Excerpts Concerning Sententiae* and the *Excerpts Concerning Conspiracies*. The *Excerpts Concerning Embassies* fall into two parts: *Excerpts Concerning Embassies from the Romans to Foreign Peoples* and the *Excerpts Concerning Embassies to the Romans from Foreign Peoples*. Each entry begins with the Greek word *hoti* (that) and appears to be quite faithful to the original, except at the beginning of the extract where the syntax is adjusted to take account of the introductory formula, and the end. Occasionally the excerptor also changed the wording of the bulk of the text as well, a point that makes it hard to establish any general rule concerning the value of these texts as records of what was written by the original author.[185] The order in which the excerpts appear reflects the order of events in the work from which they were drawn. This gives the editor an idea of the relative position of given extracts, but not the relationship between extracts in different books, or actual location within the original text. Two further collections of extracts, made at a different time, survive with the titles *Concerning Stratagems* and *Concerning Military Speeches*. The former, preserved in a manuscript at Mount Athos, contains extracts from ancient authors; the latter simply offers samples of military rhetoric.

The Constantinian Excerpta may be supplemented with the results of another project. This is the *Inventory and Enumeration of the Books that we have Read, of which our beloved Brother Tarausius requested a General Analysis*, compiled by the patriarch Photius sometime around AD 843 (probably), and commonly known today by its more convenient sixteenth-century title, the *Bibliotheca*.[186] This enormous work includes entries for 280 books. The contents reflect books above and beyond basic school texts that the learned patriarch had read (and one that he had not). For each book, Photius includes a summary of the contents, and occasionally some remarks on the style and value. These entries vary enormously in length and quality. Some appear to be descriptions composed from memory, others are descriptions composed by referring back to manuscripts that he had already read or to notes that he had made while reading, and still others seem to have been composed while reading.[187] These categories can be further subdivided, and the process as a whole serves as a warning against making the simple assumption that just because Photius says something, he need necessarily be believed or disbelieved. One has to look at the overall context of the statement.

A third source of information is the tenth century lexicon known as the *Suda*.[188] The word "suda" (often misrepresented in earlier literature as the name of an individual who was dubbed Suidas) means fortress, and in Byzantine terms, the *Suda* is a sort of fortress of culture. In our terms it is a cross between the *Encyclopaedia Britannica* and *Webster's Dictionary*.[189] It is organized alphabetically with articles on words drawn, ultimately, from lexica, collections of scholia and historians. Various entries may attempt to sort out various authors of the same name, or provide information that a certain word was used by a particular writer. The literary historical articles are based on the best earlier scholarship that was still available in the tenth century, and remain a major, if not ideal, source of information about many writers from antiquity.

Between them, the *Suda*, Photius and the Excerpta preserve a great deal of what we can know about Greek historiography relevant to the Roman world even if the quality of this knowledge is problematic, since these texts "reflect the interests of the authors who cite or summarize lost works as much or more than the characteristics of the works concerned."[190] This problem may perhaps be seen most clearly in the work of Cassius Dio, whose history has been painstakingly reconstructed by Ursulus Philip Boissevain, one of the truly great textual critics of the late nineteenth and early twentieth centuries.

There is no single textual tradition for Dio.[191] As with, for instance, Livy or Polybius, different sections of the work have their own textual histories. In this case, Books 1–35 have to be reconstructed (principally) from the twelfth century *Epitome of the Histories* by John Zonaras, and the Constantinian Excerpta; Books 36–60 survive in two manuscripts (one containing 36–60, the other 46–54) of uneven quality (55–60 are incomplete); and Books 60–80 are (again principally) reconstructed on the basis of an epitome (summary) of Books 36–80 by John Xiphilinus of Trebizond (a monk who worked in the second half of the eleventh century), Zonaras, the Excerpta, and the *Suda*.[192] For this section we also have a palimpsest that contains portions of Books 79 and 80.

The diversity of sources, and their different techniques of reporting (Xiphilinus retains first person statements, the Excerpta change them to the third person), is only part of the problem. Another problem, and one that bedevils anyone trying to find something in the most readily accessible edition (M. Cary's nine-volume Loeb) is that the first "modern" edition of Dio, published thirteen years after the death of the editor (Leunclavus) offered a division into books that was retained by Cary (who published as Boissevain was finishing his work) even after Boissevain had shown that it was inadequate. Cary had the good sense to include Boissevain's new book divisions in his margins, and Boissevain himself included Leunclavus's numbers on the left-hand page of each pair of facing pages where the two editors had differing reconstructions of the text, while his own divisions are indicated on the right hand page. The readers of Dio thus must keep their eyes trained on the margins of the Loeb or the right hand pages of Boissevain to figure out where they are. This is more than mere editorial inconvenience. It is a constant reminder that most of the time we are not reading Dio, but rather, incomplete summaries of what he had to say.

Boissevain decided, in conjunction with the German scholar Alfred von Gutschmidt, that the history was organized into fifty-one books from Romulus to the battle of Pharsalus, and thirty-nine books from Pharsalus to Dio's second consulship in AD 229.[193] This may be the wrong way of thinking about the work. Dio himself appears to have marked a significant break in his history at 31 BC, when he asserted that the sole reign of Augustus should be measured from the battle of Actium, and another break at 27 BC when Augustus reordered the government of the Roman state (Dio 51.1; 53.19). In Dio's view, therefore, Augustus rather than Caesar was the pivotal figure in Roman history. Books 45–56, one-seventh of the entire history that spans a thousand years, is devoted to the fifty-eight years from the death of Caesar to the demise of the first *princeps*. Augustus's own career is divided by Dio into three parts: Octavian as Caesar's heir, Octavian

Caesar as the victorious dynast, and Augustus the emperor.[194] No other figure in Roman history occupies anything like this amount of space, or receives anything like so nuanced a treatment. The observation that Augustus receives this amount of attention because he is regarded as the prototypical "ideal" ruler for the early third century may be one of the most secure about any aspect of his work.[195] As Augustus became a truly "great ruler" after the civil wars, it could be hoped that the same might be true of others.

In addition to the larger interpretive problems caused by the state of the text, there are basic difficulties that stem from the way that the text had to be reconstructed. Not the least of these is the fact that there is only one certain book division between the end of Book 59 and Book 80 (the division between 78 and 79).[196] Furthermore, if we divide the surviving text up into books (not knowing where one begins and the other ends), we also have to determine the relationship between the different sources for the text. One way to avoid this difficulty would be simply to print all the material relevant to different emperors according to the different sources and not to attempt book division at all: thus all the Trajanic material would be followed by all the Hadrianic material and so forth, counting on the fact that the excerptors all keep the relative order intact. This was not the solution adopted by Boissevain and his predecessors, who created an extraordinary quilt of different texts. The first ten years of the reign of Trajan, as reconstructed by Boissevain, is broken down in the table on page 77 in order to illustrate the problem (the reason that the chapters do not follow numerical order is that the numbers are those assigned by Leunclavus, which were retained even though the fragments were rearranged).

The mixing and matching of different texts offers an outline of what Dio once had to say, but it is not the same thing as the text of Dio.

If we are to understand the narrative historians of antiquity, we must first understand the way that they have come down to us. The fact that their texts are not complete offers special problems, and prevents us from saying things about them that we might like to be able to; but it does not mean that we need simply treat their works as curious artifacts, or that we can simply ignore what they have to tell us, or that they have nothing to say.

The technical problems and interpretive issues raised in this chapter are only a start. If I have stressed some problems above others, it does not mean that one sort of difficulty necessarily besets one sort of text more than another. What I hope I have done is to suggest that we need to be aware of problems that can arise with our own analytical

Chapter	Source	Event
68.4	Xiphilinus	Accession
68.5	Xiphilinus	Dream, dispositions after accession
68.15.2	Excerpts, *Foreign Embassies*	Embassies from foreign kings
68.6–7	Xiphilinus/*Suda*/Excerpts, *Concerning Virtues and Vices*	First Dacian War/character of Trajan
68.8	Xiphilinus/Tzetzes, *Chiliastes*	Events of the first Dacian War
68.9.1	Xiphilinus/Excerpts, *Foreign Embassies* (Dio 47) with Excerpts, *Foreign Embassies* from Petrus Patricius 5, assumed here to be quoting Dio.	Dacian embassy to Trajan
68.9.4 (with 68.3)	Excerpts, *Foreign Embassies* (Dio 47)/Xiphilinus	Dacian embassy to Trajan, in same section of the *Excerpta* as the preceding, but shown by Xiphilinus to be on a different occasion
68.10.1–2	Xiphilinus	Trajan's victory celebration
68.10.3	Xiphilinus	Dacians break treaty
68.11.1–2	Excerpts, *Foreign Embassies* (Dio 47)[197]	Dacians send embassy to Trajan, attempting to kill him.
68.11.3	Xiphilinus	Same story as in 68.11.1–2
68.12	Xiphilinus/Excerpts, *Foreign Embassies* (Dio 48)[198]	Decebelus captures Trajan's general Longinus, sends embassy to Trajan to negotiate his return, embassy fails. Decebelus throws Longinus in chains, Longinus promises to poison Trajan if released, but drinks poison himself. Negotiations over the body.[199]
68.13	Xiphilinus	Trajan's bridge over the Danube
68.14	Xiphilinus	The defeat of Decebelus
68.14.5 (end)	Xiphilinus	Annexation of the province of Arabia
68.15.1	Xiphilinus/Excerpts, *Foreign Embassies* (Dio 49)[200]	Embassies to Trajan in 107, celebrations in Rome.[201]

paradigms, and with the texts that we use. I have so far avoided saying much about another series of difficulties. One is the way that Greek and Roman authors sought to establish the "truth value" of the evidence that they cited. The other is the tension between "truth value" and presentation.

Chapter 3

Scholarship

Standards of research

'Why did he say that?" This question underlies the study of ancient texts. It demands a variety of different answers, ranging from literary convenience to "because he did not know any better." All these answers, however, will still leave unaddressed what many have seen as a crucial, logical flaw to any historiographic endeavor. How can anyone give a fully objective account of an incident at which a he or she was not present? Even with the aid of modern technologies like the video tape, we must realize that factors such as camera angle, light or timing may (and do) prevent the production of a record that is "completely accurate." And even if one could obtain a flawless visual record of some moment in time, it would need to be supplemented with material to assist the other senses: what was heard, felt, smelled, thought or tasted as something happened. It would also be meaningless (even when supplemented with materials to assist the other senses) without the aid of some further explanation. A tape of a person walking down the street will mean quite different things if we know that the person is going to purchase some milk, or some cocaine, is returning home from work, or is heading towards an adulterous liaison.

Historiography, in the Greco-Roman context, should be seen as the process of acquiring knowledge and explaining it rather than as a record. Critical discourse in antiquity defined the object of this exercise in terms of "the true." The point of the current chapter is to look behind this ideal, to examine the expectations that readers and writers of history might have about their task. How did a person approach the truth?

Our survey of the varieties of literary evidence from antiquity has suggested that the nature of literary production cast a number of obstacles in the path of research. Anyone familiar, as all ancient historians would be, with the way that written evidence came into being would be skeptical of the "truth value" of much that was available to be read. From the very earliest period of Greek historiography, it was obvious that all historians could hope to talk about were the stories that people told. They could compare these accounts with each other and, very occasionally, with surviving documents. As the habit of recording became more common, the opportunity to check one account against another also increased.

The use of prose for the distinct practices of checking one account against another and creating a systematic record of phenomena developed in the course of the fifth century BC. As this happened, a dialogue arose between historiography and other endeavours. The relationship between historians and these other systematic recorders of events is deeply problematic, both in antiquity and in the present. It is quite plain that people, beyond the circle of those who wrote history, had an idea of what constituted scholarship, or the process of accurate data collection, and that historians were judged as scholars as well as literateurs.

In our century, the problem of describing the relationship between historians and other professional recorders has led to the problem of whether or not history can – or should – be defined as a science. Does history have a logically coherent *techné* or method? What is the relationship between the methods of collection and those of presentation? In antiquity, the great advances that were made in the collection and arrangement of material were not made by historians any more than they have been in more recent periods. No historian in antiquity was as systematic in the collection of evidence as the doctor, grammarian or scientist, and it is arguable that the same is true today. But, as the history of science has shown, the simple collection of data does not, inherently, yield results beyond the fact of the new database. The historian, like the scientist, is responsible for explaining the value of the data as well as for assembling it. The historian need not know every possible thing about an event, and will have done his or her job if, on the basis of the evidence collected, he or she can produce an explanation that will not be overthrown by evidence that the historian does not know. This process is facilitated if the historian does not make mistakes in the collection of evidence. Thus, while questions may help define the "truth value" of a statement, they cannot define the nature of the effort expended in recording what is in the statement. The tension between the mechanics of data collection and the deployment of its results has been, and will remain, a persistent one.

The question of how an ancient historian went about gathering and deploying information is thus intimately connected with the question of using literary sources to write Roman history. The central issue is the way that historians treated their sources. The Deutero-Tacitus whom we met in the introduction might have one way of discussing this issue; Pseudo-Ammianus might do so very differently. At the heart of the dispute between these practitioners, if they should meet in some historical purgatory, might be the status of the written document. Attitudes towards the documentary record differ from period to period, and from genre to genre of historical writing. The range of opinions on this matter can be tested in a variety of ways. One is to explore the relative standing of oral versus written testimony from author to author; another is to examine the methods by which different authors created narratives from the material at their disposal. Two other avenues of exploration are offered by the Near Eastern tradition of historiography and the study of other forms of classical scholarship. Critical historiography, that is to say historical writing that acknowledged the existence of varient accounts and sought to judge one as superior to another, is attested in the Near East. But classical authors appear to have been deeply suspicious of these efforts, usually deploying ostensibly aesthetic and ethical reasons to justify their reaction. In doing so, they might take comfort from the finest technical scholars of the ancient world, the grammarians who edited texts. Historical and philological method had a great deal in common, sharing the view that it was possible to determine a better version from a worse, and that one criterion for making this decision might be ethical.

Once one of our putative historians had decided what sources to use, he was then faced with the problem of actually producing a text. The process of composition is every bit as important as the process of publication for the dissemination of knowledge. Classical techniques are recoverable, and their study may help to explain why things appear the way that they do in our texts. In what follows, we shall follow the process of a classical historian from the search for evidence through the creation of a draft. It is a journey into the shadowy land of text and discourse.

Historians and records

Polybius regarded a history of the time in which he was himself alive as superior to that of the past because he had a greater capacity to investigate events for which eyewitnesses were available, and thus a greater capacity to evaluate whatever he heard.[1] He also had recourse to original documents such as the inscription detailing Carthaginian forces at the beginning of their invasion that Hannibal left behind when he departed from Italy, a text of a content so astonishing that we must still wonder how it avoided immediate destruction.[2] He was also able to quote verbatim from the treaty that Philip made with Hannibal, a document that may have been available at Rome since a copy had been intercepted on its way from Greece to Campania (7.9). Did he consult the autograph? We cannot know, but the fact of the treaty certainly points in the direction of a public records office as an obvious source of information. We know that he found treaties that others no longer cared about in the treasury of the aediles on the Capitol, presumably hanging on the wall with treaties made between Rome and other states.[3] Polybius also read very widely, a point which makes his evident unwillingness to distinguish between a documentary record and finished books particularly interesting. They both fall into a category of record of the past that he separates from eyewitnesses; within this category, he does not draw generic distinctions. In his disquisition on the proper methods for an historian, he says that Timaeus was an energetic student of documents, but that:

> one is able to make a study from books without danger or suffering, if one has taken care to find a town that is rich in *hypomnemata* and has libraries nearby. After that, one may research in perfect ease and compare the accounts of different writers without hardship of any sort. Personal inquiry requires great hardship and expense, but it offers much and is the most important part of investigation (*historia*).
> (12.27.4–5)[4]

Others might not have seen things in quite this way. Timaeus evidently wrote that Athens was a particularly good place to write because it was well equipped with libraries (Pol. 12.25d 1; *FGrH* 566 T 19). Hundreds of years later we get a picture of an ideal historian gaining access to the Ulpian library in the *Historia Augusta*.[5] In so far as a library was a repository for older books, it appears to have been treated as a sort of alternative to the public records office, and indeed, the putative author in the *Historia Augusta* would be going to the library to consult *libri lintei*, linen books of great antiquity written on the subject of the emperor Aurelian (whose death was less than thirty years before the alleged encounter).

Polybius was not the only historian who knew that public records were there to be consulted. At Rome, it is clear that the *acta* of the Senate were considered a resource: Tacitus plainly used them as a source, and used historians who had done likewise.[6] Suetonius observed that decrees of the Senate could be mendacious, so it was better to look to what was on record from other levels of society (chiefly the equestrian

order).[7] Roman public administration depended heavily upon documentation; governors confronted with troublesome cases would naturally turn
to prior records (or records at Rome) for guidance, so it was not surprising
that when a member of the governing class turned to the writing of
history, he might turn to the public records office for material.[8] A person
familiar with these sources might also be familiar with their drawbacks,
and know better than to put absolute faith in them.

Public records could be transformed into a sort of history if people
were interested. From the early Hellenistic period onwards, we have
"history walls" coming into existence in the cities of the Greek world.[9]
These include series of reinscribed decrees or letters from famous
people, often with the wording summarized or with redundant matter
cut out. Under the empire, after records of hearings took on the form of
a verbatim transcript, two forms of literature developed to mimic
precisely this style. One variety is known as the *Acta Alexandrinorum*,
offering accounts of discussions between notable Alexandrians and
Roman officials.[10] The other is a variety of Christian martyrology (not
the earliest, which were in the form of letters) where an actual transcript
could be used on its own or grafted (possibly without great literary
success) into an account of the martyr's deeds that had become common
centuries later.[11]

A records office offered source material, but not all of it was worth
reporting. The good historian had to be selective. Dionysius of
Halicarnassus even says that archives were full of unreliable information, being the repository of *mythoi* about cities (*De Thuc.* 7). At the other
end of the era of Roman domination, Ammianus Marcellinus states that
details of camps established by the emperor are dull, and not the matter
of the *celsitudines* of history (to be found in his own work). It was not in
accord with the precepts of history to seek out such things, and the sort
of person who was interested in them might as well "set himself to
counting those individual little particles that fly through the void which
we call atoms" (26.1.2). In one of the most important critical discourses
on historical writing, Lucian complains of one author whose detail is
poorly chosen, concentrating on the adventures of a Moorish cavalryman
while omitting serious discussion of a major battle (*Hist.* 28). It is significant that exclusion of detail is a noteworthy theme in ancient historical
writing. The problem with Herodotus, in Plutarch's view, is not that he
failed to do his homework but that he selected the stories that would
reflect most badly upon his subject from the mass of available material
(866d). Polybius felt that minute reporting of detail (at least by a historian whom he did not like) was silly (12.26a).

Tacitus makes his view abundantly clear in his comments on the construction of Nero's amphitheater (*Ann.* 13.31): there was lots of material there that no decent historian would bother with. Similarly, he is willing to admit that some of the things that he records might be thought a bit dull (and unworthy of record) by some (*Ann.* 4.32) and that he feels that some things are important, even though others did not (*Ann.* 6.7.5). Still, his text is littered with references to, and versions of, speeches that were given in the Senate, and to letters sent either by or to the emperor.[12] He plainly had a sense of the value of the written document as an historical source, but he was not wedded to the notion that history could, or should, be based solely upon a documentary record: he had plenty of personal informants who could offer him information on various points that interested him. He would then decide what he wanted to use and how to use it. The fact of a documentary source does not mean that Tacitus could not cast judgment upon what he read as he saw fit.[13]

Tacitus does not appear to have privileged documents over eyewitnesses, and he was not alone. Thucydides did not try to report everything that he heard – so much is plain from his own statement – and he did not inspect documents with care. He could learn what he needed through interviews without recourse to the accounts of the Athenian State. Dionysius of Halicarnassus singles out his interviewing of witnesses as a particular strength (*De Thuc.* 6). Lucian states that a good historian knows who to talk to, selecting people who are capable of telling an unbiased story even if they were not eyewitnesses (*Hist.* 47). Polybius, as we have seen, while admitting that wide reading is valuable, stresses that encounters with eyewitnesses are more useful, especially if the historian is a person with enough experience to conduct a proper interview. In his view:

> It is inevitable that the inexperienced person will be deceived in this matter. For how is it possible to judge well about a battle or siege or sea fight, how can one understand the details of an event if he does not know about these matters? The inquirer contributes to the account no less than does the informant, for the suggestion of the person following the account guides the account of the narrator in each particular.
>
> (12.28a.8–9)

Documents are obviously not unimportant, but they are not regarded as being, *a priori*, better than other sources.

The third century AD: Dio and Herodian

A century after Tacitus, the histories of Cassius Dio and Herodian suggest a devaluation of the document as a source: one senses that Dio used them when he had to, but that they were not his first choice, and that Herodian pretty much ignored them.

In Dio's case, the break in his history (or what is left of it) around the beginning of the reign of Commodus (AD 180–92) is striking, for Dio seems to have used an author who had a great interest in the specific terms of treaties between the Romans and northern peoples up until the end of Commodus's campaigns on the Danube, and then turned to his own memory.[14] This leads Dio to make a claim about the disjuncture between the policies of Marcus and his son that is simply false on the basis of the evidence that he himself had already presented (that Marcus intended to create new provinces north of the river). But, Dio has already warned his readers that good information was hard to come by and that they should not believe whatever they were told. Without claiming that he could produce an ideal product, or even necessarily the truth, he wrote that he would follow the stories that he found in official communications and correct them in light of hearsay, reading and the evidence of his own eyes so that his work would represent an independent judgment on what had transpired (53.19.6). He was aware that "a great number of things began to happen in secret and to arise from hidden causes and if anything were by chance made public, it was not believed because it could not be proved" (53.19.3). All things were said and done at the behest of those in power, and thus "much that never happened is babbled about, and much that did is ignored" (53.19.4). Moreover, because the empire was so large, no one except the participants in events could have accurate information about them, and many never knew that they took place (53.19). This statement stands in evident contrast to another in the history where he says that:

> I will describe the events of my own lifetime in detail, and I will describe them in more detail than those of preceding times because I was present at them, and because I know of no other person who is able to put a more accurate account of them in writing than I am.
> (72.18.4)

When Dio displays a solid command of detail it often appears to be the result of his personal proximity to events (or to those who participated in them) or because he had a special interest in the subject. The history of

Septimius Severus's early wars was one of the first things that Dio wrote, and the account that survives in his mature work suggests that he was dissatisfied with the product that he felt to have been mendacious. In the new work he presented the crucial battles of Issus (AD194) and Lyons (AD 197) as close-fought affairs, disastrous to the Roman state, and ones in which fortune played a greater role than the genius of the victor.[15] At the conclusion of his account of Lyons, he even says that he has tried to write something like the truth and unlike the lies to be found in the account published by the victor (Dio 75.7.3). He also seems to have done a conscientious job in finding out what transpired outside of Antioch in AD 218, when the army of Elagabalus defeated that of Macrinus (Dio 79.38.3). He may well have been able to make use of the fact that the victorious army spent the winter in his home city to do so. However, the same ability to get at the facts is not obvious in his tale of Macrinus's war with the Parthians (AD 217), Severus's British campaign (AD 208–11) or Caracalla's operations on the Rhine (AD 213). In the first of these he appears to have decided that what may have been a fair Roman success was a failure because Macrinus refused the title *Parthicus*.[16] On the domestic front, his account of the fall from power of the powerful praetorian prefect Plautianus in AD 205 is simply a record of the report that Severus sent to the Senate, and a record of his reasons for disbelieving it, reasons stemming from his feelings about Caracalla and from common sense.[17] It is interesting that he also says that no one knew that Plautianus had castrated a hundred Roman citizens of noble birth until after he was dead (75.14.4). Since he clearly did not like Plautianus, it appears that he was willing to believe this, even though it bears all the marks of being a posthumous slander put about to justify the murder. Similarly, despite the circumstantial detail that Dio provides, it is somewhat difficult to believe that Aurelius Zoticus became *a cubiculo* because he had the largest penis in the empire, and that he lost his job when he lost his capacity to penetrate the emperor on their wedding night (allegedly because of the love potion his enemies had given him) (80.16.1–6).[18] On the domestic front, his

In general terms, Dio could often provide a good deal of information about events that took place in the Senate house, and, because he lived in Rome and Capua for much of his life, he can also provide a good deal of information about events and characters that he might have noticed or met in these areas. It is notable that all but one of the portents that presaged the death of Caracalla that he lists were reported precisely in the area around the twin poles of his Italian existence. So too, all that he can tell his readers about an alleged conspiracy against Severus is that one of the alleged conspirators was bald, that he was uncovered by

Severus in the Senate house, and that everyone checked the tops of their heads when the emperor made this announcement (76.8.4). He was also in a position to provide his readers with a special view of the spectacle that Commodus made of himself in the Colosseum when he waved the head of an ostrich at the senate during the games of AD 192 (72.21.1–2).

Herodian does not seem to have had access to many documents, and it is obvious that he made no effort to collect them in any systematic way. There are a number of cases where his narrative breaks down into a series of panels suggesting that his descriptions were based on pictures. One of these places is the description of the campaigns of Maximinus Thrax on the northern frontiers. The text is chronologically vague, and would lead the reader to believe that the whole business consisted of a single crossing of a river on a large bridge, the burning of barbarian villages, a battle in a swamp, the flight of the enemy, and various displays of personal courage by the emperor. The bridge is especially interesting. As David Braund has shown, the mental geography of the average Roman (or the average Roman who thought about such things) involved a world that was wrapped round by water, and it was thus natural to depict departure from this world as a crossing.[19] Such crossings are, in fact, central to the depictions of Roman campaigns on both the columns of Trajan and Marcus Aurelius. So too is stress on the personal intervention of the emperor at decisive moments.[20]

A rather more complicated case involves the murder of the emperor Caracalla (AD 217). Here Herodian tells us that Caracalla had to leave Carrhae to visit the temple of the moon, which was some distance away, and that when he left his cavalry escort to relieve a stomach distress, they all turned their backs. The murderer, who had been looking for his chance, then rushed up to Caracalla as he had his tunic around his waist, and stabbed him under the ribs. Caracalla's German guards killed the murderer, and then, "as the rest of the army saw what had been done, they all rushed up, and the first one there was Macrinus, who stood over the body pretending to weep" (4.13.7). Some of this is significant: there were several temples in the vicinity of Carrhae, and for the plot to make any sense, Caracalla must have set out from the city to visit one of these temples. The stress on the soldiers looking away might well be a detail that an artist would include, but what about the "rest of the army" (*ho loipos stratos*) and Macrinus? Macrinus seems to have been in Edessa when all this took place, along with the bulk of the army. His presence in Herodian's story is again likely to be an artistic convenience, depicting the official line that Macrinus was deeply sorry about what had happened, and that it was the act of an embittered individual.

Herodian's approach was to research was fundamentally undocumentary in so far as he does not seem to have regarded written documents stored in archives as a significant resource. When he was present at an event he narrates, he is a remarkably able reporter; when he was not present he appears to have been satisfied with whatever he could learn through the public channels of communication. The fact that his history seems to have been quite highly regarded suggests that his view of Roman history conformed rather well with that of the educated community, and that this same community was not greatly distressed by his method of collecting evidence. The early third century AD may represent a low point in the use of written documents in the composition of a history, representing a rather interesting shift in standards.

A startling shift occurred in the early fourth century in the Palestinian city of Caesarea. It was here that Eusebius wrote his *History of the Church*, in two *ekdoseis*, one completed very shortly after 313 AD, the second very shortly after 325.[21] While Christian historiography plainly owed something to the ideals of universal history in the polytheistic tradition and thus to the mainstream of classical historiography, Eusebius's habit of quoting his sources at length is what sets his work apart from his non-Christian contemporaries, and attached it to a different tradition.[22]

Before writing his *History of the Church*, Eusebius had produced apologetic literature in which he had followed earlier authors by quoting long extracts verbatim from polytheistic writers, to prove either their idiocy or their closet Christianity. Christian apologetic had ample models amongst polytheists and Jews for this use of direct quotation. Furthermore, as Eusebius also tells us, he would use material as he had already done in his *Chronological Canons*, where he had quoted long extracts, again verbatim, from various earlier chronographers; this again was a work connected with the apologetic tradition. The exact quotation of earlier writers likewise has a place in philosophic discourse, and in certain forms of biography, as may perhaps be best exemplified in Diogenes Laertius's volumes on the lives of philosophers. Just as Diogenes sought to illustrate the successions of philosophers, Eusebius set himself the task of collecting the scattered remains of the successors of the apostles and "giving them form through an historical treatment" (*HE* 1.4). The result was that Eusebius established a particular style of historiography distinct from that of contemporary polytheist narrative history in its direct use of documents.

Centuries earlier, another historian, also something of an outsider to the mainstream tradition, had also included direct quotation from documents. Flavius Josephus's *Antiquities of the Jews* is littered with verbatim quotation of senatorial decrees and letters from important Romans testifying to the preferred status of his people. Like Eusebius, Josephus had experience of apologetic writing, a form of discourse where appeal to direct quotation was important, and like Eusebius, he had a point to make. Josephus wrote the *Antiquities* while he was in Rome after the failure of the Jewish revolt in AD 70. At that point the Jews were subject to legal liabilities, and he was concerned to set the record straight. Judaism was a respectable form of worship with a long history; individual Jews – a disreputable minority, as he is at pains to point out in his earlier *Jewish War* – were responsible for all the trouble.[23] The point of the *Antiquities* was to reconcile nations and remove the causes of hatred, a point that he makes in the midst of an extensive citation of documents (*AJ* 16.175). He had already said that:

> I say these things of necessity since the purpose of the account of our deeds is chiefly to go to the Greeks, showing them that in former times we were treated with respect by all people, and were not prevented by our rulers from practicing any of our ancestral customs, but, having their cooperation, we preserved our religion and our way of honoring God.
>
> (*AJ* 16.174)

Direct quotation of documents evoked the proceedure in a court of law. In such a proceeding it was important not only to have one's own documents in order, but also to be able to prove that your opponent's documents were fraudulent. In his defense of Judaism, the *Against Apion*, Josephus is at pains to demonstrate that the unfavorable accounts of his people offered by Greeks are simply lies concocted by poor historians.[24] In this context it is particularly interesting to see that he quotes Greek sources to prove that Greek states kept inadequate records so that they simply could not write about other people's antiquities in an informed way.[25] The texts that he cites in his favor are quite literally described as his witnesses (e.g. *Contra Ap.* 1.70; 127), and he is at pains to assert that he has not invented them (*Contra Ap.* 1.112).

The distinction between history and apologetic, transgressed by Josephus, was shattered when Eusebius sounded the call of triumphant Christianity to establish a new style of documentary history. Perhaps the most firmly documentary and archival of all historians emerged in North Africa during the next generation, again in a plainly agonistic and Christian context. This remarkable character is Optatus of Milevis, a city in Numidia.[26] Optatus's mission was to prove that the Donatist church emerged from the self-interested scheming of dishonest clerics prior to the victory of Constantine over Maxentius in AD 312. In his first book, he cites a series of letters and other documents to build his narrative, and he added an invaluable appendix of texts with which to prove his case. The struggle between the orthodox and their Donatist rivals had been waged in court, and it is this background that enabled him to compile the dossier upon which he bases his case.

For Optatus, verbatim quotation was the way to the truth. But his context is partisan and offensive; the other side is not allowed to speak, its documents are buried in obscurity. Possibly the antagonistic aspect of verbatim transcription was a strike against its incorporation into developed classical narrative. The document needed to be tamed, all sides to be heard. If the classical historian stood before the bar of history, it would be as a judge defending a decision rather than as an advocate. It is to the taming, the training of sources, the combination of multiple perspectives that we must now turn.

Quellenforschung

The historical lion tamer indulges in *Quellenforschung*, the study of sources. The word itself can be a dirty one in some circles, suggesting an obsession with identifying lost historians behind the ones that we have, a lack of interest in evidence that survives in favor of that which does not. And, since one is trying to unearth something that does not exist, there is endless room for assertion, and little for definite proof. Indeed, discomfort with *Quellenforschung* is similar to discomfort with fragments (often the medium or result of the study) when it is seen as an end in and of itself rather than a means to an end.

Quellenforschung should not be a dirty word. The recognition that diverse sources lie behind existing texts, and that it is possible to break down the texts that we have to think about how they came together, was once the historiographic equivalent of Darwinism; it enabled historians to see the surviving texts as part of a tradition.[27] Nissen's inspired analysis of Livy, leading to his "law" that an ancient historian could only follow one source at a time, still has value even if his main point is wrong. But the search for lost sources has also led to some real absurdities, of which the greatest was perhaps the notion that Tacitus derived his histories from a lost (and unknown) "great annalist" of the early Principate.[28] On the other hand, review of what other historians had to say, especially as their views were reported by Suetonius and Cassius Dio, has not suggested that Tacitus was taking an eccentric line in his portrayal of the emperors of the Julio-Claudian house.[29] Similarly, comparison of his account of the civil wars of AD 69 with those in Suetonius, Dio and Plutarch has shown a remarkable decree of coherence, which suggests the use of a common source.

The purpose of *Quellenforschung*, properly done, is as follows:

1   to reduce the number of potential witnesses to a single event by showing that parallel accounts in different authors do not reflect different witnesses to the same event;

2   to explain how an author can be an authority for events that occurred in his own lifetime to which he was not a witness;

3   to find a source close to the events for narratives that appear in texts that were written centuries after the events that they narrate;

4   to reveal the connection between the research and compositional techniques of an author;

5   to enable a reconstruction of the general outlines of genres that are represented by a very small surviving sample.

To some extent, much of this book has already been an exploration of aspects of *Quellenforschung*, but to illustrate these points further it is worth looking at their application to two historians of the Roman empire. The first of these is Ammianus Marcellinus. There is perhaps no author whose account of Roman history is more personal, but he could not be everywhere, and the value of his history stems from his ability to channel diverse streams of discourse into a unified river of information. The exploration of these tributaries reveals something of his own attitudes to events.

Ammianus appears to have been inspired by the career of Julian, but it was some thirty or more years after the death of Julian that he completed his history.[30] He had done a lot of work in the meantime. His travels around the empire had enabled him to meet a wide variety of people who could tell him things that he was in no position to know on his own. One such person was the eunuch Eutherius, a high official of Constantius II, who had retired to Rome where Ammianus met him. Ammianus says that he was a man of prodigious memory, suggesting that Ammianus had experienced the benefits of this memory himself, such as some remarkable things about the conduct of secret meeting with Constantius II.[31] But he did not rely on personal informants alone, and he could be influenced by his surroundings.

Ammianus admired Julian greatly; hence, it seems, his willingness to trust what Julian had to say about his seizure of power at Paris in AD

360. Ammianus's account is closest in form and tone to Julian's *Letter to the Athenians*. What makes this so important is not just that Ammianus was aware of the problems with documents of this sort – he is scathing about the compositions of Constantius II – but rather that Ammianus had access to a better account, one that suggested a bit more intervention on Julian's part to move the events forward, and rejected it.[32] This account is known to us through Zosimus's *New History*, a work of the sixth century AD that Photius says was little more than a summary of Eunapius's history. Eunapius wrote, in his *History*, that he was inspired to write his history by Oribasius, Julian's doctor, who gave him his notebooks.[33] Ammianus's knowledge of Eunapius's history is evident from his account of the Persian expedition of AD 363, where he uses it to supplement his own memory. There is no reason to think that he only read it for the Persian expedition, and a clear allusion to things that Eunapius had to say about Julian appears in the narration of events after the proclamation in Paris.[34] Ammianus simply wanted to believe that Julian was a better source for himself than was Eunapius.

Another case where it seems that Ammianus rejected an account in Eunapius to follow one from official sources is the account of the conduct of Procopius in the months prior to his revolt in AD 366 (26.6.1–10). According to Zosimus, Procopius returned to Jovian (emperor AD 363–4) the imperial insignia that he had received from Julian before the latter departed for the invasion of Persia, and retired to Caesarea in Cappadocia. It was there that troops of Valens and Valentinian, Jovian's successors, came to arrest him. He escaped and headed off to the Crimea, from whence he returned to Constantinople to claim the throne (Zos. 4.4.3–5.2). Ammianus has Jovian try to arrest him, and knows nothing of the sojourn in the Crimea, saying only that Procopius lived the life of a wild beast in hiding and then, when he had tired of this, that he embarked on his bold enterprise. The retrojection of responsibility for the persecution of Procopius upon Jovian, and the depiction of Procopius as a desperate beast, looks very much like an account that serves the purposes of Valens. Zosimus's account, which provides a picture of Procopius's continued residence in the context of aristocratic life, is easier to reconcile with the facts of the rebellion. If, as we have seen, Ammianus has knowledge of the Eunapius/Zosimus tradition for Julian, there can be no doubt that he had it for Procopius as well, and that he simply chose to ignore it.

A final case, where Ammianus may be seen to be influenced by documents, is in the story of the alleged persecution of the aristocracy of the city of Rome under the *vicarius urbis* Maximinus in AD 370/71.

Maximinus was elevated to the rank of praetorian prefect after his stint in Rome, and was executed by Gratian in AD 376.[35] A speech of Symmachus in the same year as the death of Maximinus mentions the restoration of peace to the innocent and the abrogation of the power of slaughter stemming from foreign customs (*Or.* 4.13). Ammianus's point about Maximinus is that he was a Pannonian social climber who sought advancement by persecuting the wealthy at Rome. It is not necessary to assume that Ammianus knew Symmachus's speech, but it is worth considering the possibility that the persecution of Maximus was a construct of AD 376 that he took over.

In the case of Ammianus, then, reflection on sources reveals habits of thinking and work. In turning to Tacitus, it is possible to gain similar insight into his views and habits by comparing what he has to say not only to the work of other historians who describe the same events, but also to documents. In this case, pride of place must go to the recently published *Decree of the Senate concerning Gnaeus Piso senior.*[36]

The later half of the second book of Tacitus's *Annales* and the first nineteen chapters of book three are devoted to Germanicus's mission in the east, his death, and the subsequent trial of Gnaeus Calpurnius Piso on the charge of treason for (allegedly) poisoning Germanicus, waging civil war to regain his province, and behaving in a generally obnoxious manner. Tacitus plainly regarded the tale of the death of Germanicus and the trial of Piso (which ended with Piso's suicide) as part of a connected story, and in this he was almost certainly not alone (Tac. *Ann.* 3.19.2). Although we now know that the decree containing the honors for Germanicus and that containing the disposition of the case against Piso were not intended to be seen as a pair – the provisions for publica- tion are noticeably different in the two texts – provincials, and even Roman governors, might still take them that way.[37] Taken together they might tell a tale of grief, remembrance and revenge.[38] When he concludes his account of these events, Tacitus writes:

> this was the end of avenging the death of Germanicus; it has been discussed with various rumors not only amongst those who were involved, but even in the times that followed. Many things are still ambiguous, while some people hold gossip that they have heard somehow as true, others turn truth into falsehood, and both errors gain strength with posterity.
>
> (3.19.2)

For Tacitus the tale is, at least in part, a case study in the perversion of truth in its manifold forms, a crucial theme to the *Annales* as a whole.

In the course of his narrative, Tacitus shows knowledge of the documentary record, either directly or indirectly. He uses technical language to describe the nature of Germanicus's mission, and the nature of Piso's appointment; he summarizes the text that we now have on bronze tablets from Heba in Etruria, Rome and Siara in Spain. He quotes speeches of Tiberius that we do not have, and describes events in the Senate that are plainly reflected in the wording of the *Decree of the Senate concerning Gnaeus Piso senior*.[39] However, he also leaves out some things that modern historians would regard as important, such as the charge that Piso tried to start a war with Persia in the interests of the exiled Parthian king Vonones, sundry details of Piso's conduct in Syria (the crucifixion of a centurion and the distribution of donatives in his own name) and the cases against various of Piso's associates, whose names he never mentions.[40]

Intensive analysis of the circumstances surrounding the trial of Piso now supports the case made by Judith Ginsburg that Tacitus does not abide by the structuring of the annalist year as it was established by Livy (if not well before) with its strict tripartite division into internal affairs–external affairs–internal affairs, a structure that was dictated by the civil and military calendar at Rome.[41] The test case at that time was the decree of a triumph to Germanicus in AD 15 mentioned by Tacitus in *Annales* 1.55. It was felt that this should come at the end of the summer rather than at the beginning of the year. This feeling was wrong, the triumph related to events in AD 13, but that is not the issue here; the handling of material surrounding the trial of Piso (if not the trial itself) confirms that Tacitus moved the material around within his years as it suited him.[42] It is worth noting that he is explicit about this in the context of foreign affairs at one point, and that he had theory on his side, at least in the form of Dionysius of Halicarnassus who stated that complicated narratives should be given as unities (*De Thuc.* 9).

The study of Tacitus's sources is the key to understanding what he did to make the narrative of Tiberius's reign his own. It is not simply a question of identifying lost annalists, or documents, it is a question of authorial technique that calls attention to what it is that the author is trying to do.

Tacitus is explicit that no one source can guide readers to the truth. Matters that are important emerge from careful study and reflection. Documents lie, and so do people:[43]

> In describing the death of Drusus, I have reported the story as told
> by the majority of authors, and those of the most authority, but I
> will not pass by a rumor that was circulating in those days…the
> reason that I have reported and discussed the rumor is that I wish to
> refute false stories with clear examples, and I entreat those into
> whose hands our cares have fallen, that they should not prefer
> stories even if they are commonly told and avidly received, nor that
> they should prefer truth turned into marvel.
>
> (*Ann.* 4.10–11)

For Tacitus, the task of history is to teach (4.33), and one of the lessons
that he has to teach is how to evaluate what you are told.

Historians, ancient and modern, delimit the meaning of their analysis through the sources that they select, by what they chose to include or
omit. Edward Gibbon dragged the history of the Roman empire into
the late eighteenth century through the liberal use of ethnography and
all manner of then contemporary theory, using his notes to establish
himself as a trustworthy authority, and thus to teach his contemporaries
a lesson about the internal causes of imperial decline. So Tacitus, moving
from the works of other historians to the gossip of his own day, to the
decrees of the senate, to books (or a book) that others had missed, tried
to teach his readers a lesson from the past about a critical issue in their
own times.

The way that those sources were used by others depended upon a
number of factors. Some of these may broadly be described as cultural,
others as personal, still more as technical. In all cases, issues of what is
said and recorded are intimately bound up with the question of the
nature of scholarship in the Roman empire.

Near Eastern records of the past and the Roman imagination

> I must also fulfill the requirements of those who do not believe
> anything written in the chronicles of barbarians, but hold that only the
> writings of Greeks are to be believed.
>
> (Jos. *Contra. Ap.* 1.161)

The Greeks were not the only people to write history, nor was their
history the only one that might potentially have an impact on the historical consciousness of the Roman empire. Indeed, it was the record of a

people who were long subject to others, be they Assyrian, Babylonian, Greek or Roman, that ultimately came to restructure historical consciousness in much of the Mediterranean world. Other ancient societies had their own records, and linear narrative accounts are by no means a universal method for communicating those records to future generations.[44] But Mesopotamia, Egypt, Anatolia and, most famously, Palestine all saw the creation of narratives concerned with past and contemporary events.[45] The question of how, and under what circumstances, these records might come to be of interest in the ancient Mediterranean thus requires some attention in this context, for it reveals something of the working of cultural prejudice in determining what might count as valid historical material.

The most famous narrative is contained within the Hebrew Bible (Deuternomy–2 Kings). These books form the narrative of the people of Israel, from the "return" to Palestine to the Babylonian exile, and present themselves as inspired literature, the work of an editor rather than a primary investigator. The purpose of this composition was, arguably, to justify claims to hegemony by a group of exiles who had returned from Mesopotamia, bringing with them a radically revised version of a temple cult whose claim to legitimacy they had to assert against local traditions. The Bible was one vehicle for the assertion of that claim, demonstrating how proper worship of Yahweh alone ensured the prosperity of his people. In compiling this record, the editor had access to earlier accounts that dated to the period prior to the exile; to suggest that there were no such accounts would be wrong. Both this editor, the Deuteronomist, and his successor, the author of Chronicles, were heirs to literary traditions that they sought to preserve rather than to question.[46]

Typical features of the sort of composition used by the Deuteronomist historian, and his successor, are badly reconciled, and often contradictory accounts reported without an ostensible effort to establish the "truth" value of one account against the other, repetition, and errors in reconciling numerical calculations.[47] To the author, who was interested in stories from the past to validate a theological message for the future, these were not likely great concerns: stories from different sources about the same event that demonstrated the importance of respect for Yahweh were equally valuable. For the author it mattered more that Yahweh created the Universe than that at one moment he took six days to do it while at another (in the succeeding sentence no less) he accomplished the feat in one (Gen.1–2:2; Gen. 2:4). From the point of view of historical research, the great interest of the Hebrew Bible is that the Deuteronomist, and the author of Chronicles, both read a range of earlier texts; their critical criteria seem to have been defined by the usefulness of the story rather than by a desire to isolate a "true" version or to report variants as such.[48]

The Hebrew Bible obviously had its readers in the Roman world, both in the original languages and in Greek translation, and it is probable that the selection of books was only canonized after the fall of Jerusalem in AD 70.[49] But who were these readers and why were they reading? The most obvious answer to the first question is members of the diverse Jewish communities around the Mediterranean and, later, Christians. But was it a source for conventional historiography concerning the Jews outside of the Jewish community? Here the answer seems to be no. The presentation of Jewish history down to the beginning of the Hasmonean period in Josephus's *Jewish Antiquities* is little more than a pastiche based upon books of scripture, but his point in writing them is to introduce non-Jewish writers to Jewish history (Jos. *AJ.* 1.5; 20.261; *Contra Ap.* 1.54). What would be the point if they were inclined to read it in the books that Josephus was using? It was his task to dress them up with the forms of classical historiography in order to make them more palatable to non-confessional readers.

The past was a source of authority in ancient Mesopotamia as well; the surviving archives of both Babylon and Assyria provide evidence for the research into archives as well as the collation of divergent accounts.[50] Perhaps the most interesting of these texts are those recording the restoration of ancient buildings or institutions. Thus Nabonidus, the last king of independent Babylon, proclaimed when he restored the rites of the High Priestess at Sippur:

> Because for a very long time the office of high priestess had been forgotten and her characteristic features were nowhere indicated, I bethought myself day after day. The appointed time having arrived, the doors were opened for me; indeed I set eyes on an ancient stele of Nebuchadnezzar, the son of Ninurta-nadin-sumi, an early king of the past, on which was depicted the image of the high priestess; moreover they had listed and deposited in the Egipar her appurtenances, her clothing and her jewelry. I carefully looked into the old clay and wooden tablets and did exactly as in the olden days.[51]

Nabonidus's use of archives is anything but exceptional. Contemporary history was a feature of palace decoration in Assyria, while the great libraries of the palaces could be, and were, exploited to reform a record of the past that would suit contemporary circumstances.

The most important text of this sort is the so-called *Synchronistic History*, which appears to have narrated the history of relations between Assyria and Babylon from the middle of the fifteenth century BC to the end of the reign of Adad-Nerari III in 783 BC. While the contents are notable for mendacity, the process of composition, manifestly in the early part of the eighth century BC, led the author to consult archives selectively from some seven hundred years. Divergent traditions are ironed out (always to the advantage of Assyria), making this in principle, a true work of historical investigation, that was retained in three copies over a century after its composition.[52] On the Babylonian side, we have the so-called Chronicle P, a source for the *Synchronistic History*, which derives information from a wide range of texts, including historical epics.[53] Such texts stand apart from the Babylonian Chronicles that run from the eighth century to the early Seleucid period in that the Chronicles are contemporary records, while these are the result of archival research composed to make a point. The exclusion (and deliberate falsification) of material in the *Synchronistic History* reveal the nascent techniques of historiography. It is somewhat ironic that it is a manifest piece of propaganda designed to deceive.

For the purposes of an historian of the Roman Empire such texts are valuable as memorials of a tradition that continued to live on into the Roman world, for it was in the reign of Seleucus I, that a priest named Berossus essayed to translate the historiographic tradition of Babylon into Greek. Berossus had few contemporary readers, and few readers after that; although it does appear that he was used as a source by two historians of the first century BC, Alexander Polyhistor and Juba of Mauretania, both figures who were arguably on the fringes of mainstream literary society. Alexander, a freedman of Sulla, seems to have specialized in rescuing little-read historians from obscurity, and Juba, the husband of Cleopatra Selene (daughter of Mark Antony and Cleopatra) two generations later, seems to have specialized in what the mainstream regarded as recherché learning. Berossus was ignored by Timagenes, the author of what appears to have been a most influential universal history in the reign of Augustus, and also by Pompeius Trogus, the author of a large-scale universal history in Latin at roughly the same time. Berossus's history only attained importance several hundred years later when Christians came to study the Hebrew Bible. Unlike the sources preferred by classical readers, Berossus had a good deal to say about characters who also appeared in the biblical Kings and Chronicles, and he had a creation myth that was stuck in the deepest depths of time whose truth needed to be refuted in order to validate the Hebrew creation account.

The pre-Christian avoidance of Berossus is particularly interesting in light of a continuing interest in the powers that dominated Mesopotamia, both ancient and contemporary. Herodotus may have set the stage for the misunderstanding of Mesopotamian history by attributing an enormously long span to the Assyrian empire prior to what he thought was its conquest by the Medes, and showing no knowledge of Babylon as a great power in its own right. His error was compounded by Ctesias of Cnidus, whose twenty-three-book *Persika* opened with a five-book account of Assyrian history in which he attributed to their empire a 1,300-year span, a number that bears no relationship to any known Mesopotamian chronology.[54] Possibly stemming from Ctesias's authority as an eyewitness (he was the court doctor to Artaxerxes II), Assyria came into the western tradition as the first great empire, to be succeeded by the Medes, Persians and, according to later traditions, the Macedonians. The scheme of four empires that thus emerged may owe something as well to the four ages of Man in Hesiod's *Theogony*, representing thereby a rather interesting fusion of myth with historical understanding. This understanding changed somewhat by the second century BC, when Rome was added to the list as the fifth and final kingdom.[55] The scheme of successive world empires then became a topos, useful for organizing world history. Dionysius of Halicarnassus exploited the notion of the five empires in the preface to his *Roman Antiquities* as a way of pointing out that Rome was superior to the four previous kingdoms, and Pompeius Trogus adopted it to give structure to his universal history.[56] In the second century, Appian used it in the preface to his collected histories of Rome's wars and civil wars in a way that was very similar to Dionysius.[57]

The legacy of Herodotus and his place in the educational curriculum may be seen in another way: the persistent interpretation in official propaganda of Parthian and, later, Sassanian history in terms evocative of his description of the Achaemenids. While it is just possible that a Parthian monarch may actually have claimed Achaemenid hegemony (including the eastern provinces of the Roman empire) in the reign of Tiberius (AD 14–37), the attribution of Achaemenid aspirations to rule all lands as far as the Hellespont or beyond by the first Sassanians is a western myth.[58] The sources of information for this claim produce in one case (Cassius Dio) no evidence to support it, and in the other (Herodian) an alleged letter from Ardashir that he could never have seen. What is more important, their statements are not supported by the self-presentation of the second Sassanian monarch, Sapor I, in the massive inscription that he commissioned to describe the causes and results of his wars with Rome. A later statement that the Sassanians aspired to the empire of Xerxes, allegedly in a letter from Sapor II to Constantius II (AD 337–61) in 356, rests upon hearsay.[59]

Roman fantasies about Persia are of further interest because the Roman state actually had reasonably good access to information about Persian ambitions. The collection of intelligence from beyond the frontiers depended upon a wide variety of informants ranging from merchants (the least reliable) to highly placed traitors (the most reliable) and exiles (problematic, with a tendency to being self-serving).[60] Roman attachment to the image of the empire as the defender of civilization along the lines of the Athenians in 480 BC was widely advertised, and is a sign of the curious double vision inherent in a culture that was devoted to ancient literature.[61] While precise knowledge of Persian affairs was available, it tended to be exploited in a context saturated by the history of classical Greece: nonsense and knowledge could coexist, the available tools of learning would not necessarily supersede cultural assumption.

Egypt was different. The scribes of Egypt produced no chronicles to compare with those composed in Babylon or Nineveh. The royal inscriptions on temples that form such an important part of our understanding of various reigns seem not to have played a fundamental role in an ancient Egyptian's understanding of his or her own history. Perhaps this is inevitable in a land where history began anew with each new pharaoh. There were texts that were composed at court for broader dissemination, and some of these were along the lines of the more literary inscriptions, featuring scenes where the Pharaoh turns away bad advice and sees his way to direct his armies to victory. There were dynasty lists, and there were works of fiction that served to form a historical consciousness through the presentation of ideal figures.[62] But we have no evidence of a systematic effort to join the works of different traditions together to form a coherent narrative of the past before the reign of Ptolemy I Soter, and when this happened the choice of source material is extremely revealing.

Manetho probably wrote somewhere around 280 BC. His text married a dynastic list with texts known to modern scholars as *Königsnovellen*, novelistic texts based upon the encounter between a king and a sage, and other works that would fit the modern (or even the Greek) notion of fiction.[63] Narratives were joined to the king-lists as he had them; not all (or even most) kings were the object of any discourse. A representative section of the history (in terms of style, if not content) ran as follows:

after the expulsion of the shepherd folk, the king who expelled them, Tethmosis, ruled for another twenty-five years, four months, and died, and his son, Chebrom took the throne for thirteen years, after him Amenophis for twenty years, seven months, his sister Amesses, twenty-one years and nine months, her son Memphres, twelve years, nine months…[12 more kings]…his son Sethos, also called Rameses, who had a powerful force of horse and foot. He made his brother Harmais governor of Egypt, and gave him all the royal prerogatives, ordering him only not to wear the diadem, and not to be unjust to the queen, the mother of his children, and to stay away from the other royal concubines. He himself campaigned against Cyprus and Phoenicia, and then, again, against the Assyrians and the Medes…(FGrH 609 Fr.9)

The style of the passage just quoted is typical of Manetho, a point confirmed by a howl of protest from Josephus when he wrote, very shortly after quoting the passage quoted here, that "up to this point he followed the Chronicles, then he gave himself liberty to offer to record legends and gossip about the Jews, interpolating nonsense, wishing to confuse us with a crowd of Egyptian lepers and other diseased people" (*Contra Ap.* 1.228). The content of the passage about Rameses, while showing some dependence upon Egyptian legend, is in fact a piece of Ptolemaic propaganda intended to offer a model for Ptolemaic campaigns against the Seleucids, and to join the traditions of Egypt with those of Argos, an important point because of Ptolemaic dynastic claims.[64] The reference to the Medes, who did not exist as a people until the very last years of the Assyrian regime, shows a clear dependence upon the pseudo-history of Mesopotamia invented by earlier Greek authors. The legend of Rameses here proved, it seems, to be one of the more influential developments in his whole history. Herodotus had attributed conquests of this sort to Sesostris, but when Germanicus arrived in Egypt in AD 18, it was a colossal statue identified as Rameses that he sought as the place to receive an account from Egyptian priests, an account that seems to have been modeled on this very passage of Manetho (Tac. *Ann.* 2.60.3).

Manetho's success with the story about Rameses, a success that probably stemmed from his introduction of contemporary Greek material into the Egyptian account, was exceptional. In what looks like a quotation from the introduction to his history, it appears that he claimed to have translated accounts from "sacred texts," and that Herodotus had made errors through ignorance. The choice of Herodotus as a target is not accidental, for Herodotus must by then have replaced Hecataeus of Miletus as "the" authority on Egyptian matters. But Herodotus was soon replaced by Hecataeus of Abdera, and it is his work rather than Manetho's that forms the basis of Diodorus Siculus's narrative of Egyptian history in the second book of his *Universal History*. Diodorus is something of a touchstone for taste in the mid-first century BC on this matter, since he elsewhere appears to have sought information from acknowledged classics. It is revealing that, aside from Josephus, who discussed Manetho because Manetho had rude things to say about the Jews, we do not have a single quotation from any classical author prior to the emergence of the Christian chronographic tradition. Christians, of course, had great difficulty in finding any studies of Biblical history written by Greco-Roman authors, and it is as a result of that difficulty that they rescued Berossus and Manetho from oblivion.

The treatment of Near Eastern histories by Roman authors in the classical tradition represents a form of treatment for a source tradition that was influenced by cultural tradition rather than close analysis. The logic that Egyptian texts could tell you more about Egyptian history than Greek texts does not appear to have been self-evident. Likewise it is interesting that where we do see Egyptian texts, including the *Königsnovellen*, entering the Greek, and then the Roman tradition, their fusion with invented traditions also depends upon cultural stereotyping. "Eastern Wisdom" was much valued in the Roman world, and some actual Egyptian texts such as the *Oracle of the Potter* were translated and read in this context.[65]

Grammarians and historians

How, in the ancient world, did you go about determining what is true, and how is it that technical expertise and morality were considered equally valid critical tools? So far I have suggested that cultural prejudice and personal background are significant factors. But they were not the only factors, and neither factor consciously informs the discourse of criticism in antiquity. The paradigm of research to which authors might appeal (even if not doing it very well) was determined in another context.

Modern historians have tended to draw upon an analogy with the physical sciences for their notion of what is true. The result has not been wholly without cost, and has led to the belief that history is an "objective" enterprise, that truth emerges simply from the bare record of facts. In the United States, appeal has long been made to the authority of

Leopold Ranke and his dictum that it was the historian's duty to simply tell the story "as it actually was" (*wie es eigentlich gewesen*), a statement that looks very much like a reference to a lecture on history delivered by Wilhelm von Humbolt three years before Ranke's *History of the Latin and Germanic Peoples from 1494–1514* (in the preface to which the famous statement occurs) saw the light of day.[66] The decline of strong positivism amongst later twentieth-century historians does not stem so much from an engagement with what Ranke was trying to say, as from an unfortunate assumption that he supported a view that the fact offers its own meaning.[67] Such a view means that there can only be one truth about an event.

Classical historians (and, indeed, their successors down to the end of the eighteenth century) did not have an "authoritarian" understanding of the meaning of the fact. The fact (for which there is no good Greek or Latin word) is a "true" thing that the historian knows, and uses in the construction of a useful discourse. But how did one know that what one had was true? What, in the absence of modern physical science, could offer historians in ancient times a paradigm for establishing a "fact"? To answer these questions, it is necessary to turn once again to the grammarians.

Grammarians, not historians, were the real scholars of antiquity. History as a discipline emerged in the Greek world in the context of the systematic (if somewhat silly) study of all phenomena (including speech), that began in the sixth century BC. In the fourth and third centuries BC, with the establishment of the great library at Alexandria and then the library at Pergamon, critical scholarship reached a new level. Textual scholarship led the way, and the leaders in the field were three third-century BC librarians at Alexandria: Zenodotus, Aristophanes and Aristarchus. Their work, as will be seen, combined objective collation of variant reading with subjective judgments concerning the suitability of specific readings. The dividing line between the objective and subjective is not altogether apparent in all cases.

In the generation after Aristarchus, definite efforts were made to define *grammatikê* as an actual *technê* with specific rules (the point attacked by Sextus Empiricus) under the influence of Aristotelian and Stoic linguistic theory.[68] The key figure here appears to be Dionysius Thrax, and one crucial part of the process appears to have been the development of a technical vocabulary for describing linguistic phenomena, or the division of *lexis* (diction) into its constituent parts. Coincidental with the description of *lexis* was the description of *hellenismos*. According to Asclepiades of Myrleia, the starting point of all languages of communication was Attic

Greek. Attic was thus the "common usage" of all Greeks. One determined common usage through usage, analogy, etymology and, according to some, literary authority. This theory of proper Greek appears to have been fully developed by the beginning of the first century BC, and, possibly, to have influenced Latin theory (especially as represented by Varro) in the definition of *latinitas*.[69]

The study of text and language under these conditions could thus be an objective science, or attain the status of one. Such was the authority that accrued to the trained grammarian that Galen waited until a *philologos* could be summoned in order to determine if a book that was found in a bookshop was really by him, or was a fake. He wrote a lot, and evidently could not remember everything that he had done in detail. But the language with which the *philologos* proclaimed the work in question a fake raises again the issue of subjectivity. He said that a man as well-educated as Galen could not possibly have produced the stylistically weak work that he had in front of him. His judgment was thus based upon his view of Galen's reputation rather than any obviously close study of the great man's work. Likewise, it is interesting that Galen makes extensive use of the techniques of textual scholarship, while his view of the value of "history" appears to be limited to case studies in the work of other doctors. In his implicit hierarchy of disciplines, that of the grammarian rated imitation, while that of the historian was not evidently regarded as being on the same level.[70]

Textual scholarship in the Roman empire was based upon three principles: collation, usage and "the appropriate" (*to prepon*). The nature of textual transmission made the close study of variant traditions an obvious course to take for those who sought to establish *grammatikê* as a discipline in its own right: textual variants could be explained by scribal error, and the validity of observations could be sustained by empirical observation (either the words were in the text or they were not). Galen once again offers an excellent insight into the process when he writes that, in the case of unclear passages, "nothing prevents a person engaged in this business either from adding what is left out or straightening out what is wrong. Just as it is reckless to change old readings, so too the removal of difficulties by some small addition or change is the work of good writers of commentaries" (*De diff. resp.* 3.2 [VII 894.5–10 Kühn]).[71] While we have no explicit statement of this sort from any of the three great editors of Homer, it is plain that they worked in the same spirit. Thus Zenodotus, while he wrote no commentary, can be seen to have omitted many lines from his edition. We cannot be certain (although some have argued that this was the case) that he did so on the basis of collation of the manuscripts, though it is clear that he recognized problems in transmission and that his text was shorter than the *koine*, and shorter than the one that Aristarchus later produced.

Aware that his choices were controversial, Zenodotus recognized that he needed to justify his decisions, probably through notes written in the margin of the text, and he evolved a series of criteria for doing so. Often the choice would be made on grounds of diction. At *Iliad* 3.364 he read "heaven on high" in place of "broad heaven" on the grounds of usage in Pindar; at *Iliad* 2.484 he read "Olympian daughters with deep folded dresses" in place of "having homes on Olympus," again on the basis of Pindar and, it seems, the usage in the Hymns. Aristarchus attacked him on the grounds that Greek women in Homer do not wear "deep folded dresses," while Trojan women did (*Il.* 18.122; 339; 24.215).[72] The important point here is that there is no reason to think that Zenodotus was resorting to conjectural emendation; rather, he was deciding between variants in the tradition. In his criticism of Zenodotus, Aristarchus was doing the same thing. The logical problem with Aristarchus's criticism of Zenodotus is that Greek women in Homer would wear "deep folded dresses" if you accept the reading that Zenodotus accepted. Neither Aristarchus nor Zenodotus could appeal to a "superior" manuscript tradition to make the decision for them, since such a tradition did not exist.

Another determinant was *to prepon*, the suitable. The debate over this criterion stems from differing views in Plato and Aristotle. Plato argued that "unsuitable readings" should be removed from the poets. In Aristotelian terms, solutions to "problems" could be found through historical or philological learning, and the statements of poets could be justified on the grounds that they were true, as they were said to be, or as they ought to be.[73] Zenodotus seems, more often than not, to be working within the Aristotelian tradition when he, for instance, accepts a different beginning to the *Iliad* on the grounds that the wrath of Achilles is not a function of the plan of Zeus, and, arguably, when he says that Helen would not offer Aphrodite a seat on a small stool since this is not the way that people treated gods in Homer (*Il.* 3.421 fol).[74] On the other hand, there are plainly cases where he seems to be closer to the Platonic norm.

The importance of literary critical practices to historians is evident throughout the classical period of Roman historiography. Likewise, the vocabulary of literary criticism seems to come naturally to those not indulging in historical writing, which suggests that these were the standards by which factual records were evaluated. When the Younger Pliny contemplated writing a history, and considered doing one of the past, he observed that the material was all there but that the collation of accounts was hard, *onerosa collatio* (5.8). This is the explicit language of the grammarian. The rather remarkable statement of Tacitus regarding his procedure in chronicling events under Nero participates in this same discourse. He says that he will follow the consensus of the authors (three of them), and reveal differences in their accounts under the names of each (*Ann.* 13.20). If he had been editing Homer he might have said that he would offer a text based on the consensus of the readings available. The particular oddity of Tacitus's statement is that we know that he made full use of sources well beyond the three writers that he mentions.

Polybius knew that things got lost, and that, when he was dependent upon historians, he was in trouble. Polybius's history depended upon autopsy, collation, documents and common sense. Thus when his great rival, Timaeus, accused Ephorus of an error in addition he noted that this had nothing to do with Ephoran numeracy, but with the stupidity of a scribe: Timaeus should have recognized a textual problem when he saw it (12.4a). A sense of what was appropriate was also important. When Timaeus describes Demochares, an Athenian politician of the late fourth century, as a rogue, this was simply inappropriate because the Athenians were respectable people, and respectable people would not have selected an unworthy leader (12.13). Polybius's discussion is in very similar terms to that offered by Dionysius of Halicarnassus in his discussion of Thucydides' Melian Dialogue. Here the sentiments of the Athenian speaker are judged unworthy of the speaker. They are wrong not because Thucydides could not have heard what was said, but because, in attributing a statement to the Athenian, he had selected sentiments that were unworthy of a representative of such a city (*De Thuc.* 41). Discourse on the determination of verity as defined by appropriateness, which might strike us as being simply stupid, is important in that it is mingled with the sort of technical analysis that we would all respect. But to the ancient mind, the careful scrutiny of original documents and criticism on the basis of moral appropriateness were both technical disciplines, having been established as such by the grammarians.

The physical process

It is impossible to consider research without considering the physical process connected with the final product, the *ekdosis*. Galen makes it abundantly clear that he regarded failures of the physical process of transmission as a fundamental problem in the production of an edition, and that problems could creep into a text at a very early stage. There were no note cards, no computer databases, no texts on disc to be manipulated until they could form a readable text.

Roman historians did not necessarily take notes in their own hand. Cassius Dio records that he heard things, manifestly in written accounts, about the Rome of the Julio-Claudians and Flavians a century before he was born or began to write history himself.[75] He is not talking here about personal informants as he was when he said that his father had unearthed embarrassing truths about the accession of Hadrian in AD 117 (Dio 79.1.3). He is plainly using a word that came naturally to him in the course of composition. He heard it because his slave reader was reading to him.[76] His process was scarcely exceptional. The Younger Pliny offers the following picture of his uncle at work:

> he gave whatever spare time he had to his studies.(10) After lunch (which was usually light and simple after the custom of our ances-tors), if he had a chance he would often, in the summer, lie in the sun while a book was read to him, make notes and extracts. He never read anything that he did not make extracts from; he was accustomed to say that no book was so bad that he could not profit from some part of it.(11) After his time in the sun he would usually take a cold bath, eat, and then have a short nap; then he would work as if it were a new day until dinner time. A book was read aloud over dinner, and he took rapid notes.(12) I remember one occasion upon which one of his friends, when the reader pronounced something incorrectly, compelled the reader to go back and pronounce the word correctly and my uncle said to him "could you not under-stand him?" When he admitted that he could, he said, "then why did you make him go back, we have lost ten full lines through your interruption."
>
> (3.5.9–12)

The reader or *lector* is the ubiquitous figure on the Roman literary landscape. He, sometimes she, is found at dinner parties, accompanying the master on walks, and even as an aid to sleep; the emperor Augustus was evidently fond of having someone read to him if he woke in the night so that he could go back to sleep.[77] Despite some pictures of litera-teurs sitting in rooms full of books talking to each other without the aid of the intermediary, the overwhelming impression of the personal contact between a man of letters and any piece of writing is that there is another person in the room. While it is true that aristocrats might read things for themselves, especially private documents or texts of no literary merit, we often find the *lector* present even for this process. Before writing a letter to Atticus, Cicero says that he had the last two from his friend read to him as soon as it was light (*Att.* 16.13=SB 423). Juvenal asks who will give the historian as much as he gives the person who reads the *acta* to him (7.104). Cicero appears to have had a *lector* reading out passages of the *Republic* when his friend Sallustius came over so that he could suggest improvements.[78] In another context he suggests that people would come to watch him read or write, presumably neither activity was without sound (*Fam.* 9.20=SB 193).

Public places were rather noisy. An orderly city was one where a person could hear children reading their lessons (Livy 6.25.9) or, it seems, the monuments. Ennius speaks of a talking column that announces the glory of the Scipios. The column talks, one may assume, because people are reading the inscription on it out loud.[79] It is this that makes Tiberius's statement to the Senate that he wished the scroll he had composed concerning the virtues of Germanicus to be inscribed, so that it would be of use to the young of future generations, all the more interesting (*Tab. Siar.* Fr.b col. 2, 16–17). His readers would be speaking his words out aloud as they read them. A library was another place to read, making it an intensely sonorous spot; the *lectores* are presumably patrons in this case rather than performers.[80] They might also be dictating the contents of books to scribes. Lucian suggests that the purchasers of books would read them aloud in the bookshop (*Ind.* 2).

Not everyone read aloud all the time, though what may be the most famous instance of silent reading suggests that it was a rarity among the rich. Augustine thought it was amazing that Ambrose should do so (*Conf.* 6.3.5). It was presumably amazing not because Augustine was an upstart from North Africa unfamiliar with the ways of senators, but rather because, based on his experience with the upper classes, it was unusual for such a person to be seen reading rather than being read to. For Augustine, it may also have been a mark of personal spirituality, for at the decisive moment of his life, he too read silently to himself (*Conf.* 8.12). In a rather less spiritual context, Gaius Fannius dreamed that Nero sat down in his study and read his three books on the crimes of Nero. There is no suggestion here that Nero read the book so that Fannius could hear it (*Ep.* 5.5).[81] Likewise one might be expected to read private letters silently in public, as Caesar did when he received a love letter from Cato's sister during the debate over the fate of the Catilinarian conspirators (Plut. *Brut.* 5).

Most reading appears to have been aloud in upper-class circles, though this was not a hard and fast rule. People obviously could, and did, read without moving their lips if they wanted to. Cicero may have favored readers precisely because he had trouble with his eyes for much of the period of his life that is covered by his extant correspondence.[82] As Bernard Knox observed, it is also rather difficult to believe that Aristarchus collated manuscripts out loud.[83] The importance of divergent tastes in encountering literature is great for evaluating the actual practice of research simply because it suggests that there may have been more than one model.

What then does it mean when the listener takes a note? Cicero says that he made a note of a solution to a legal problem when he had been drinking. Was he reading the book himself? Almost certainly not: when he heard the point, he had a slave copy it out and send it to his friend Trebatius (*Fam.* 7.22=SB 331). The same process appears to be followed by the Elder Pliny (possibly minus the drink). There is no suggestion that he wrote things down himself, or that the massive notebook of quotations that he created was in his own hand. Aulus Gellius seems to have written things out on his own, for he says:

> Whenever I took some Greek or Latin book in hand, or I heard something worth remembering, I wrote down whatever interested me, of whatever sort it might be, with no clear plan or order, as an aid to my memory, a kind of literary storehouse... The result is that there is the same disparity in these notebooks as there was in those original notes that were made briefly with no rhyme or reason as a result of various instructive encounters or readings.
>
> (*NA* proem 2–3)

The first distinction here is between what he found in books that came to hand (*in manu*) and things that he had heard. The contents of the *Attic Nights* makes it plain that things he classified as heard were just that, conversations involving some one whom he regarded as worth quoting. He implies that his reading is on his own, not, as we have seen, an impossible situation. The notes that he took may therefore be in his own hand, unless we are to believe that he kept a secretary with him as he read to himself. The next distinction is between the *adnotationes* and the *commentarii* that he wrote up on the basis of those notes. He does not suggest that he went back to the books from which he was quoting as he organized those notes. Quite the opposite, since he says that he used his notes when he did not have the books with him, and all that he did was to put the notes in some order. His explicit description of the final product as *commentarii* shows that he regarded the *Attic Nights* as falling one step short of a finished piece of work.

Other evidence for scholarly research reveals different habits. Polybius stressed the importance of personal autopsy, and gives the impression of having consulted much evidence first hand. Cicero often depended upon the research resources of Atticus. But when he had a question for Atticus, did Atticus look up the answer? In one case Cicero suggests that Atticus can get information himself, either from the principals or from Satyrus and Syrus, slaves or freedmen who would surely know the answer (*Att.* 12.22.2=SB 261.2). On another occasion Cicero writes "will you see to it that he looks it up in the book of senatorial decrees from the consulship of Gnaeus Cornelius and Lucius Mummius?" (*Att.* 13.33.3=SB 309.3). But in the case of both Polybius and Cicero it appears that they end up working from notes (*adnotationes*), whether in their own hand or that of another. Polybius's journeys took place in some cases well before he recorded the results in his history, and Cicero is explicitly asking for notes to supplement information that he seems already to have had in insufficient form. Cassius Dio says that he researched for ten years before writing, which took him twelve years.[84] The final draft must then have come from notes made earlier. Plutarch, who researched his biographies in groups, would likewise seem to have composed from notes taken on various authors.[85] Lucian said that the historian should start from notes (*hypomnemata*) and work up the history on the basis of them later (*Hist.* 47–8).[86]

With Dio and Plutarch, as well as with Cicero in his philosophic works, the question then arises as to what language these notes were in. They are explicitly dealing with translations from Latin into Greek or Greek into Latin. Pliny's manifold researches took him (and his reader) through vast quantities of Greek; so too Livy, who worked with the Greek history of Rome by Fabius Pictor, and the Greek history of Polybius. Cicero claims that he could compose fluently in Greek, hence his history of his consulship in that language, and, like other Romans, would have learned to write the language through doing translations.[87] Some Greek translations of Latin works that have survived on papyri in the east from the first century AD may have their origin in similar efforts at self improvement.[88] Aulus Gellius mingles Greek quotation easily with his Latin, suggesting that the bilingual aristocrat might only change the language of his notes in the last phase of composition.

Only in the case of Livy, alone of extant Latin historians, can we detect anything of the process of bilingual adaptation, in those sections of the history where he is translating sections of Polybius. The first point that emerges is that he is not making a translation. The art of formal translation had its own rules, certainly formalized by Livy's own time, and there is no sign that Livy was interested in appearing to be a Polybius Latinus. There are some places where he made mistakes. At one point he has Romans and Aetolians fighting each other underground with doors; at another, he has the Macedonian army drop its pikes before charging the Romans. The first of these points may be a simple error in transcription, reading *thuras* (doors) for *thureas* (shields); the other might be a failure to appreciate the meaning of the technical expression *katabalousi tas sarisas*, which means to lower the sarissa.[89] Both errors might have been corrected from context if Polybius was being read directly, a possible indication that Livy was using notes that were in Greek rather than the original text. Three other mistranslations may point in the same direction: the failure to distinguish between Boeotian and Phthiotic Thebes, the statement that the summer was a good time to attack a city (rather than that a river was useful in supplying troops besieging a city in summer), and the identification of the Aetolian assembly in the Thermaic gulf as being at Thermopylae. The geographic errors would again be readily correctable if the full text was in front of him, especially as Livy gets the identity of Phthiotic Thebes correct on two other occasions.[90] It is certainly better to see all such errors as stemming from a procedural problem rather than from fundamental problems with Livy's Greek, especially as it has been demonstrated that he was capable of translating Polybius with extreme accuracy elsewhere.[91] It would be interesting to know if Livy, like Cicero, worked with scribes who specialized in dealing with Greek texts (*Fam.* 16.21.8=SB 337.8).

The movement from notes to draft varied from author to author, and might not even be consistent within the work of one person. Galen expresses a preference for writing drafts in his own hand, including variant versions in the margins that scribes did not recognize as such. At other times he says that he dictated things. Cicero's physical problems towards the end of his life, the bad eyesight that he blames for causing him to send personal letters in the hand of a secretary rather than his own, suggests that the greatest Latin prose author may not have set pen to parchment himself for a significant part of his career. Letters of Augustus existed in his own hand to be read by Suetonius (who notes trouble that he had with spelling) (*Aug.* 88).[92] Julius Caesar wrote to his friends in his own hand (sometimes using a code that he had developed), and is said to have been able to read or write one thing while dictating another, and listening to something else.[93] It is thus possible that he wrote some of his major works himself, and he seems to have left notes for books of *commentarii* that he did not finish before his death (in whose hand we cannot know).[94] Horace is scathing about poets who dictated hundreds of lines while standing on one foot before dinner; Vergil is said to have dictated a large number of lines in the morning and to have worked them over again in the afternoon, reducing the number (Hor. *Sat.* 1.4.9; Suet. *Verg.* 22.).

There was no one system of producing a draft. One might dictate or write it out depending on choice. For a specific case connected with an historian, there is C. Fannius, to whom Nero appeared in a dream. Fannius plainly visualized himself as working alone in his study (5.5). Petronius visualizes the fictional poet Eumolpus sitting alone writing, just as Horace, Persius and Martial suggest that they did.[95] Cassius Dio, as we have seen, clearly had someone with him.

The physical construction of an autograph manuscript, meaning a manuscript produced under the direct supervision of the author, has now been analysed with great care on the basis of a carbonized papyrus from Herculaneum, containing an early working draft of a work on philosophers by the Epicurean philosopher Philodemus. Philodemus's process, which appears to be similar to that of other authors, was as follows:[96]

1   Philodemus provided a list of texts that he wanted to have copied, marking out sections of other texts, dictating the shorter ones, or handing over *pugillares* (wax or wooden tablets) to be copied.
2   Philodemus dictated his introductions to the different passages and other linking material.
3   A scribe produces a first draft where longer passages were continued onto the back of individual sheets.
4   Additions, supplements and correction written on the front, back, margins or any other empty space on the sheet are collated.
5   The corrected text is copied out or dictated.

The papyri used in the first stage of the compositional process were not connected rolls. They were individual sheets that could be gathered up and glued together to make a roll, readily identifiable as such in the surviving record by the fact that they might contain writing on both sides of the papyrus along with other marginalia. Indeed, the surviving record has now shown that the supposition of R.G. Prentice on Thucydides's compositional process was correct. He had written:

But how was it possible for Thucydides to be continually revising and enlarging his book, how could he have acquired certain "docu-

ments gradually and stuck them in his manuscript to work up later,"
if his manuscript was on papyrus rolls? Such a procedure can be
imagined only if the author wrote on flat sheets, which he kept
together in a bundle or in a box....The original manuscript
consisted of a pile of loose sheets with many corrections, alterations
and insertions.[97]

The point of examining the physical process by which information came
to be reported is not simply to understand how books came together
over a long period of time. It is also to get a view of the distance
between source material and finished draft. At every stage of transmission there were fresh opportunities for error to creep in, for tone to be
altered, for information to be garbled. Perhaps the most important point
of all is the ubiquity of notes. The passages excerpted at the beginning
of the process appear to be the basic material from which later narratives were constructed. An author might (would) have close copies of a
source made at this stage, but it would not be the whole thing, and it
looks as if much of the work with a text would be on the first reading. It
is then that decisions would be made about what to include, and what to
leave out.

The draft that emerged at the end of the third stage of the composition process outlined above could be the basis for later developments in a
work. Indeed, in the case of three historians it is possible to observe
something of the connection between the draft at this stage and the final
product. The first of these is Thucydides, whose importance as a model
for historiography in the Roman empire makes him relevant here. In an
appendix to the fifth volume of the unrivaled commentary on his history
that was completed in 1981, Antony Andrewes analysed indications of
incompleteness in the surviving text to show how Thucydides composed
extended prose drafts on the basis of extensive earlier notes. He had, for
instance, a long account, made at the time, of the escape of the
Plataeans from the Spartan siege, and texts of the various documents
that have come down in Books 5 and 8 which he would probably have
shortened in a final draft (unless he was in the process of changing his
working methods). The continuous prose draft came to an end where
Book 8 now ends, and Book 8, with its many inconsistencies awaiting
rectification, represents the earliest extant phase of Thucydides's
compositional practice. It is at this stage that the basic form of the
account is reached, "in many cases, perhaps in most, it would not be
necessary to alter his first draft, though from time to time we see from
the reflection of later events that he must have done so."[98] Finally, it is

Figure 3 An autograph text. The recto (on the left) is written in a very good hand, giving us the first two lines of a poem and the opening of a work on "What Hesiod would have said when he was inspired by the Muses." The verso (right) is part of an encomium, and at the lower left we can see substantial

changes written in the hand of the author. It is possible that
the author of the verso also wrote the text on the recto,
using his best handwriting for the finished product.

Source: P. Oxy. 3537 46 5B.51/E (1–2)b. © The Egypt Exploration Society, London

worth noting that the final stage of composition, where speeches were added, removed the text farther from the actual source material than the first draft. It is of considerable interest that in antiquity these differences were explained as a result of a change in plan (*proairesis*), suggesting that a final plan for a work was not obtained until a very late stage (Dion. *De Thuc.* 16)

A careful examination of Livy's compositional technique reveals habits very similar to those that may be deduced for Thucydides. T. J. Luce has argued, with great conviction, that Livy did not compose one book at a time, or even necessarily in groups of five books. Compositional units could be as great as fifteen books, and for these books Livy read his sources, took his notes, determined key themes and manipulated his material as he saw fit. Thematic divisions between units do not necessarily indicate that groups of books were composed at different times; they can be interpreted as predetermined subdivisions within the larger whole, so that the preface to Book 6 can be seen as marking a thematic turning point within a fifteen-book account of the rise of Rome prior to the First Punic War.[99] On the question of the manipulation of material within narrative sections, a key test case for Luce's view emerges from the narration of events in 182 BC, where Livy draws material from Polybius's account of Italian affairs at 40.3.3, and in the immediately following clause uses material from Polybius's account of affairs in Macedonia, which would have been separated from the Italian affairs by the account of matters in Sicily, Spain and Africa.[100] The extent to which Livy followed one author at a time was simply that which was dictated by the choice of notes that he had available. The choice of what notes to use was not made in ignorance of other accounts of the period.

With Tacitus the clearest evidence of practice may emerge from the hand of Pliny the Younger. When Tacitus wrote to him, asking for information about the death of the Elder Pliny at the eruption of Vesuvius, he seems to have worded the request in a way as to suggest that he had already made decisions about how to treat the event (Ep. 6.16). Pliny suggests that Tacitus asked for the account so that he could write about the eruption more accurately (Ep. 6.16.1). How much did he add on the basis of the pages that Pliny wrote him? We obviously cannot know, but the fact that he then decided to say something about the Younger Pliny as well suggests that the draft was still in a state of some flux, just as we have seen that Thucydides's must have been. It is well known that the eight-book division of Thucydides's history is not necessarily Thucydidean. A thirteen-book edition was known in antiquity, and the eight-book edition does violence to Thucydidean grammar at a crucial point.[101] If Tacitus was expanding his account of Vesuvius as new information reached him, does this mean that he had not yet decided on book divisions while the work was in draft stage?

The division of a history into books plainly meant more to historians, and writers of all sorts, after the emergence of professional grammarians. Vergil, for instance, seems to have composed far more lines than ultimately found their way into the *Aeneid*, but he also produced a first draft in prose. It may have been when he had done this that he determined the shape that the finished product would take. Similarly, might Tacitus and Livy have decided upon the division of their material when they had already done most of the research for major sections? While we cannot answer these questions with certainty, the compositional habits of antiquity, varied though they were, do suggest that caution is in order when discussing the shape that a book would have taken.

When an author had developed a final draft of a work, he would then circulate it amongst friends and/or offer recitations to the public. This process has already been examined, and there is no need to rehearse that discussion here. The process of circulation involved checking for stylistic problems for the most part, rather than for points of detail, and it was then that the author might lose control of the product.

Conclusion

Classical historians were not the only scholars in the ancient world, and they did not set the scholarly standards of their culture. These standards emerged from the study of text and language, and came to influence the historian's view of the way that "true statements" could be assembled. There was a clear awareness of the availability of first-hand documents, but there was a tendency to place these at a secondary level in compiling an account. An educated gentleman like Aulus Gellius or the Elder Pliny might specialize in the compilation of extracts from earlier writings, the assemblage of *commentarii* that could form the basis for a later work, or even be offered to the public as the sum total of one's labors.

When it came to handling primary materials, two widespread cultural biases are apparent. The first of these is that representatives of mainstream culture are preferred to outsiders even when outsiders might well have better information. Lucian of Samosata or Justin Martyr might obtain a literary hearing in the second century AD because they had become members of that literary culture. There can be no question but that Jesus Christ himself could not have found a broad audience for works that he had composed in Aramaic unless (as is possible) such writings or, more likely, recorded sayings were put into a more acceptable literary framework by someone else. Berossus and Manetho, to say nothing of the authors of the Hebrew Bible who wrote things that, for all of their best efforts, read oddly, were avoided before the rise of Christianity. The movement of the Hebrew Bible from the fringes of educated society to the center marks a major cultural shift that accompanied the rise of Christianity. But even then the shift was not total; liturgical works written in languages other than Greek tended to stay in those languages, and the victorious church was marked by linguistic as well as doctrinal divergences.

The second cultural prejudice is in favor of the personal informant over the document. Herodian almost never quotes documents directly and Cassius Dio, in writing about his own time, has a tendency to regard them as dubious guides at best. It never seems to have occurred to him to make a detailed investigation of archives in the writing of contemporary history. This is all the more striking as archival research was a feature of Roman administration. Even if archives were organized in awkward ways, we can see both Roman governors and provincials appealing to documents to make a point. But they were not privileged above other sources in the composition of learned works. Tacitus, for instance, used them not in the way that a modern scholar might, to correct accounts received from other sources, but to fill in around the edges, to add depth to the account, to change emphasis. It may be that this preference was conditioned by the practices of Herodotus and Thucydides, who had exalted the eyewitness to the level of primary importance in the writing of history.

Personal informants were valued on an equal level with documents, as were other literary works, it seems until the rise of Christianity. It may be that the apologetic tradition that developed in the second century AD had something to do with this. Christian apologists valued direct quotation of documents to make points about pagan belief, and Eusebius quotes directly from countless texts in his history of the Church, just as he did in other works.

The physical process of scholarship is critical. An author would start from notes, but as a work progressed he would move further and further from the texts upon which he based his account. It was a process that could (and did) lead to the accidental alteration of details; final checking of a text did not, it seems, include recourse to the original sources on a regular basis. The shape of a work seems to have been in flux up to a very late phase in composition, but when a draft was ready to be circulated, the issue that concerned the author was style, not accuracy of detail. Pollio's statement that Caesar would have corrected errors in his *Commentarii* if he had had a chance is remarkable for its isolation in the tradition (Suet. *Caes.* 56.4).

Scholarship in the ancient world cannot be measured by modern standards. So much is obvious. To argue that the process left much to be desired would, however, be to miss the more basic point. There were cultural standards of critical research, and these standards exercise a profound effect over the surviving literary record. It is now to the final stage of presenting that research that we turn our attention.

Chapter 4

Presentation

The problem

Rome

It was Thucydides who drew the distinction between a history that would be a possession for all time and a lightweight bit of writing to win immediate applause (1.22.4). However, this did not mean that he approved of bad writing, or dull presentation. What he never did do was to offer a formula by which excellent research could be presented to the public in an interesting way. Instead, he created a critical vocabulary of abuse. Josephus imitated Thucydides's style as best he could in his *Jewish War*, and found that he was attacked in very Thucydidean terms:

> Certain disreputable characters have attacked my history as a prize essay for boys in school, an astonishing and wicked charge...I wrote my history of the war, being a participant in many of the events, and an eyewitness to most of them, I was ignorant of nothing that was either said or done.
>
> (*Contra Ap.* 1.54–5)

Elsewhere he levelled very similar charges against Greek historians in general, saying that, despite claims to the contrary, they did not rush to history to discover the truth, and they chose their topics simply so that they could outshine their rivals (*Contra Ap.* 1.24). But is this an admission that he wrote badly? Not in the least. The problem was to balance fact and style; good history could not be badly written.

Ammianus Marcellinus wrote in very much the same vein in the concluding lines of his history when he invited a successor to be a person who had no fear of discovering the truth, and who knew how to write in the high style demanded of the subject (31.16.9). If our putative Deutero-Tacitus and Pseudo-Ammianus could leave the purgatory of their research and emerge into the fresh air of composition, it was precisely the issue of style that would concern them. How could they display their literary accomplishments while also maintaining the standards of accuracy that were desired, however those standards might be defined? It is not an issue that has ceased to trouble historians in the centuries since the end of the classical period.

Historiography, style and the American historian

When Hayden White reintroduced the American historical profession to the study of historiography in 1973, he was staking out a particular turf for himself in the ongoing struggle against the then retreating "objectivist" school of thought. The debate within the American historical profession about the "true" nature of history had already been raging for half a century, and given rise to a vast range of discourse. In and of itself, this discourse is of considerable interest, but it also has a tendency to be highly self-referential, depending on a series of images that have occasionally had a less than precise correlation with what they claim to describe.

In recent years, White's work has come to exercise some influence over the discourse of ancient historiography.[1] Again, this is no bad thing; as I will suggest, the importance of this work may well be that it freed discussion from earlier paradigms, rather than providing a practical paradigm in and of itself.[2] In any case, it is still necessary to see developments out of the American school of historiography within their own context. This does not mean that similar debates have not existed, and do not exist, amongst historical professionals in other countries (or all countries where free discourse is possible). But university systems have very different histories, and debates within them have different starting points. It is worth noting, for instance, that E.H. Carr and G.R. Elton, whose works may be taken as defining very similar positions within the English system to those of the "objectivists" and "relativists" in the United States, have virtually nothing to say about American debates, and that Fernand Braudel, looking back to Lucien Febvre and Mark Bloch, has nothing to say about anglophone movements.[3]

In the United States, "objectivism" is intimately connected with the rise of the university. The university, a quite distinct entity from the colleges of previous generations, developed in the second half of the nineteenth century. The point of the university was not simply to educate young men and women of good breeding, it was to train other university teachers, and to provide a forum for advanced research. One of the challenges that faced members of the emerging American academic professions, and even more so their successors in the next generation, was to establish that they had something to offer that the gifted amateurs who had dominated various fields of learning in previous years lacked. They had to prove that advanced research was in fact a useful thing. The tack of historians, who had to contend with the legacy of non-academic giants like Francis Parkman and William Prescott, was to claim a new methodological superiority based upon the teaching of history in German universities. In doing this, they elevated the figure of Leopold von Ranke to the status of a virtual divinity. In the words of an early leader of the profession in the United States:

> While an admirable critic of sources, Niebuhr read into his version of Roman history a variety of moral and philosophical views unwarranted by the existing evidence....Ranke, on the other hand, determined to hold strictly to the facts of history, to preach no sermon, to point to no moral, to adorn no tale, but to tell the simple historical truth. His sole ambition was to narrate things as they really were "wie es eigentlich gewesen." Truth and objectivity were Ranke's highest aims....He did not believe in the historian's province to point out divine providence in human history.[4]

It would be hard to get further from the way it actually was than this.[5]

Leopold von Ranke

> The task of the historian is both learned and literary, for history is at once both art and science. It must fulfill the same demands of criticism and learning as a philological study, yet offer the educated person the same pleasure as the most accomplished literary production.
>
> (Leopold Ranke)[6]

The European academy to which Americans turned was very much the German one. The German professor became the model for the American, professionalism was tinctured by the experience of the German seminar, and, amongst historians, the professor of Modern History at Berlin was the presiding genius. The influence of this professor was much less pronounced in France and England,[7] and it is arguable that his influence over American thinking grew with the passage of time, as he was transformed from human being to symbol in debates that raged a half century after his death.[8] But he is important, both in his own right and in terms of what became of his legacy nonetheless.

Leopold von Ranke, for this is the professor in question, was born in Saxony on 21 December 1795. Descended from a long line of Lutheran priests and educated within his native principality, Ranke obtained a doctorate on the basis of a thesis about the political doctrine of Thucydides, submitted to the University of Leipzig in 1817.[9] Deciding then not to pursue a priestly career, he took a job at the Gymnasium at Frankfurt on the Oder, teaching classics.[10]

Although his reputation in later years was as a master of archival research, Ranke was not a straightforward technician. He was deeply religious, interested in philosophy, devoted to the ideals of the German nation and, at heart, a romantic. His romantic side (as well as his taste in literature) emerges from his statement that he chose his period as a result of his irritation with Walter Scott's description of Charles the Bold in *Quentin Durward*.[11] He thus betook himself to the library in Frankfurt where he is said to have annoyed the librarians with his constant demands for books (he was a nobody at the time). The result was his first book, the *History of the Latin and Germanic Peoples, 1494–1514*, published when he was twenty-nine. It established his reputation.

It is in the introduction to the *History of the Latin and Germanic Peoples* that Ranke made his famous statement about method (*wie es eigentlich gewesen*). It is worth quoting that statement here in somewhat fuller context than is the norm, as it is part of a rather broader program of analysis than the simple statement might suggest:

> This book seeks to comprehend all these and other related events in the history of the Roman and Germanic nations as a unity. History has had assigned to it the office of judging the past and of instructing future ages. To such high offices the present work does not presume: it seeks only to show what actually happened...[discussion of sources].... Aim and subject shape the form of a book. We cannot expect from the writing of history the same free development as is, at least in theory, to be expected in works of literature...a strict presentation of facts, contingent and unattractive though they may be, is the highest law. A second, for me, is the development of the unity and progress of events.[12]

Bare narrative of fact is here, but it is not fact itself that offers the interpretation. In his view, the all-important history of Europe took its shape from the clash between Teutonic and Roman peoples (people speaking Romance languages). This clash lead to the creation of a number of different nation-states, each embodying a particular ideal.[13] The truly important history was thus the history of the nation, of those who built it, and the concepts that shaped it.[14] Ranke himself saw the key development in European history to be the emergence of the nation-state, and the adjudication of relationships between what he saw as the constituent elements, people, church and national government. But while he could, and did, write histories of individual nation-states, he remained attached to the notion that they were part of the greater whole of Europe, each contributing something to European culture.[15] It was this vision that set him apart from historians obsessed with the history of their own nation.

Nations were themselves subdivisions of greater unities that he called states. In a bizarre dialogue published in 1835, Ranke wrote that each state had "not merely their roots, but also the spirit that links past and present and which must also animate the future" and that just as "the spirit of each particular language creates an infinite variety of modifications. Similarly, by the principle of the state we must not understand a theoretical construction, but its inner life."[16] In another essay, he went so far as to state that:

> World History does not present such a chaotic tumult, warring, and planless succession of states and peoples as appear at first sight. Nor is the often dubious advancement of civilization its only significance. There are forces and indeed spiritual, life-giving creative forces, nay life itself, and there are moral energies whose development we see. They cannot be defined or put in abstract terms, but one can behold them and observe them.[17]

It was this mystical belief in the spirit of the state that seems to have driven him. The fact that he allowed each state to have its own unique history removed his work from the realm of the purely nationalistic outburst, and gave him his reputation for even-handedness; in the preface to his history of England, he wrote that German historical scholarship "expresses the genius of the nation in attempting to comprehend the history of all other peoples with the same trouble and effort as its own."[18] What is perhaps more interesting, he appears to have been aware that his efforts were part of an ongoing process. His would not be the last word, historical research would continue once he was done: "historical works of great reputation and usefulness become obsolete. This is especially true of modern history…facts which later come to light reveal the attempted reconstruction to be erroneous."[19] The essence of Ranke's historiography was the search for God's plan through the study of fact. Without God's will, his work would have no direction.

While the romantic side was important, it should also be noted that Ranke was a very fine technical scholar, with a very good sense for nonsense in what he was reading. A brilliant appendix on Italian historiography in his first book shows how literary form can distort reality, and it was this, rather than the narrative, that made his scholarly reputation in 1824. Likewise he shows a definite awareness in his own works of the tension between factual representation and style, suggesting that the one has a tendency to distort the other.

A well-trained classical philologist, Ranke admired Niebuhr's *History of Rome*, which he read as a student in Leipzig, and appears to have known Wolf's work on Homer. These were crucial texts, for Ranke's great accomplishment would be to establish a rational basis of criticism for the sources of later periods. At first glance, this looks like it may be no more than a simple application of Niebuhr's methods to another era, a point that Ranke himself denied, writing that "my work was not based upon Niebuhr, who was really engaged in giving significance to a tradition, nor completely with Gottfried Hermann, who had criticized particular details of authors, although I had hopes of gaining applause from men such as these."[20] There is some truth here, for Ranke had discovered what could be done with archives, documentary material that Niebuhr lacked, to correct the accounts of narrative historians, but there is also a certain lack of candor. The memoirs in which this statement appears were dictated by Ranke when he was ninety years old, and his memory does not jibe particularly well with the letter that he wrote to Niebuhr at the time that his first book came out. In that letter, he allowed that Niebuhr had provided him with a model for his endeavours.[21]

The letter to Niebuhr raises a very interesting issue about Ranke's own understanding of his accomplishment. As an ambitious young man, he might well write in such flattering terms to a person who, then holding an ambassadorial post, could open doors to the archives that he longed to visit. But there may be more to it than that. Ranke did not discover archives, nor was he the first person to exalt the primacy of documents over secondary narrative. Indeed, the young Ranke disliked footnotes – he begged his publisher not to mar the text of his first book with them – and he would never really take to them.[22] He preferred to print documents in appendices and his citation of secondary scholarship was stunningly incomplete. Compared to Gibbon, one of whose great strengths was the ongoing defense of the views that appear in the main text through an extraordinary apparatus of scholarship at the bottom of the page, Ranke might appear to be stepping back from standards established in the eighteenth century.[23] Moreover, compared with his contemporaries, Francis Parkman and William Prescott in the United States, his zeal to travel to the site of his sources is anything but extraordinary. There is nothing in his account of travel to the archives of Italy to compare in danger or adventure with Parkman's journey along the Oregon Trail in 1846.

What Ranke did was to institutionalize the study of documents. He taught as well as he wrote. Students who wished to learn how to be historians need not domesticate "in a village of the western Dahcotah, on the high plains between Mt. Laramie and the range of Medicine Bow."[24] All they had to do was go to Berlin. The archives that Ranke visited himself were not opened because he wanted to see them, they were opened as a result of the Napoleonic wars. While Ranke did not invent the use of such material in history, it was his great accomplishment to democratize it.[25] He transformed historical study from the pastime of the gentleman to the occupation of the professor, enabling students to follow in his path.[26] It was in this way that he represented a decisive break with the past, and it may be the sense that the University in which he died was so different a place from that in which he had studied that led him to create an image of his own development, one which could fall victim to his own methods of criticizing a deceptive source. He is all the more interesting as a result.

Objectivism and relativism

For the Americans who had gone to Europe to encounter the new educational environment, the formulation *wie es eigentlich gewesen* attributed to Ranke "was fitted into the great conception of natural science – cold neutrality over against the materials and forces of the physical world."[27] The key to new learning lay in archives, the accumulation of as much new data as was possible that could then be allowed to explain itself. This was not a particularly accurate representation of Ranke's own thought, since he saw archives as providing the material for research rather than the end product, and never reduced the role of the historian to that of a mere redactor. Nonetheless, archival research became the domain of the "new" historians, scientific writing their aim. The implicit disparagement of a Francis Parkman or William Prescott was unfortunate, for while Parkman could write plushly of an army marching "into the thickest gloom of the woods, damp, still, and cool as the recesses of a cavern, where the black soil oozed beneath the tread," his histories were marked with a superb command of the available documentary sources and, as we have seen, remarkably adventurous habits.[28] Prescott's command of archives was equally impressive. The author of a highly regarded recent history of Cortez's conquest of the Aztecs has allowed that very little is now available that Prescott did not know, and Winfield Scott's army of invasion that marched from Vera Cruz to Mexico City in 1848 was able to use his work as a guide.[29] Yet Prescott too was given to the purple passage. The modern technical historian (at least after the turn of the century) had to exclude such language, to appear the scientific reporter. A reaction set in during the 1930s, associated with the names of Charles Beard and Carl Becker.[30]

Beard, whose *An Economic Interpretation of the Constitution* marks the first significant application of prosopography to a major historical problem, provided an eloquent ultimatum in his presidential address to the American Historical Association in 1933.[31] In "Written History as an Act of Faith," Beard argued that "it is history as thought, not as actuality, record, or specific knowledge that is really meant when the term history is used in its widest, most general significance."[32] In his view, "the historian who writes history, therefore, consciously or unconsciously performs an act of faith, as to order and movement, for certainty as to order and movement is denied to him by knowledge of the actuality with which he is concerned"; but, within this world of uncertainty, the "scientific" approach to fact as "the chief safeguard against the tyranny of autocracy, bureaucracy and brute power," remained a "precious and indispensable instrument of the human mind."[33] Two years earlier, Carl Becker had introduced the historical profession to "Mr. Everyman," the remarkably middle-class gentleman who wandered through his life paying coal bills (after looking up the fact in his book), making golf appointments and worrying about General Motors stock. "Mr. Everyman" was an historian for himself, the professional historian was the historian for "Mr. Everybody." In performing his function (always "his" for both Beard and Becker) the historian had to establish the facts; the establishment of fact was "the first duty of the historian; but to suppose that the facts once established in all their fullness, will 'speak for themselves' is an illusion."[34] For Becker, the historian was to modern society what the bard or storyteller was to primitive, "the history written by historians…is thus a convenient blend of truth and fancy, of what we commonly distinguished as 'fact' and 'interpretation'."[35]

The relativist position, as it came to be known, was open to ready assault as the dividing line between scientific collection and bias was hard to define or determine on any reasonable theoretical basis; "when absolutes in history are rejected the absolutism of relativity is also rejected."[36] But there were other reasons for rejecting what Beard and Becker had to say. T.C. Smith, whose answer to Beard's address is a masterpiece of misrepresentation, upheld the spirit of "scientific" and "objective" historiography as the bulwark against the situation in "countries where history, under the sway of precisely these ideals [his version of what Beard had to say], has become so functional that it is systematically employed as a means for educating people to think as the ruling authority wishes them to do."[37] A second line of attack, represented by the medievalist C.H. McIlwain, was that Beard's approach suggested that methods borrowed from other fields might be used to solve historical problems. In his view (and that of many others), historical problems were best solved by a better understanding of the periods wherein they existed, and hence by implication, Beard and Becker were advocating the writing of bad history based upon inappropriate assumptions, or worse, urging a council of despair by suggesting that genuine historical progress was not possible.[38] Faced with new challenges in the wake of the Second World War, historians tended to close ranks against relativism as a menace to any sense of positive social values; their arguments were somewhat more sophisticated than Smith's, but they had the same result. If everything was relative, then one could not tell the difference between the accomplishment of Stalin and that of Roosevelt.[39] It was safer, better and socially responsible to assert the positive, intrinsic value of the fact that explained itself. Such views did not survive the Vietnam era in the United States, and White was simply staking out a new position, albeit an extreme and highly provocative one, on a field where the "objectivist" orthodoxy was already in flight.[40]

In White's view, as adumbrated in his 1973 book, *Metahistory: The Historical Imagination in Nineteenth-Century Europe*, historical writing can be defined in terms of a series of styles that represent "a particular combination of modes of emplotment, argument, and ideological implication. But the various modes of emplotment, argument, and ideological implication cannot be indiscriminately combined in a given work. For example, a Comic emplotment is not compatible with a mechanistic argument, just as a Radical ideology is not compatible with a Satirical emplotment." The affinities that White sees are represented by him as shown in the table overleaf:[41] The choice of styles is limited to four, which mirror the four tropes of poetical language: metaphor, metonymy, synecdoche and irony. There is no strict correlation between the different tropes and the four modes of historical argument; for while metonymy, metaphor and

mode of emplotment	mode of argument	mode of ideological implication
romantic	formist	anarchist
tragic	mechanist	radical
comic	organicist	conservative
satirical	contextualist	liberal

synecdoche may have respective affinities to formism, mechanism and organicism, irony is different. White suggests a connection between irony and satire, as the latter is opposed to romanticism, comedy and tragedy, but then maintains that it is transideological, tending "to engender belief in the 'madness' of civilization itself and to inspire a Mandarin-like disdain for those seeking to grasp the nature of social reality in either science or art."[42] The key feature of White's analysis is that the four terms of discourse are not evaluated in terms of "truth" but rather on moral and aesthetic grounds.[43]

Metahistory continues on from its theoretical introduction to a discussion of enlightenment thinking about history and extended analysis of eight writers, four philosophers of history, and four historians from the nineteenth century. The philosophers in question are Hegel, Marx, Nietzsche and Croce; the historians are Michelet, Tocqville, Ranke and Burkhardt. The four historians are selected on the grounds that, unlike other great historians of the nineteenth century whose work defined (and defines) individual fields of study, they are paradigmatic for modern historical consciousness.[44] In this they also separated historiography from an enlightenment background that placed emphasis on the philosophy of the subject. "Method" replaced "philosophy" in the theoretical construction of the subject; it led to new developments in the philosophy of history, now separated from what might be termed (though not by White) practical historiography. The curiosity is that it is possible to detect a similar development in both areas from the "primitive" tropes of metaphor, synecdoche and metonymy to irony.[45] Much of the book involves extended discussion of the relationship between the selected authors and the tropes that White would have them represent. The stress on trope rather than evidence, on representation rather than process, has made, and continues to make, White's work a powerful symbolic tool, and White something of a symbol for what may be described as the "new relativism" in American historiographic thought. His successors may not find the theory of tropes very useful (it was itself deployed as a metaphor for the development of nineteenth-century historical thought), but it opened the way to the broader application of critical theory to all aspects of historical discourse.[46] This is especially the case with the far more flexible tools made available through various forms of postmodern criticism, which enable an analysis of both the forms of discourse and the world that they attempt to describe.

Fact and presentation: Dionysius of Halicarnassus and Lucian

If White's work is detached from its context within American debates, it remains the case that he is arguing, as Beard and Becker had before him, for consciousness of the non-factual aspects of historical writing. Presentation counts: facts matter because of the context in which they are placed by the historian. These are views that would not have surprised any historian in antiquity. But as is the case with the early relativists such Beard and Becker, much more than the later descendents of White and Dominick LaCapra, a real tension was felt between the requirements of factual accuracy and the rhetoric of presentation. As Nancy Partner has put it:

> only the narcissistic shortsightedness of a rather too self-flattering professionalism prevents historians, as a discipline, from recognizing that the basic literary forms and authorial intentions established in Greek and Latin antiquity have continued, with astonishingly few alterations, into modern times.[47]

There are two works that are of particular importance for understanding the classical approach to the issue of fact and representation in historical writing. These are Lucian's *How to Write History* and Dionysius of Halicarnassus's critical essay on Thucydides. In both cases, it is striking that the authors emphasize the tension between fact and presentation. Dionysius is also notable because he is not concerned with correcting Thucydides's facts, but rather in commenting on the way that he presents them. Lucian casts his net rather wider; his essay belongs to the debate over the borderline between truth and fiction that is such an important feature of the general literary discourse of the second century AD.

Dionysius's work on Thucydides is one of a number of literary critical works composed for the benefit of Quintus Aelius Tubero in the last decade of the first century BC. As Dionysius himself puts it, the very notion of criticizing Thucydides might be taken as a sign of arrogance, since Thucydides is regarded as the model of *pragmatikê historia*, and the pinnacle of political oratory.[48] The view of Thucydides as a model for rhetoric is anything but original. Demosthenes is said to have learned his history by heart, and Cicero, repeating commonplace views, likewise recommends him to the aspiring orator. As a branch of rhetoric, the historian who wanted to be taken seriously had to have a notable style. Such views can be traced as far back as Theophrastus in the late fourth century BC.

After an introduction that sets Thucydides in the context of earlier historians, Dionysius goes on to deal with the moral issue (important as ever). He must show that Thucydides was a man of good character because he wrote as was appropriate about the characters in his history (*De Thuc.* 8). Where he falls down is on the "more technical side" of his business, the arrangement that is expected of philosophical or rhetorical works (*De Thuc.* 9). The object of his criticism here is the division of the history into winters and summers, which he says breaks up individual narratives so as to ruin the general flow of related events. Pragmatic history, in his view, ought to be presented as a series of unbroken narratives when it deals with a large number of complicated stories (see also Dion Hal. *Ep. ad Pomp.* 3). A second problem is that Thucydides did not choose an appropriate starting or finishing point, since an appropriate beginning is the point where nothing can be imagined as preceding it, and an end is the point where nothing can be imagined as following it (*De Thuc.* 10). The point about the conclusion is ostensibly so stupid as to require no comment (Thucydides obviously did not mean to leave off in the middle of a sentence), but the theory behind it is significant, betraying an Aristotelian interest in unity of theme, the notion that a complete work is a self-contained whole (*Poet.* 1451a 30–5).

The next point of criticism is the unequal treatment of individual subjects. Why do some battles get a full description and others a mere mention; why do the catastrophes of some cities get detailed discussion and others only a passing reference (*De Thuc.* 14–15)? Dionysius recognizes this as a matter of judgment; Thucydides clearly thought that some things were more important than others. The problem is that the justification for this judgment is not always clear. Likewise in the placement of speeches, Dionysius notes that there is a problem of consistency; the first books were filled with rhetorical displays, while the last was not. This again is seen as a clear case for rational selection of detail. The Funeral Oration is placed where it is, while there is no mention at all of the public funeral for those who died at Pylos, so that Thucydides can make full use of the character of Pericles (*De Thuc.* 18). The point that he is raising is not related to truth or falsehood here, but rather to appropriate rhetorical choice.

Dionysius's final section is concerned with the style of individual passages. It is style at the level of the construction of the period and individual passage that sets the great historian apart from the bad, style that made Herodotus superior to his predecessors and that set Thucydides apart from Herodotus (*De Thuc.* 23). Individual passages such as the great naval battle in the harbor of Syracuse come in for particular praise, while others such as the discussion of revolution on Corcyra are condemned (*De Thuc.* 26–9). Where Thucydides writes like a normal person he is to be praised; where he descends into stylistic peculiarity and harshness of expression, he should have thought again.

Dionysius's discussion of speeches in Thucydides is of great importance as the most extensive exposition of a theory of the speech in an historical author. Here again, Thucydides can be seen as the model for later practice. There is no question of the theoretical propriety of his decision to write speeches for people as he thought appropriate to the circumstances. In discussing the Melian Dialogue – which he did not much like – Dionysius observes that "from what he writes about himself in the previous book, the historian was not a participant in these discussions, nor present at the meeting, and did not learn what was said from either an Athenian or a Melian…it remains to see if he composed the dialogue in a way that was suitable to the facts and in keeping with the characters who were present" (*De Thuc.* 41). The sentiments of the Melians are judged appropriate, those of the Athenians are said to be unworthy of the city – possibly Thucydides was having a bad day, bearing a grudge against the city that had exiled him.

Elsewhere it is explicitly stated that the historian may make use of the rhetorical technique of *prosôpopoiia*, or the putting of an imaginary speech into another's mouth, provided that the speech is appropriate. Quintilian wrote that Livy had "accommodated all that was said with the events and people involved" (*Inst.* 10.1.101) and that the art was of great value to poets as well as to future historians (*Inst.* 3.8.48). According to Polybius, a bad speech was one that neither set down the words spoken, nor the sense of what was really said, but was a completely invented piece of rhetorical display (Pol. 12.25a.5). A good speech summed up events and held the whole history together (Pol. 12.25a.3).[49] Indeed, while Polybius's strictures often look as if they are demanding a higher degree of accuracy in reporting than other historians could manage, close reading of his text suggests that he is in fact following closely upon Thucydides's practice of making things as much like reality as he could (Thuc. 1.22).

When it comes to other speeches, determining what constituted, "as much like reality" as possible was, of course a very slippery process, and it appears that the grammatical principle of *to prepon* was often used as the standard for measurement. Dionysius wrote that what went into speeches ought to be *prepon*, suitable to the situation (*ad Pomp.* 3.20). Dionysius also offers a list that "historians should take for emulation" (*De Thuc.* 42). This is a critical point. In Dionysius's view a historian should give speeches that are stylish, suited to the subject and look both to the events of an historian's own subject, as well as to the models of the literary record. In no other place does his theory of history as a form of literary mimesis come through so clearly. Mimesis is not simply free composition; the speeches have to be appropriate to context, but because history is a branch of rhetoric, so too its speeches must fulfill the dictates of that discipline. It is also significant that he divides the speech off from the narrative as a constituent element of an historical discourse. Thucydides is both good at recording detail, and at providing it with flair, but there are limits. When he writes with controlled moderation, he is in a class by himself, but when he is excessive, he deserves censure (*De Thuc.* 51).

Dionysius admits that while no one might want to talk like Thucydides to one's friends, or in a law court, "those who are writing *pragmatikê historia*, in which an impressive, dignified and striking style is required" might find Thucydidean style appropriate (*De Thuc.* 50). In its fullness this is a mistake, for by limiting their readership to a very small class of educated people, they are removing a crucial subject from human beings in general, making it the property of a few, like a government under an oligarchy (*De Thuc.* 51).

For Dionysius, history is a defense of humanity against autocracy that needs to be written clearly and well. Narrative sections should be clear and well-balanced, speeches should be appropriate to their subject and speaker. He takes factual accuracy for granted in discussing a great historian so as to concentrate on points of presentation that have an impact on his comprehensibility. Successful history demands a proper style while recording events, and he sees no contradiction between these two demands. History should give pleasure as well as it should inform.[50]

Lucian's work situates itself precisely in the aftermath of Lucius Verus's Parthian war, an event that appears to have given rise to a mass of adulatory historiography.[51] Lucian himself was, of course, no historian and it is unfortunate that we have no way now to get at the texts that informed his critical vocabulary, but there is no reason to think that he was being particularly original. Indeed, there is considerable similarity between the canons that he describes and those implied by

Dionysius's discussion of Thucydides, and expressed in numerous places by Polybius.

The first fault that Lucian condemns is the excessive praise of generals and rulers. Praise and blame had always been a feature of history, the absense of such praise is central to Dionysius's assertion that Thucydides was a reliable source, and to Plutarch's that Herodotus was not, but there were limits. In Lucian's view the dividing line between history and pane-gyric was not "a narrow isthmus…but a great wall," and while there was room for some praise (or blame) it needs to be kept within reasonable limits (*Hist.* 7; 9).[52] Likewise, Tacitus had asserted that he could offer dispas-sionate judgment because he was not a participant in the events of the *Annales*, while pointing to excesses in both directions as faults in the work of his predecessors (*Ann.* 1.2). In discussing his treatment of the Achaean politician Philopoemon, Polybius wrote that a youthful work, "being in the style of an encomium, demanded a summary account with amplifica-tion of his deeds" while his *pragmatikê historia*, that distributed praise and blame equally, "seeks the truth, offering an account supported by reasoning and the considerations accompanying each action" (10.21.8).[53] For Lucian, failure to recognize this limit turned history into a sort of *kolakeìa*, or flattery; using the techniques of poetry without meter detracted from the pleasure of reading it (*Hist.* 8; 10).

Just as Dionysius criticized Thucydides for excesses of expression, so too Lucian observed that there must be a general unity to history, a head well matched to the body. One aspect of this balance was simply getting things right. Historians who lacked a sense of geography were useless, as were historians who invented in bad taste: the story that the general Servianus killed himself with a large piece of a crystal bowl was just as tasteless as the ensuing encomium by a centurion that sounded like Pericles. Neither was believable (*Hist.* 25–7).

The ideal historian was a person who came to the task with real polit-ical understanding and power of expression, the one being a gift of nature, the other the result of long practice; he must be devoted to the truth, having a mind like a mirror to display the shape of things as he receives them (*Hist.* 34; 40; 50).[54] Lucian's ideal writer is, in fact, Thucydides, who wrote not for the pleasure of the moment but rather to offer a gift for all time, who left behind an account that could guide future generations if they ever found themselves in situations analogous to that which he described (*Hist.* 42). Of equal importance to a devotion to the truth was power of expression. Like Dionysius, Lucian prefers the historian who will use language that people can understand, giving way neither to a desire for archaism, nor to the language of the street; the sort of language that any reasonably educated person could be expected to understand (*Hist.* 44). He must also have an eye for the reliable informant and take good notes, points which he shares with many other commentators.

The ideal product of the ideal historian begins with a preface that outlines the main events, moving then into a clear narrative. The narrative itself should proceed smoothly, moving from topic to topic, avoiding disjuncture between related events and ensuring that one topic leads logically to the next. The historian also needs to know what to leave out, for brevity everywhere is a virtue, and needs to recognize limits to the expected set pieces: descriptions of rivers, fortifications and the like. If a speech is needed, let that person speak as is appropriate, in words that suit both himself and his subject. Here again we see no expectation that there will be a verbatim report, but rather, as with Dionysius, that limits of taste will be observed. The same is true with praise and blame: keep it short and to the point, and write always with an eye to the future audience rather than the present (*Hist.* 54–61).

Fact and presentation: Cicero

The foundations of history, so thought Cicero, were that the historian would not dare to lie, and that he would not fail to say something that he knew to be true. The superstructure that rested upon these foundations consisted of style and events. Events and style have different requirements. In the case of the former:

> The nature of events requires chronological order and the description of geography, it even desires – since in the case of great events worthy of memory, first plans, then deeds, and finally results are expected – something to be said about the plans that the writer approves, and in the narration of events a discussion not only of what was said or done, but also of how; and in the discussion of the result, that all the reasons be explored, whether by chance, design or rashness, and not just the deeds of the men themselves who excel in fame and reputation, but even something about the life and character of each.
>
> (*De orat.* 2.63)[55]

The nature of style and form of discourse is to be diffuse and full, flowing with an agreeable moderation, lacking the harshness of expression that characterizes the rhetoric of the law court. The critical feature of Cicero's discussion is the separation between the nature of events and the nature of style. The narration of events has its own set of rules, the style employed along with the narration does also. Just as the *fundamenta* of a work of history have two distinct elements so does the *exaedificatio* that is erected upon them. The completed structure is not simply a piece of rhetoric like a speech in a law court, but an independent form of narrative facilitated by a pleasant style. It is this that the orator well-trained in the use of language is admirably fitted to provide. It is not Cicero's suggestion that the orator who turns to history should write history as if it were a speech, but rather that the orator use the skill that he has acquired through learning how to manipulate the language (*De orat.* 2.36–7). After all, *historia* is the "true witness of time, the light of truth, the life of memory, the guide of life, the messenger of the past" (*De. orat.* 2.36). History is not oratory, but another art that an orator can learn to practice (*De orat.* 2.37).

The first requirement of history for Cicero, as with Lucian and Dionysius, is that the author be of good character, of a sort who will attempt to tell the truth. The presentation of the narrative cannot be limited to a simple listing of events, but requires explanation as it goes along. All three concur that the style must also be agreeable, avoiding the harshness to be found in other forms of rhetoric (or in some passages of Thucydides) (see also Cic. *Brut.* 287). It is precisely style, or the lack of it, that Cicero reprehends in his discussion of earlier Latin historians in the *Laws*, which he wrote in the last year of his life. The earliest historians tend to be stylistically lifeless; more recent authors show a lack of taste. Only Cornelius Sisenna, who wrote on the disasters of the Sullan age, was really any good – "but he was never an orator of your rank," says Atticus. It is this phrase that explains Atticus's earlier observation "that you should be able to fill in the gap [the lack of a well-written history in Latin] since you have always thought that this form of literature is most like oratory," for the point is that Cicero should be able to write a history with ease since he has already mastered the stylistic side, and his historical work promises to be much better than Sisenna's since he, Cicero, is better than Sisenna as an orator.[56]

The discussion of history in the *Concerning Oratory* comes at a time when history seems to have been much on Cicero's mind. A few years earlier he had written a commentary on his consulship in Greek, and a poem on the same subject.[57] At about the same time as he was finishing *Concerning Oratory* he wrote to the historian Lucceius, asking him to produce something that featured Cicero as the hero (*Fam.* 5.12=SB 22). Cicero here contemplates two possibilities. One is a decision by Lucceius to continue his *History of the Italian and Civil Wars* through 57 BC (and the

return of Cicero from exile), an *historia perpetua*, or systematic chronological narrative. The other option is that Lucceius write up a special work,
on the model of various Greek histories of individual wars, concerning
the conspiracy of Catiline. Cicero is aware that he is asking Lucceius to
do something that might offend the sensibility of the historian, because
he presumes that Lucceius will judge that his deeds really were worth
praising (5.12.2). But, having passed the bounds of good taste, Cicero
goes on to ask explicitly that this is what Lucceius do. There are several
points that he thinks Lucceius might want to consider. First of all, as an
acknowledged expert on civil disorder, he will have much material for
interpretation – giving the reasons why he will praise or assail some act –
and plenty of the extraordinary changes of fortune that readers love to
hear about (5.12.4). Interesting history is not a simple record of events,
but it takes as its theme the rise and fall (and resurrection) of some
statesman. The story that Cicero offers is like a play, with distinct acts
and scenes, and if Lucceius will only consider it, Cicero will send his
own *commentarii* to help him so that he can describe it as accurately as
possible (5.12.6; 9–10). Throughout, Cicero plays with the distinction
between *historia* and panegyric that so concerned Lucian in later years.
The point that he wants to make is that his deeds are such that they
would justify an encomium. Elsewhere in his writing, Cicero shows the
same comprehension of the distinction between what is the matter for
historia proper and other forms of representation. In his poem about
Marius, he says that he could include stories that would have no place in
a serious history; in a letter to Atticus he says that he treated people not
"as in a panegyric, but rather as in a history in the book that he wrote
about his consulship."[58]

  If an orator turned to history he would be expected to change his
ways. Thus in the *Brutus*, Cicero disagrees with Atticus's presentation of
the death of Coriolanus (making it less spectacular). Atticus responds
that it is all right for rhetoricians to lie in history, but, by implication, it is
not for historians (*Brut.* 42). In another place, Cicero states that encomia
on famous men have distorted the early history of Rome, returning here
to the dichotomy between historical and rhetorical standards that is so
evident elsewhere in his writings (*Brut.* 62), and that Demochares wrote a
history of Athens that was less historical than oratorical: *earum rerum
historiam…non tam historico quam oratorio genere perscripsit* (*Brut.* 286). Asconius
used similar vocabulary years later, in commenting upon Cicero's *Against
Piso*, saying that when Cicero claimed that no Roman had ever had his
property restored at public expense, he was speaking like an orator

rather than an historian (*oratorio more, non historico*) and promptly adduced several examples from ancient history to prove the point (Asc. 13C).

From the persistence of the distinction between what is suitable to an orator, and what is suitable for an historian, questions must arise about the validity of assuming that definitions offered as instruction for the preparation of a speech are viable as definitions for features of the narrative within a history. Thus, when Cicero offers a definition of *narratio* for use in an oration, is he de facto offering a definition of *narratio* that applies also to history?[59] If Cicero saw no distinction between history and oratory, the answer must be yes. But he does see the two as different forms of representation. Thus when Cicero writes that the *narratio* of a forensic speech will be convincing if it appears to contain elements which customarily appear in real life (*Inv.* 1.29), he is not talking about the qualities to be expected of *narratio* in a work of history. They will have aspects in common, but they will not be identical, or, at least in theory, they should not be identical. The qualities to be expected from good historical narration were discussed by others, both before and after Cicero, in remarkably consistent terms, suggesting that he would be well within the intellectual framework of his time in feeling this way.[60]

In Cicero's view, history is a form of representation that is distinct from other forms. His view is similar to that evident in Dionysius and Lucian, and may be derived from theories of historical writing that were propounded in the Hellenistic world. No one claims that everything in a history will necessarily be true, or that the historian should remove his personality from what he writes.[61] Rather, the historian should cast judgment on events and should produce speeches that entertain so long as they are appropriate to the circumstances. The core narrative should be based on the best evidence that can be found, and that evidence should not be distorted. It is this that sets *historia* apart from *plasma*, or fiction.

Other forms of presentation: chronicles and chronographies

Historical exposition took the form of a narrative based upon the collation of accounts by first-hand informants, or upon reading in accounts of a period. It included passages of analysis in which the historian might speak in the first person, and speeches in which the participants would comment in character on the situation that was being described. In some cases the author might include short quotations (ordinarily no more than a sentence or so) from his sources.[62] Other features of narrative might be ethnographies (usually based on written sources), descriptions of famous places, or battle scenes. Finally there would be points where the historian let the reader know if one should think that a person or course of action was worthy of praise or blame. In the ideal world, this would all be offered to the public in a reasonable prose style.

Figure 4 P. Oxy. 12: the text of a chronicle including both Greek and Roman history. The surviving portions cover the period from 355/354 to 316/315 BC. A *diple oblismene* marks off each Olympiad, and *paragraphoi* (single lines under lines of text) mark off years within Olympiads. These are sometimes inserted incorrectly, as is the case with the second *paragraphos* in the central column.

Source: P. Oxy. 12. © The Ashmolean Museum

Historical exposition was not the only form of narrative discourse, and it was not the only form that a record of the past could take. A work such as Aulus Gellius's *Attic Nights* could be given to the public as a collection of notes, *commentarii*. Varro's account of the Latin language includes quotation from older books to illuminate the meaning or derivation of a word; Valerius Maximus's collection of memorable deeds and sayings and Polyaenus's book of great stratagems are likewise little more than organized *commentarii* given to the public with no pretense of style. There was plainly a great deal of space in the Roman literary world for this sort of record of the past. Another way in which the past could be represented was in the form of a chronicle, whereby events were presented according to some universal organizing principle.[63] Several such texts have been preserved on papyri and stone, enabling us to appreciate the visual impression that they would make on readers.[64] One of the first papyri published from the finds at Oxyrhynchus contains a chronicle of Greek history from 355/354 to 316/315 BC. Paragraphoi (Figure 4) mark the entry for each Olympiad, and the entry then runs as follows:

> In the one hundred and seventh Olympiad, Smicranas the Tarentine won the stadion race. The archons at Athens were Aristodemus, Thessalus, Apollodorus, Callimachus. At Rome, in the third year of the Olympiad censors were first elected from the people.
>
> (*P. Oxy.* 12; *FGrH* 255)

A slightly different format is employed on the papyrus that preserves a chronicle treating events of the early third century BC (Figure 5). Here the number of the Olympiad is written in the middle of the column, a long list of all Olympic victors, with their records follows, and then we get, "in the first year…" (*P. Oxy.* 2082; *FGrH* 257A). For the period prior to the first Olympiad, the record would be based on various king lists. Another format, used on two inscriptions offers a chronological list dating backwards from the present, again with clear indications of the changing year (*IG* 12.5, 444; *FGrH* 239; *IG* 14, 1297; *FGrH* 252).[65] The amount of material for each entry varied according to the tastes or learning of the author.

The organization of Greek history by Olympiads appears to have been the invention of Eratosthenes of Cyrene in the third century BC. But how did one deal with earlier events, and how was earlier history laid out? In the second century BC, Apollodorus of Athens seems simply to have used a Spartan king list to get from the Trojan War to

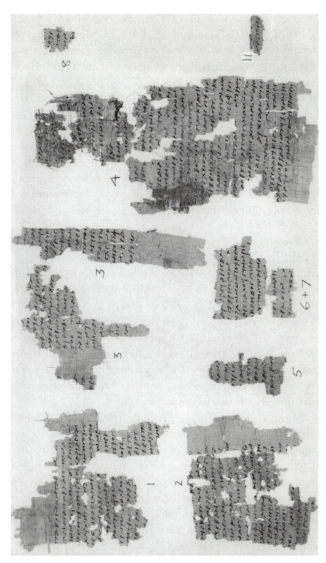

Figure 5 P. Oxy. 2082: a chronicle organized by Olympiads attributed to Phlegon of Tralles, who wrote it in the second century AD. The text we have is reconstructed from eleven fragments. Next to the number 4 on the left-hand side, the number of the Olympiad can be read in the middle of the column. Significant entries (not years) are marked by *paragraphoi*.

Source: P. Oxy. 2082. © The Ashmolean Museum

the first Olympiad (*FGrH* 244 F 62).[66] The next critical development appears to be connected with an author of the mid-first century BC named Castor of Rhodes. Castor introduced synchronisms between a list of Assyrian kings that he had found in Ctesias of Cnidus with Greek king lists and that of Rome.[67] The loss of the original text makes it impossible to know how this was laid out on the papyrus: was there a single list of Assyrian kings with entries indicating synchronism with lists that followed, or were the lists laid out side by side? We cannot know for certain, but it is most likely that they were laid out consecutively rather than side by side, and that arrangement in parallel columns was perhaps the critical contribution of Eusebius to the visualization of world history.[68] Nonetheless, Castor's connection between "barbarian" and Greek history was of fundamental importance, for he offered a model for the reconciliation of diverse traditions. It was thus to Castor that Sextus Julius Africanus, the first author of a Christian chronography, turned as a model.

Africanus wrote, probably in Palestine, a five-book chronology of world history from creation to the year AD 221.[69] Africanus's great achievement was the reconciliation of biblical history with that of the classical world, fitting it into a scheme based upon the theory of the Sabbatical millennium, whereby human history would last for 6,000 years (1,000 years for each day of the creation).[70] Earlier Christians, as well as Jews, had argued that Biblical history was much older than any other, but it was Africanus who gave this point a clear visual demonstration.[71] Africanus's work, in turn, provided a model for Eusebius's great *Chronicle*.[72]

Eusebius's *Chronicle* is known from an Armenian translation, Jerome's Latin adaptation of a part of it, quotations in later Greek authors, and two Syrian epitomes.[73] It was divided into two parts: the first, the Chronology, offered a scholarly discussion of different chronological schemes; the second, the Canons, offered a graphic depiction of the history that was reconstructed in the Chronology. The first section of the Chronology was concerned with the great kingdoms of the Near East, the second with the chronology of the Jews, the third with Egypt, the fourth with Greece, and the fifth with Rome. King lists are appended to each section, and a list of Olympic victors is added to the Greek section that ends in AD 217. The Roman history is perhaps most interesting in that Eusebius discusses the kings, and then simply borrows Castor's number of years between the expulsion of the kings and the consulship of Valerius Messala and M. Piso (61 BC) to link the kings with the succession of monarchs from Julius Caesar to his own day.

The Canons which follow the Chronology were a masterpiece of organization, evidently made possible by Eusebius's characteristically Christian preference for the codex over the papyrus roll. Down to the refoundation of the temple at Jerusalem, dated to the second year of Darius I, the Canons were spread over a double page. On the left side of the left-hand page there was a column of numbers representing the years of Abraham, with a numeral underlined every tenth year. Next to the column listing the years of Abraham there was a column listing the years of the leader of the Jewish people. On the right-hand side of the page there was a column for Assyrian history (again with a mark under every tenth number). Between the columns there was space to record significant events in Old Testament history. On the right-hand page were the lists of the kings of Greek states and Egypt (on the far right); between the columns with space for entries on significant events. Accessions of new kings were marked and the number of years that they reigned were included at relevant points. For especially important events, such as the fall of Troy, a full line was left. From the second year of Darius onwards, Eusebius required only a single page (Old Testament History having come to an end).[74] Years of Abraham once again occupied the extreme left-hand column, and each Olympiad was marked on a separate line. There was then a column of regnal years, first Persian, then Ptolemaic and finally Roman. Notes on important historical points occupied the center of the page, and on the extreme left were columns for other royal houses. After the fall of Jerusalem to Rome in AD 70, Eusebius used this space for a list of Christian bishops.

The inspiration for Eusebius's form of historical representation appears to have come from textual criticism, for it appears to have been modeled on Origen's *Hexapla*, an edition of the Old Testament in six columns.[75] The left-hand column contained a Hebrew text, the column next to it a transliteration into Greek, and the next four contained four Greek translations, those of Aquila, Symmachus, the Septuagint and Theodotion.[76] Here again, a critical development in historical representation was borrowed from another discipline.

As a recorder of the past, Eusebius stands apart from the mainstream of polytheist culture in a number of ways. As a chronicler, he appears to have devised a new form of representation, as an historian he included long verbatim quotations from earlier texts. What he has in common with these traditions is, however, much more important. His view of the historian's task, of the task of the scholar who was interested in the past, was accurate reporting of what he could find out about it. This did not rule out editorializing commentary, or expressions of open hatred for specific individuals. But he did not see that this was at odds with his activity as a collector of information. Indeed, the whole chronographic tradition as we have it represents an alternative form of presentation to narrative history, but it would scarcely be reasonable to assert that it represented an alternative view of the historian's primary task, finding out what was true. Some of the authors of these works may qualify as professional intellectuals; certainly this would be a fair description of Eratosthenes and Apollodorus, and indeed, of Eusebius. But they are not professional historians if that term be taken to indicate a devotion to history alone as an intellectual activity. Such a definition would exclude virtually all writers of history that we know of from antiquity. The image of the task of the recorder of the past, in whatever form that record should take in the end, was not formed by any single university or school; it was the product of literary culture. The vast array of forms made available by that culture was exploited in different ways by different writers as it suited their taste. The one thing that was not a feature of these writings, if they were to be considered as records of the past, was the conscious falsification of fact for literary effect.

Factual record, or a record of things that happened rather than of events as they might have been, events that imitated life, was not of course to everyone's taste. Nor was a recorder of the past limited to that as a sole activity. Tacitus was of course a great orator, and the author of a work of fiction as well as of history. The *Dialogue on Oratory* is a *plasma*, a representation of something as if it were true rather than something that was true. So too are Cicero's philosophic works, the dialogues of Plato and Petronius's *Satyricon*.

Verisimilitude

It is notorious that there is no definition of the novel in ancient writing, even though there are novels. Works of history were a form of *mimesis* based on a set model, accounts of witnesses or documents; the *mimesis* of the *plasma* was based on everyday life. The line between the two forms of *mimesis* was permeable; works of fiction could be dressed up to look like real events, and they could be used in place of works of historical *mimesis*. Such works are of importance in the context of this chapter for the light that they cast on cultural assumptions about the way that a historical record would look.

Undoubtedly the most important works of *mimesis* that survive from the Roman empire are the Christian Gospels. Whatever view one takes of the actual composition of these texts, there are a couple of points that are indisputable. All were written well after the events that they narrate;

all tell the story in different ways, deploying alleged statements of Jesus, often with minor textual variants, to make slightly different points. Yet they all place Jesus in the context of identifiable historical figures, and imply a "real time" chronology for his career, although only one of them, the Gospel of John, provides a narrative of the crucifixion that bears a factual relationship to the workings of Roman justice.[77] It is arguable then that the Gospels imitate the form of a literary biography in that they profess to offer a narration from the birth to the death of a man, that they derive their force from the imitation of a form of literature that was regarded as veridical, while being essentially fictional in content.

Chief among the techniques employed by the authors of the Gospels in their effort to convey an impression of authority is the use of direct quotation, which implies, as we have seen, direct access to a tradition and the use of documents. In this case, however, the documents are of a rather unusual sort: they are prophetic texts of the Jewish tradition. While this is not the place to review the extensive evidence connected with the interpretation of the divine through prophecy, or the reinterpretation of the mundane with the assistance of this medium, there can be little question that the word of a reliable prophet could be used to guarantee the truth value of a statement. Finally, in Luke and John there is the invocation of a widespread tradition based on eyewitnesses. Thus Luke writes that he will follow "many writers" who have written on the basis of "traditions handed down to us by the original eyewitnesses and servants of the Gospel" (Luke 1.2). John asserts that he is giving testimony on the basis of an actual statement by a disciple, "it is a fact that he wrote it, and we know that his testimony here is true" (John 21.24).

The Gospels do not stand alone. In the late fourth or early fifth century, an author, probably at Rome, composed a series of imperial biographies, professing his product to be the work of six people writing in the period of Diocletian and Constantine, the *Historia Augusta*. The fraudulent claims to authorial diversity and date confused scholars until Hermann Dessau demonstrated that many names that appeared in the work attached to people for whom an actual existence was highly doubtful. All evoked the atmosphere of the 390s rather than the period around 300.[78] Subsequent work has convinced all but a few that Dessau was correct.

Although the introduction to the *Historia Augusta* has been lost, it is reasonable to assume that it began with Nerva, the point where Suetonius left off, and came to an end with Carinus, who died defending his claim to the throne against Diocletian. We have no idea why the author decided to identify himself as six different people, or to backdate his composition by nearly a century. Nor, despite more than a century of debate, is it at all clear why he wrote. Some scholars have sought to find a serious purpose, one proposal being that what becomes, by the end, a virtual satire of imperial institutions is intended as a commentary on the sad state of affairs in which the empire very rapidly found itself after the end of the reign of Theodosius (presuming that the work postdated 395). Others have seen the work as an elaborate scholarly fantasy.[79] These two views, and others, are not mutually exclusive.

The crucial issue, for present purposes, is that the author decided to equip his biographies with the apparatus of scholarship. Lives based on a work that appears to have been readily available to the author's audience, a collection of the lives of the twelve Caesars after Domitian by Marius Maximus, appear to be little more than epitomes of what Marius had to say, with the occasional example invented by the author for good measure. Where Marius was not available for direct comparison, the author had recourse to other works in Latin that appear to have been in the form of relatively short summary histories.[80] One such work, uncovered on the basis of detailed *Quellenforschung* at the end of the nineteenth century, is known as the *Kaisergeschichte* (Imperial History).[81] Other works that we know to have existed, works by the Greek authors Herodian and Dexippus, are quoted but it is doubtful that they were quoted directly from the Greek by the author, who elsewhere shows no propensity for reading in that language.[82] A generous soul might simply put much of this up to sloppiness. The problem is that the less than perfect citation of real sources is accompanied by what is at times a virtually endless string of citations of authors who did not exist, and of documents that are fake.

The citation of documents is a feature of Suetonian biography that has its roots in the tradition of books about famous people to which Suetonius had contributed before turning to the lives of the Caesars.[83] The tradition is usually referred to as antiquarian, which tends to evoke a mindless accumulation of fact for its own sake. This may not be the best way to characterize work that employs direct quotation of documents to make a point, but it is a useful term to distinguish records that stop short of full literary style in their presentation of evidence, while bringing original materials, through direct quotation, to readers. It is also, of course, a feature of learned discourse on literature. The most famous example may be Athenaeus's *Deipnosophistae* in which the literary heritage of the Greek world is ransacked for comments, course by course, on good dining; or nearer to the author of the *Historia Augusta*'s own time, a work such as Macrobius's *Saturnalia*. The author of the *Historia Augusta* treats his readers to all manner of learned discourse of this sort. He reports a conversation about whether or not Firmus was really a usurper that is solved by the production of a coin; he produces critical discourse under one of his assumed names about his production under another; he indulges in learned commentary on the possibility that an emperor of military background might actually quote comedy while splitting a rival in two.[84]

The documents assembled by the author of the *Historia Augusta* cover a full range of official discourse. There are acclamations and speeches of the emperor Tacitus that fill pages, possibly modelled on the real acclamations commemorating the death of Commodus that the author seems to have from Marius Maximus, and recalling Suetonius's statement that acclamations, which express real opinions, are a reliable source.[85] There are testimonials from one emperor on the character of another at an early point in his career that suggest early recognition of excellence. There are letters to the Senate, and letters from kings.[86] Most of this occurs in sections for which there was no biography by Marius Maximus, though some bogus material was included in lives that the author had decided to write of defeated rivals or obscure colleagues of emperors about whom Marius had written (lives of Pescennius Niger and Clodius Albinus, the doomed rivals of Severus, a life of Avidius Cassius, the short-lived usurper under Marcus Aurelius, and so forth). It is as if the author deliberately invokes the apparatus of scholarship to mark his fictions.

A further curiosity is that the *Historia Augusta* survived, and that it was treated as an authoritative text for imperial history before the end of the western empire (Jord. *Get.* 83). Then again, this may not be so curious: all manner of texts that existed in the misty region between the bright light of fiction and the dark night of reality were accepted as authoritative. The key factor in winning such acceptance appears again to have been the adaptation of the stylistic furniture of veracity. The fourth century AD also saw the emergence of Christian hagiography and the evolution of martyrology into new forms, none of them strictly factual in content.

The concept of "witnessing" to the truth of Christ's revelation through the endurance of torture, prison and death appears very early in Christian theology (the word *martys* in Greek means a witness). It is plainly established by the time that Luke wrote his account of Stephen, the "proto-martyr" in (probably) the 90s AD (Acts 7.29–60) even without using the word *martys* in that sense, while Clement of Rome, writing at roughly the same period, did use the word of Peter and Paul, who had met their end under Nero (AD 54–68) (*Ep. ad Cor.* 5.4–5). Accounts of martyrdom by contemporaries and witnesses begin to appear in the mid-second century AD. The earliest extant is the *Martyrdom of Polycarp* at Smyrna in AD 157, though the observation in the letter describing these events that he was the twelfth in the "succession of martyrs at Pergamon" should indicate that there were earlier texts (*Pass. Pol.* 19).

The martyrdom of Polycarp, as we now have it, is in the form of a letter from the Church of Smyrna to other churches, with a coda at the end that describes some of Polycarp's other accomplishments and the copying of the text from an old version in Corinth by Pionius, who would himself be martyred in AD 250 (*Pass. Pol.* 22). By the beginning of the third century different kinds of texts begin to appear. Some of these are based on actual *acta* (records) of trials, or written in such a way as to suggest that this is what they are. Others are based on a combination of diaries by Christians while in prison and eyewitness accounts of their demise. At no point in the first three centuries AD can we say that there was a specific genre of "martyr act"; rather there is a habit of recording martyrdoms, and the form that this record could take varied enormously from place to place, and time to time. Into this chaos of texts stepped Hippolyte Delehaye, who sought to bring some order to it by imposing a standard of reality for categorizing texts.[87] In doing so, he suggested that there were basically six kinds of martyr literature:

1   official records of trials;
2   accounts of eyewitnesses and contemporaries reporting eyewitness accounts;
3   accounts based upon written documents of varieties 1 and 2;
4   historical romances, including accounts derived from other accounts of martyrdom;
5   imaginary romances in which even the martyr is an invention;
6   forgeries composed with a conscious intention to deceive.

Delehaye's classification is immensely valuable, and offers a starting point for any reasonable effort to understand the enormous literature that survives on the subject. But there are times when it is perhaps a little too schematic, and where one may perhaps need a type 3a, the text based a combination of eyewitness material and fiction, neither romance nor documentary record, a record that relies upon the canons of veridical representation to make a claim for itself. One such text is the *Martyrdom of Theodotus of Ancyra and the Seven Virgins.*[88] It represents, perhaps better than

most, the marriage between history and fiction to provide a context for
the relics that had come to occupy a place at the heart of a Christian
community.

The tale of Theodotus and the seven virgins, which survives in but
one manuscript, presents itself as the work of a gentleman named
Nilus, who claims to have been a companion of Theodotus while he was
imprisoned. The story itself is placed in the reign of Maximin Daia, and
the chief agent of the persecution is an officer named Theotecnus.
Theotecnus is a real person, well known from Eusebius for having urged
Maximin on in his hatred of the Christians with the aid of an oracular
statue; his administration in Galatia is a real event, and his particular
antipathy to Christianity is obvious.[89] Theodotus too was a real person,
and so were the seven virgins. The problem is that Theodotus appears to
have been all too real a person. He seems to have worked in food supply,
probably running some kind of inn. He also appears to have been an
overseer of the finances of his church, which appears to have been of a
rather hard-line Montanist variety.[90] Nilus is concerned to defend
Theodotus's reputation, which he says is under attack solely because of
his occupation. To do this, he needed to improve on what appears to
have been a detailed account of both the death of the seven virgins and
the rather problematic story of the delivery of the relics of Theodotus to
the village of Malos near Ancyra. He has also, it seems, to defend
Theodotus from the charge that he was a voluntary martyr, and thus not
entitled, in the view of some, to the crown of a martyr, as well as from
the charge that, as a Montanist, he has no place in the orthodox church.

The tale of the transportation of the relics appears in two parts. The
first, in sections 11–12, tells how Theodotus came to the area to collect
the remains of a martyr named Valens, met some Christians hiding in
the hills, and had a premonition of his own impending martyrdom,
which he revealed to Fronto, the priest of the town. The second part
relates to the miraculous transportation of the remains of Theodotus
after his death through the agency of Fronto and his ass (sections 32–5).
Prior to the encounter with Fronto, there is an account of the question-
able martyrdom of a man named Victor, who had broken under torture
despite the great moral support offered him by Theodotus. Nilus says
that the fact that he asked for time to rethink his devotion led to controversy about his real status (*Mart. Theod.* 9).

The account of the martyrdom of the seven virgins occupies sections
13–15. The story is remarkable in its detail. We are told that as they were
taken to their death, Theodotus hid in a small house near the martyrion of
the Patriarchs, and was given an account of the proceedings that led to

their fatal immersion in a lake a few miles from the city (*Mart. Theod.* 15). Circumstantial detail suggests very strongly that this portion of the martyrdom is the work of an eyewitness. We are told who accompanied Theodotus on his vigil, and that he received news of the death precisely in the sixth hour from a woman who had been present. The lake where the martyrdom occurred has been identified as lying three hours from the center of town, which would have given the witness precisely the right time to see what transpired and return to the city.[91] The recovery of the bodies from the lake occupies sections 16–19; it is filled with visions and miracles (not the least being the parting of the waters so that the bodies could be retrieved), and works with quite a different time frame from that suggested by the previous story of the martyrdom of the seven virgins (it takes all night to get there). Sections 20–31 deal with the actual martyrdom of Theodotus, who is said to have turned himself over to the authorities after his identity was revealed by a "traitor," as had been predicted in a vision. It is filled with long speeches, some of them delivered amidst horrendous tortures that Theodotus does not seem to feel.

Nilus stresses the fact that he is an eyewitness, that he knew Theodotus prior to his martyrdom, and he spoke with him in prison (*Mart. Theod.* 1; 36). He names other eyewitnesses as well, and gives remarkably personal details of Theodotus's conduct, quoting him verbatim on many occasions. Nilus's account of this is thus built upon the techniques of the historian, claiming validity for itself through an appeal to method. Technique and the admixture of independently verifiable fact thus validate fiction.

Conclusion

"Now the Greek and Roman historians advertise a debt and an affinity to poetry, to the epic and to drama. Is it certain in this late season the writing of history must forfeit its claim to belong as a province of literature?"[92] The distance that separates Nilus and Leopold Ranke may not be as great as the sixteen centuries that stand between them, for both feel the tension between what it is that they wish to represent and the literary means available.

Historical narrative and the recording of facts are not, and were not in antiquity, the same thing. Thus the different styles of representation that were reviewed above. Historical narrative such as that produced by a Tacitus or an Ammianus had its own rules: it needed to be grounded upon authentic testimony, but it needed also the personality of the historian to make sense of it. The form of the historical narrative gave rise to imitations whose aim was likewise to convince, they might be *plasmata* in technical definition, but the division between representing the world "as it is" and "like it is" can become a very thin one indeed. The existence of narratives such as the one Nilus wrote is perhaps the best testimony to the importance of the standards discussed by Lucian, Cicero and Dionysius, for without them, could the fiction that was designed to persuade obtain its force? History cannot stand apart from other forms of representation. Historical writing may influence these other forms, just as those forms influence it. The study of historical representation, in whatever form it takes, is integral to the study of the values of the society in which it was, or is, produced.

Epilogue: the discourse of dominance?

Classical historiography was a form of literature with its own rules and methods, defining its ideal practitioner as well as its ideal audience. The ideal historian had time to travel. The ideal historian had access to archives and libraries. Good libraries and interesting archives were not to be found everywhere. The historian who could not get to a city with good libraries, public or private, had no access to public records offices, and had no substantial library of his own (or no friend with one) would have a problem.

The ideal interviewer was a person who knew what it was like to command an army and to direct the operations of a state. The ideal author had slaves to take notes and make copies. In short, the ideal historian was rich and lived in a big city.[1] Friends and money carried a great deal of weight. With money and powerful friends, a freed slave could obtain the "restoration of free birth" through a legal fiction, and might even obtain the right to wear the gold ring that was a signifier of high status.[2]

The ideal audience for such a discourse should contain people who were able to appreciate a good prose style. They ought to be well read enough to pick up allusions, to catch adroit deployment of stock opinions, *sententiae*, which gave them fresh meaning. Such people must then have received a good rhetorical training. Members of the audience should have an interest in foreign places, in the experience of generals, in the fate of important people. They ought to care about the conduct of the governing class, to worry about the restraint of the ill-educated. They should be people for whom the lessons of history were meaningful. Members of the ideal audience should be rather like the ideal practitioner: wealthy residents of urban areas.

Narrative history was thus the discourse of the rich and powerful. Those with access to power shaped the literary tradition about their world.[3] At Rome this was a world where virtuous aristocrats, dedicated to the preservation of *libertas* (the ideal of the *Res publica*) and the social order, sacrificed themselves for their community. Their values became enshrined in the historiography of Rome as the values of the society, never mind the misguided souls who undertook to improve the condition of the less fortunate without prior agreement. It was the Senate that conquered Italy, the Senate that directed the struggles with Carthage, the Senate that oversaw the conquest of the east. The peasant soldiers who died in their hundreds of thousands over the years had no place in this history without their commanders.[4] The Roman plebs who voted on the laws had no mind of their own, at least not on a good day. It is no accident that the first historian of Rome was a senator, Fabius Pictor, and that the first historian to write in Latin, Marcus Porcius Cato, was also a prominent politician.[5] Cassius Hemina, about whom we know virtually nothing, may not have been a senator, but he appears to have been the first person to contrive an historiographic style that placed the operations of the Senate at the center of history: the annalistic year divided between internal affairs, external affairs and internal affairs mirrored the political year of the senator. It was another senator, Piso, who expanded this model, adding massive amounts of new material drawn from diverse traditions to construct what became the "annalistic tradition."[6] Successors like Claudius Quadrigarius and Valerius Antias may not themselves have been senators, but they were clearly men of good education, and attached to the ideology of the governing class. Whatever changes they wrought to the tradition, they were not inclined to write the history of the Roman plebs.

The material for Roman history came from numerous sources, all of them controlled by the governing class. First and foremost there were *commentarii pontificum*, annual records kept by the college of pontiffs. While there is no reason to think that they were "published" in an eighty-eight book edition in the second century, as one late tradition has it, there is likewise no reason to think that there were no records to be used.[7] Then there were family records, displayed in the *atria* of the house of the great and paraded by the families at public funerals. Notoriously inaccurate (and given to family aggrandizement), they were records nonetheless, and they were used.[8] There were, in addition, monuments of the great men of the past, statues, temples and so on, a physical record of aristocratic contribution to the shape of Rome.[9] The senate itself kept records of magistrates and notable accomplishments. These records may also have extended at a very early date to include information about embassies sent and received; implicit in them is a list of wars fought and won. Records of wars lost might themselves get lost in that there would be no reason to recall them unless defeat could be explained by a ritual error that might find its way into the records of a priestly college.[10] There were commentaries on laws (the earliest known to us survives from the late fourth century BC) and speeches (the earliest on record appears to be from the early third century BC), also relicts of aristocratic behavior. Finally, there was drama, in the form of plays on historical subjects, which may have provided important elements of the story to shape Roman historical consciousness prior to the development of Greek-style historiography.[11]

Historiography thus joined poetry, the festival cycle, the law and the magistracies as the province of the dominant class, the province of those who were in a position to describe to others what mattered in the world. But that the history of the Republic as presented in the historiographic tradition was a fabrication of the ruling class does not mean that it was false; rather, it offered a perspective on Roman history that was limited by class and the selection of material. It was one story, but not the only possible story.

It would thus be simple to describe Roman historiography as the discourse of the dominant, to suggest that the upper classes who supported it had stifled other voices to create a social image congenial to itself. But this would be too simple. There were alternatives to the history of Rome as it appears in the annalistic tradition, and its successors down to the end of the classical tradition of historiography in the seventh century AD. In Republican Rome, there was the much more fluid version of history that was placed before the plebs on a regular basis by orators seeking their support, deriving themes, if Cicero is to be believed, from the interests of their audience (*De orat.* 3.92). Beyond this circle there were versions of the past and present, created by men and women with special expertise in the divine who could offer something else.[12] What is missing from the description of Roman historiography as the "discourse of the dominant" is the element of choice. People could opt out, and often did.

The history of the Greek cities of the Roman world would not be the history of Rome. It would not even be a history. Rather, it would be a conglomeration of separate histories, one or more from each city, for history as a discourse is extraordinarily flexible, multilingual as well as factually diverse. But to concentrate on the histories of cities or peoples as alternatives to the history of Rome would be to miss something, for civic or ethnic history was likewise the discourse of local ruling classes who made use of this tool to establish a relationship between themselves and the governing class at Rome. The Gospels, Christian Martyr Acts, the so-called *Acta Alexandrinorum* all were histories of groups asserting themselves outside of the canon of classical historiography, at times using its canons to make their own points. And then there were records of independent associations, and oracles, oracles of all sorts, delivered from shrines, attributed to sages of the distant past, personal revelations in the present age. The incredible diversity of oracular literature in the Roman world points to an interest in a hierarchy that was not contingent upon the whims of the ruling class. Oracles could use chronologies independent of any used by the institutions of any state, and claim an authority greater than that of any mundane power. The prophet could move people to act in ways that no historian could. The discourse of classical historiography was there for those who chose, or were able, to participate; but it excluded, or did not interest, many others. Such people may have found records of charioteers and gladiators a great deal more interesting than those of the senate, or the *Annales* of Tacitus.

The theme of this book has been the construction of a discourse about the past and present by those in power. It was an extremely varied discourse, at times responding to the discourse of those who were excluded, at other times responding to itself. A very different book could have been written, concentrating instead on self-conscious fictions and the restructuring of reality in terms very different from those that have been presented here. Historiography is not simply about dominance and politics, even if the definition of "politics" is extended to include the negotiation of relationships between individuals and groups. Historiography may be limited only by the range of the human imagination, and the physical reality by which it is constrained.

Appendix

Classical authors discussed in the text

In the case of authors with very large bodies of work, only those works discussed in the text are listed. This compendium is merely intended to help readers orient themselves in the text. For more information, readers are advised to look up the relevant entries in the *Oxford Classical Dictionary*, 3rd edition.

Aelius Aristides (AD 117–after 181), highly successful Greek orator, whose extensive rhetorical output is a measure for the transmission of classical Greek themes to the second century AD. His *Sacred Discourses*, an account of his relationship with the god Asclepius, offer an extraordinary document of religious history (and coincidentally valuable for the reconstruction of Roman administration in the province of Asia). Editions: Dindorf (1824), Keil (1898, 1 only), Lenz and Hehr (1976–80, 1–16 only), Behr (1981–6, translation).

Ammianus Marcellinus (*c.*AD 330–95), the last great Latin historian of antiquity. He was born in Syrian Antioch, though he wrote his history (after 378) in Rome. The history was in thirty-one books (1–13 are lost) and carried the story of Roman history from AD 96–378, though the extant portion begins in 352. Editions: Seyfarth (Teubner, 1978), Rolfe (Loeb, 1935–40).

Antoninus, Marcus Aurelius (AD 121–180), emperor AD 161–80. His philosophical musing, the *Meditations*, have survived and are one of the most intimate diaries from antiquity. Editions: Dalfen (Teubner rev. edn 1987), Farquharson (Oxford, 1944).

Apollinides (first century BC–early first century AD), author of thirty-one epigrams preserved in the *Greek Anthology*. Editions: Gow and Page, *The Garland of Philip* (Cambridge, 1968).

Apollodorus of Athens (*c.*180–after 120 BC), author (among other works) of an important chronicle that extended that of Eratosthenes of Cyrene from the death of Alexander to his own time. It is important for its synchronisms between political and cultural history. His major preserved work is the *Bibliotheca*, an account of Greek mythology. Editions: *FGrH* 244 (chronicle), *Bibliotheca*, Frazer (Loeb, 1921).

Appian (late first century–160s AD), historian from Alexandria in Egypt, wrote a history of Rome's wars in twenty-four books, of which books 6–9, 11–17 survive, including accounts of the wars in Spain, with Carthage in North Africa, with Hannibal, Macedon, Mithridates, and the Roman Civil Wars (five books ending with the defeat of Sextus Pompey). He often preserves valuable information not found elsewhere. Editions: Viereck and Roos (Teubner 1939 1–12 with frs, revised Gabba, 1962), Mendelssohn and Viereck (Teubner, 1905 13–17), White (Loeb, 1912–13).

Arrian, Lucius Flavius (*c.*AD 86–160), consul 129 (?), the author of numerous works, of which the best known is a history of Alexander the Great (preserved intact). Editions: Roos rev. Wirth (Teubner, 1967), Brunt (Loeb 1976–83), fragments of other works in Roos and *FGrH* 156.

Asclepiades of Myrleia (first century BC), historian and literary theorist. His views on the divisions between fiction and history were influential in later generations; a critical edition of his works is needed.

Atticus, Titus Pomponius (BC 110–32), great friend of Cicero, he oversaw the publication of many of Cicero's speeches and other works. He was himself the author of numerous literary works, including histories. Fragments: Peter *HRR* 2, 6–8.

Aulus Gellius (*c.*AD 125–80), man of letters. His principal surviving work, *The Attic Nights*, in twenty books, is a collection of excerpts made from his reading and reminiscences. Editions: Marshall (Oxford, 1990), Rolfe (Loeb, 1927).

Bassus (early first century AD), author of thirteen epigrams preserved in the *Greek Anthology*. Editions: Gow and Page, *The Garland of Philip* (Cambridge, 1968).

Berossus (late third–early second centuries BC), a Babylonian priest who wrote a history of Babylonia in Greek, based on Babylonian sources. It appears to have been little read except by Christians and Jews, and is now known only through fragments. Editions: *FGrH* 680, Verbrugghe and Wickersham (1996) (translation with commentary).

Caesar, Gaius Julius (100–44 BC), most successful politician of his age, and later accorded the honor of having been Rome's first emperor. Seven books of *Commentaries* on the Gallic wars and three on the Civil War survive; the corpus of Caesarian writings in the manuscript tradition is filled out by works on the *Alexandrine War*, *The African War* and the *Spanish War* by diverse hands. The eighth book of the commentaries on the Gallic wars was written by Aulus Hirtius, who may also be responsible for the *Alexandrine War*, though not the others. Editions: editions are available from Budé, Teubner, Oxford and Loeb (the Oxford edition should be avoided) and there are numerous translations. His other works are lost.

Callisthenes of Olynthus (died in 327 BC at a considerable age), the nephew of Aristotle, wrote numerous philosophical and historical works, of which the most famous was about Alexander the Great, fragments in *FGrH* 124.

Cassius Dio (*c.*AD 164–after 229), consul *c.* AD 204 and in AD 229, the author of a history of Rome from the foundation of the city to the reign of Severus Alexander in eighty books, a critical source for many periods of Roman history. Editions: Boissevain (1895–1931), Cary (Loeb, 1914–27).

Cassius Hemina, Lucius (mid to late second century BC), the author of a history of Rome, otherwise unknown. Scanty fragments survive of an historical work, possibly annalistic in form (Peter *HRR* 12 98–111).

Castor of Rhodes (first century BC), author of an important sixteen-book chronicle that included Near Eastern, Greek and Roman history; his work was important for later chronographers, including Eusebius. Editions: *FGrH* 250.

Cato the Elder (*c.*234–149 BC), one of the most influential politicians and literary figures of his day, principal surviving work, *On Agriculture*, one book; of his other works, fragments of numerous orations survive (collected in *ORF4* 18–97) as well as significant fragments of his history in seven books, the *Origines* (Peter *HRR* 12 55–90 and Chassignet (Budé, 1986).

Catullus, Gaius Valerius (84–54 BC?), one of Rome's greatest poets. Editions: texts are readily available from Oxford, Teubner and Budé, and there are many translations.

Cicero, Marcus Tullius (106–43 BC), consul 63 BC, the greatest man of letters of his generation, and a politician of note. His views on literature were significant for the development of Roman theories of rhetoric; editions of his numerous surviving works are too extensive to list.

Crinagoras (mid-first century BC–early first century AD), almost certainly from a distinguished family at Mytilene, the author of fifty-one epigrams preserved in the *Greek Anthology*. Editions: Gow and Page, *The Garland of Philip* (Cambridge, 1968).

Dio Chrysostom (*c.*AD 40/50–after 110), Greek orator from Prusa in Bithynia; eighty speeches are attributed to him (two are by his pupil Favorinus) ranging widely in subject, offering valuable information about culture, civic life, Roman administration and ideals of king-ship (among other things). Editions: von Arnim (Teubner 1893–6), de Budé (Budé 1915–19), Cosby (Loeb, 1932–51).

Diodorus Siculus (first century BC), the author of the *Bibliotheca*, a universal history from mythological times to 60 BC in forty books. Only books 1–5 and 11–20 survive intact, though there are extensive fragments from later sections. His work stands as a touchstone of literary taste in his age and is important for the history of Rome because he attempted to integrate Roman history into Greek from the foundation of the city, as well as for the history of the period of Rome's rise to empire. Editions: Vogel and Fisher (Teubner 1888–1906), Oldfather *et al.* (Loeb, 1933–67).

Dionysius of Halicarnassus (second half of the first century BC), historian and literary critic, works include *Roman Antiquities* (C. Jacoby, Teubner, 1885–1925; E. Cary, Loeb 1937–50) and numerous rhetorical works (Usener and Radermacher 1885–1929, Usher, Loeb, 1975–85).

Ennius, Quintus (239–269 BC), the most important early Latin poet, he was the first Latin author to use hexameter verse; significant fragments survive of his *Annales* (ed. Skutch, 1985), tragedies (Jocelyn, 1967) and other poetry (Vahlen, 1903).

Ephorus of Cyme (*c.*405–330 BC) the author of a thirty-book history that recorded Greek and "barbarian" history from the "return of the Heraclidae" to the siege of Perinthus in 340 BC. Polybius regarded him as the first universal historian, and he is thought to be the principal source of Diodorus Siculus for the period down to 340 BC. He is extensively quoted by authors other than Diodorus as well. Editions: *FGrH* 70.

Eratosthenes of Cyrene (*c.*285–194 BC), one of the pre-eminent intellectuals of his day. He wrote poetry and philosophy, on mathematics, geography and literary criticism, and produced a chronicle. His geographical work was of great importance for Strabo, while his chronicle was the first scientific attempt to reconcile different Greek chronologies from the mythological period to the death of Alexander (323 BC). Among other things, he reconciled lists of Olympic victors with Athenian archon dates to provide a common chronological scheme for the Greek world. Editions: *Chronology*: *FGrH* 241.

Eunapius of Sardis (*c.*AD 345–after 414), author of the *Lives of the Philosophers* (extant) and a *History of Rome 270–414* in fourteen books, now lost but extensively quoted by later authors (and used by Ammianus Marcellinus). The date of publication for the *History* is disputed since portions obviously circulated well before the final work was done. Editions: *History*, Blockley (1981–3); *Lives of the Philosophers*, Wright (Loeb, 1922).

Eusebius of Caesarea (*c.*AD 260–339), author of numerous works of biblical exegesis, Christian apologetic and history. Perhaps his most influential works were his *History of the Church* in ten books and his *Chronicle*. His five-book *Life of Constantine* offers an important

Christian perspective on the life of that emperor. His historical works (and chronicle) are notable for the direct quotation of documents). The *Chronicle* has not been preserved in Greek; the most useful versions are the Armenian translation, ed. Karst (GCS 20, 1911) and Jerome's Latin version (GCS 47 (1956), Greek fragments are printed in Schoene 1 (1875) and 2 (1866). For the *History of the Church* see Schwartz (CGS 9.1 (1903); 9.2 (1908); 9.3 (1909); for an English translation see Lake and Oulton (Loeb 1926–32). For the *Life of Constantine* see Winkelmann (GCS *Eusebius Werke*1.12 1975), English translation Richardson, 1890.

Fabius Pictor (*c.*270–200 BC), the first Roman historian of Rome, his history, in Greek told the story of Rome's history from earliest times down to at least the year 210, and possibly to the end of the Second Punic War in 201. The work is known only through fragments. Edition: *FGrH* 809.

Galen (AD 129–216 probably), from Pergamon. He was the greatest doctor of his age, and his surviving corpus is enormous. He was doctor to Marcus Aurelius and his family. Editions: the enormous corpus was edited by C.G. Kühn (1821–33) and there are now editions of most of the individual works.

Hecataeus of Abdera (*c.*360–290 BC), author of philosophical ethnographies, regarded as an authority on non-Greek peoples; fragments in *FGrH* 264.

Hecataeus, son of Hegesander of Miletus (late sixth–early fifth centuries BC), one of the most important early Greek prose writers. His *Periegesis* and *Genealogies* are two of the best-attested works of early Greek prose (albeit both fragmentary). Fragments: *FGrH* 1.

Herodian (late second–first half of the second century AD), author of a history of Rome from the death of Marcus Aurelius to the accession of Gordian III (180–238). Editions: Müller (1996), Whittaker (Loeb, 1969).

Herodotus (*c.*484–420? BC), writer whose history exercised a profound influence over the development of historiographic thought throughout antiquity. Editions: Hude (Oxford, 1926–7), Rosen (Teubner), Godley (Loeb).

Historia Augusta (AD 390s probably), the title given by Isaac Casaubon to a series of imperial biographies from Hadrian to Carinus (AD 117–284). The work purports to be by six authors writing in the late third–early fourth centuries AD. It is in fact by a single author, probably writing at the end of the fourth century AD. Editions: Hohl (Teubner, 1927), Magie (Loeb, 1922–32).

Horace (BC 65–8), major lyric poet of the reign of Augustus; his major works, in addition to a poem that was sung at the *ludi saeculares* of 17 BC include the *Epodes*, *Satires*, *Odes* and *Epistles*, the latter being particularly important in the history of literary criticism. Editions: Shackleton Bailey (Teubner, 1985) and numerous others.

Josephus, Flavius (AD 37/38–after 94); after participating in the Jewish revolt against Rome, he was captured by Vespasian and ultimately became a valued member of his staff. His works include the *Jewish War*, an account of the great revolt against Rome in 65–72, a self-justificatory autobiography, the *Life*, the *Jewish Antiquities* in twenty books, giving the history of the Jewish people from the creation to the beginning of the reign of Nero, and the *Against Apion* in two books, justifying Judaism against critics. Editions: Naber (Teubner 1888–96), Thackery, Marcus, Wikgren and Feldman (Loeb, 1926–65).

Libanius (AD 314–93 ?), great rhetorician and man of letters at Antioch in Syria; his surviving corpus includes sixty-four orations, some 1,600 letters and fifty-one school declamations and numerous other rhetorical works. He was a committed pagan. Editions: Foerster (Teubner 1903–27), Norman (Loeb, 1969–77, 3 vols selections).

Lucan, Marcus Annaeus (AD 69–35), a prolific poet of the reign of Nero; only his unfinished epic *On the Civil War* treating the war between Caesar and Pompey, a critical exploration of the theme of *bellum civile*, remains intact. He committed suicide after his complicity in the plot to overthrow Nero in AD 65 was discovered. Editions: Shackleton Bailey (Teubner, 1996), Duff (Loeb, 1928).

Lucian of Samosata (*c.*AD 120–after 180), author of numerous prose satires that offer much information on social life in his age. His *How to Write History* (composed around 165/6), although satirical, is a critical guide to standards of historiography in his age. Editions: Macleod (Oxford, 1972–87), Harmon *et al.* (Loeb, 1921–67).

Manetho (late third–early second centuries BC), Egyptian priest who wrote a history of Egypt from earliest times to 342 BC based on Egyptian sources. His work still provides the fundamental dynastic structure for Egyptian history, though it is now preserved only in fragments. Editions: *FGrH* 609, Waddell (Loeb, 1940), Verbrugghe and Wickersham (1996) (translation with commentary).

Marius Maximus (AD170?–after 226), prefect of Rome in 217–8, consul for the second time in 226; he wrote the lives of the twelve Caesars from Nerva to Elagabalus, continuing Suetonius. His work was exploited by the author of the *Historia Augusta*. Editions: Peter *HRR* 2, 121–9.

Martial, Marcus Valerius (AD 38–104?), author of twelve books of epigrams, of great importance for literary tastes in the late first century AD. Editions: Shackleton Bailey (Loeb, 1990, based on his Teubner text).

Ovid, Publius (43 BC–AD 17), the most prolific poet of the Augustan age, his major works include *Amores* (three books, elegies, primarily erotic in theme), *Heroides* (elegiac letters from famous heroines), *Medicamina faciei femineae* (Cosmetics for the Female Face), *Ars Amatoria* (three books on erotic intrigue), *Remedia Amoris* (recantation for the *Ars*) *Metamorphoses* (epic poem in fifteen books), *Fasti* (*Calendar*, poetic description of the first six months of the Roman calendar), *Ibis* (curse poem in elegiacs), *Tristia* (*Sorrows*, five books of lamentation from exile), *Epistulae* (four books of elegiac letters written from exile). He was exiled in AD 8. The reason is obscure, though the *Ars Amatoria* was one cause. Editions: numerous editions are available; Goold (Loeb 1977–89) offers the complete works.

Pausanias of Magnesia ad Sipylum (mid-second century AD), author of a description of Greece that is full of vital information about the antiquities of Greece in his age, chiefly those prior to AD 150, though he displays some interest in the benefactions of the emperor Hadrian (AD 117–138). Editions: Rocha-Pereira (Teubner, 1973–81); Jones (Loeb, 1918–35 with translation by Frazer).

Pliny the Elder (AD 23/4–79), imperial official and polymath. His principal surviving work is *The Natural History* in thirty-seven books; numerous other works, now lost, include a *History of Rome* in thirty-one books covering the later Julio-Claudians and a *German Wars* in twenty books. Editions: Mayhoff (Teubner, 1899–1906) Rackham and Stuart Jones (Loeb, 1938–63) Budé; Historical Works, Peter *HRR* 2, 109–12).

Pliny the Younger (*c.*AD 61–112), consul 100 AD, often regarded as a guide to the sentiments of his class; principal surviving works are the *Letters* (ten books) and the *Panegyric* (originally delivered in AD 100). Editions: *Letters* Mynors (Oxford, 1963); *Panegyric* Mynors (*Panegyrici Latini* Oxford, 1964), Radice (Loeb, 1969).

Plutarch (*c.*AD 50–120), biographer and philosopher. Complete editions of his numerous works are available in Teubner, Budé and Loeb editions.

Polybius (*c.*200–118 BC), the great historian of the rise of Rome in the third and second centuries BC; his history in forty books is preserved intact for Books 1–5, and there are substantial fragments of Book 6 and Book 12 (containing extensive critiques of other historians); there is much less of the rest. Editions: Büttner-Wobst (Teubner, 1889–1904, 1905), Paton (Loeb, 1922–7).

Pompeius Trogus (first century BC), the author of a universal history in forty-four books, completed after 20 BC. The most significant work of its genre in Latin, it has not survived intact. The contents are known through the epitome of Justin (probably fourth century AD) and a list of the contents is preserved in the manuscript tradition. Editions: Seel (Teubner, 1956), and there is a good translation by Yardley (1995).

Propertius, Sextus (BC 54?–probably before 10), author of four books of elegies; the first two are primarily erotic in theme, and the fourth deals with a variety of Roman themes. Editions: Barber (Oxford, 1960), Fedeli (Teubner, 1984), Goold (Loeb, 1990).

Quintilian, Marcus Fabius (*c.*AD 35–90s), the premier teacher of rhetoric in his generation, known now chiefly from his *Institutio Oratoria*. Editions: Winterbottom (Oxford, 1970), Butler (Loeb, 1921–2).

Sextus Empiricus (second century AD, probably second half), skeptical philosopher and doctor. His chief works are *Outlines of Pyrrhonism* and *Against the Professors* (*Adversus mathematicos*). Editions: Mutschmann and Mau (Teubner 1958–62), Bury (Loeb, 1933–49).

Silius Italicus (*c*.AD 26–102), consul 68 AD, author of an epic poem on the Second Punic War in seventeen books. Editions: Delz (Teubner, 1987), Duff (Loeb, 1934).

Statius, Publius Papinius (*c*.AD 45–96), the most important epic poet of the Flavian period. His *Thebaid* survives intact, along with the finished portions of an epic on Achilles; there are also five books of occasional poetry, the *Silvae*. Editions: *Silvae* Courtney (Oxford, 1990); *Thebaid* Hill (1973), Mozeley (Loeb, 1928, complete works).

Suetonius, Gaius (AD 70–130?), biographer of the Caesars from Caesar to Domitian, and author of many other learned works. Editions: *Caesars* Ihm (Teubner, 1908), Rolfe (Loeb, 1913–4, complete works); *De grammaticis et rhetoribus*, Brugnoli (Teubner, 1973); *De grammaticis*, Kaster (Oxford, 1995); numerous translations of the *Caesars* are available.

Tacitus, Cornelius (*c*.AD 57–120?), consul 97, historian of Rome; his surviving works include the *Agricola* (about his father-in-law), *Germania, Dialogus, Annales* (history of Rome AD 14–68) and *Historiae* (history of Rome AD 69–96, preserved only to AD 70). Editions: readily available from Oxford, Teubner, Budé and Loeb; there are numerous translations.

Theophrastus of Eresus (*c*.371–287 BC), the successor to Aristotle as head of the peripatetic school at Athens, and the author of numerous works on a wide variety of topics in philosophy, natural history, and literary criticism. He was responsible for an important theory that traced the development of historiography through the evolution of prose style, a theory that influenced both Cicero and Dionysius of Halicarnassus. Editions: Wimmer (Didot 1931) is complete if dated; editions of individual works are available from a number of sources.

Thucydides (*c.*460–395? BC), regarded in later generations as the greatest Greek historian; his surviving work is the *Peloponnesian War* in eight books but incomplete, telling the story of the war from 431–411, with allusions to the end of the war at various points and a long digression on the rise of Athens from 478 to 439 in Book 1. Editions: Stuart-Jones (Oxford, 1898–1902), Smith (Loeb, 1926), and numerous translations.

Timaeus of Tauromenium (*c.*350–260 BC), the most important western Greek historian; he wrote, amongst other things, a history of Sicily from the earliest times to 289/8 and a history of the Roman wars against Pyrrhus. Fragments in *FGrH* 566.

Trajan, Marcus Ulpius (AD 53?–118), emperor 98–118; some letters to Pliny survive in Book 10 of the latter's correspondence. One of Rome's most successful rulers.

Varro, Marcus Terentius (BC 116–27), the pre-eminent scholar of the Latin language and antiquities in his generation, he is also the author of *Satires*. His main works include *Concerning the Latin Language* (twenty-five books, of which 5–10 survive), *Concerning Agriculture* (three books, extant), and *Human and Divine Antiquities*. Editions: Semi (1965–6); *De lingua latina* Kent (Loeb, 1951); *De re rustica*, Hooper and Ash (Loeb, 1935); *Antiquities* (divine) Carduans (1976), (human) Mirsch (1882), *Satires* (Astbury, 1985).

Velleius Paterculus (*c.*20 BC–after 30 AD), author of a two-book *History of Rome to the Consulship of Marcus Vinicius* (AD 30), of which the second book is preserved intact. A critical work for the ideology of the Augustan Age. The fragments of the first book are of interest as an example of the adaptation of Greek history into Latin. Editions: Watt (Teubner, 1989), Elefante (1997), Shipley (Loeb, 1924), Helleguarc'h (Budé, 1982).

Vergil (70–19 BC), Rome's greatest poet; his surviving works include the *Eclogues*, *Georgics* and *Aeneid*. Editions are numerous, as are translations.

Verrius Flaccus, Marcus (*c.*55 BC?–AD 20?), significant student of the Latin language and Roman antiquities. A critical edition of his works is badly needed.

Zenodotus of Ephesus (late second century–first half of third century BC), the first librarian of the library at Alexandria (appointed *c.* 284); wrote a Homeric Glossary, and produced editions of the *Iliad* and *Odyssey* in addition to editions of other classical authors, e.g. Hesiod's *Theogony*, Pindar and Anacreon. A collection of his fragments is needed.

Zosimus (late fifth–early sixth centuries AD), a government official and a pagan; his *New History* in six books carries the history of Rome from the mid third century AD to the sack of Rome in 410. It appears that his history is little more than an epitome of earlier pagan writers including Eunapius and Olympiodorus. Editions: Paschoud (Budé, 1971–89).

Notes

Introduction

1 D.S. Potter, *Prophets and Emperors: Human and Divine Authority from Augustus to Theodosius* (Cambridge, MA, 1994).

I Definitions

1 C.L. Becker, "Everyman his own historian," *AHR* 37 (1932), 223; 226 for both definitions, and discussion of the problems with both.

2 OED s.v. "history"; another definition offered in the same dictionary is "the study of past events, especially of human affairs."

3 The formulation here is similar to that in L. Stone, "History and post-modernism III," *Past and Present* 135 (1992), 189–90. The key study upon which Stone bases his remarks is G.M Spiegel, "History, Historicism, and the Social Logic of the Text in the Middle Ages," *Speculum* 65 (1990), 59–87. repr. in K. Jenkins, *The Postmodern History Reader* (London, 1997), 180–203. A slightly earlier discussion of these problems, with a similar perspective is offered by E. Hobsbawm, "Escaped slaves of the forest," *New York Review of Books* 6 (December, 1990), 46–8, repr. as "Postmodernism in the forest," in E. Hobsbawm, *On History* (New York, 1997), 192–200. For a broad perspective on these issues, see A.D. Momigliano, "Considerations on history in an age of ideologies," *The American Scholar* 51 (1982), 495–507, repr. in A.D. Momigliano, *Settimo contributo alla storia degli studi classici e del mondo antico* (Rome, 1984), 253–69.

4 P. Joyce, "History and post-modernism I," and C. Kelley, "History and post-modernism II," *Past and Present* 133 (1991), 204–13. Joyce seeks support from a then unpublished essay by G. Eley, that has now appeared as "Is all the world a text? From social history to the history of society two decades later," in T. McDonald (ed.) *The Historic Turn in the Human Sciences* (Ann Arbor, MI, 1996), 193–244. In the relevant section of what is a valuable survey (pp. 207–16), Eley recommends "intermediate course" between text and reality, a position rather similar to that of Stone. For a more radical critique, that places the historian in control of the reality that the historian has decided to narrate, see R. Barthes, "The discourse of history," in R. Howard (ed.) *The Rustle of Language* (Berkeley, CA, 1989),

127–40; N. Dirks, "Is vice versa? Historical anthropologies and anthropological histories," in T. McDonald (ed.) *The Historic Turn in the Human Sciences* (Ann Arbor, MI, 1996), 17–41; for a general survey, see R.T. Vann, "Turning linguistic: history and theory and *History and Theory*, 1960–1975" in F. Ankersmit and H. Kellner, *A New Philosophy of History* (Chicago, 1995), 40–69.

5   C. Geertz, "Blurred genres: the refiguration of social thought," in C. Geertz, *Local Knowledge: Further Essays in Interpretive Anthropology* (New York, 1983), 30, for the influence of linguistic theory. On various forms of social and cultural history, see the lucid discussion in J. Appleby, L. Hunt and M. Jacob, *Telling the Truth about History* (New York, 1994), 225–31 though see also the critique of the ideological tendency therein provided by M. Poster, *Cultural History and Postmodernity: Disciplinary Readings and Challenges* (New York, 1997), 47–8.

6   For this problem see, for instance, F. Jameson, *Postmodernism or the Cultural Logic of Late Capitolism* (Durham, 1991), xiii: "for the name itself – postmodernism – has crystallized a host of hitherto independent developments which, thus named, prove to have contained the thing itself in embryo and now step forward richly to document its multiple genealogies." M. Sarup, *An Introductory Guide to Post-Structuralism and Postmodernism*, 2nd edn, (Athens, GA., 1993), 1–4 points out that postmodernism may be described as a series of critiques of "the human subject," "historicism," "meaning" and "philosophy." For another lucid discussion of the evolution of postmodern approaches see L. Cahoone, *From Modernism to Postmodernism: An Anthology* (Oxford, 1996), 13–19.

7   Appleby, Hunt and Jacob, *Telling the Truth about History*, 201. For earlier debates in the context of the North American historical profession, see below.

8   Joyce, "History and post-modernism I," 208; Kelley, "History and post-modernism II," 210. See also Stone, "History and post-modernism III," 135; G. Spiegel, "History and post-modernism IV," *Past and Present* 135 (1992), 197–8. See also J. Passmore, "Narratives and events," *History and Theory* 26 (1987), 71, drawing the distinction between "narrative" as a linguistic mode and "event" as an "ontological" mode. K. Jenkins, *On "What is History? From Carr and Elton to Rorty and White* (London, 1995), 29–36, likewise admits that no postmodernist construction denies the existence of reality, but fails to see the importance of the admission to his own discussion. *Pace* Jenkins, it is unreasonable to assert that the concern is primarily to do with the future of peer review (p. 30), his evident unfamiliarity with studies of the past using material culture alone leads him to suggest that the past has only ever been accessed through textuality. The counter-argument to this point is, of course, that the material culture passes through the filter of textuality in the discourse of the past, but that is to confuse the vehicle of contextualization with the object being contextualized. Jenkins's fourth point (p. 31–3), that textualism calls attention to the "textual conditions" under which *all* historical work is done and *all* historical knowledge is produced" (his italics), would call forth few objections, and is stated by Stone with the qualification that "*all* historical knowledge" is not produced in this way. The issue is rather the way that the historian approaches "historical knowledge."

9 See for instance the responses to D. Harlan, "Intellectual history and the return of literature," *AHR* 94 (1989), 581–609 by D.A. Hollinger, "The return of the prodigal: the persistence of historical knowing," *AHR* 94 (1989), 610–21 (implying that Harlan's critique is a threat to all forms of monographic history, which it plainly is not, note particularly D. Harlan, "Reply to David Hollinger," *AHR* 94 (1989), 625 specifically pointing out that he is talking about intellectual history). The same issue informs J. Appleby, "One good turn deserves another: moving beyond the linguistic; a response to David Harlan," *AHR* 94 (1989), 1326–32, who treats Harlan as if his discussion ranged well beyond the one branch of historiography. For a very useful discussion of the relationship between text and "history" in the New Historicism, see K. Ryan, *New Historicism and Cultural Materialism: A Reader* (London, 1996), ix–xviii, especially p. xiii.

10 See Poster, *Cultural History and Postmodernity* especially pp. 14–37. For a less nuanced view, see K. Windschuttle, *The Killing of History: How Literary Critics and Social Theorists are Murdering Our Past* (New York, 1997), *passim*. Most recently, see C.B. McCullagh, *The Truth of History* (London, 1998), 13–61.

11 J.-F. Lyotard, *The Postmodern Condition: A Report on Knowledge* (Minneapolis, MN, 1984); see also J.F. Lyotard, "Futility in Revolution" in R. Harvey and M.S. Roberts (eds) *Toward the Postmodern*, (Atlantic Highlands, NJ, 1993), 91.

12 See also J. Marincola, *Authority and Tradition in Ancient Historiography* (Cambridge, 1997), 258–66. Marincola's volume appeared after the present text was largely complete. I have taken account of his excellent and well-informed discussions as far as is possible under the circumstances.

13 C. Geertz, "Commonsense as a cultural system," in C. Geertz, *Local Knowledge*, 73–93. For the importance of Geertz's work to the New Historicism, see Ryan, *New Historicism and Cultural Materialism*, 1–4.

14 Sarup, *An Introductory Guide to Post-Structuralism and Postmodernism* 2nd edn, 59 for a lucid summary.

15 Chantraine, *Dictionaire etymologique* sv. οἶδα. E. Floyd, "The sources of Greek "istor," "judge," "witness"," *Glotta* 68 (1990), 157–66, suggests a different etymology, from *izô*, "to sit." This view has not gained assent.

16 W.R. Connor, "The *histor* in history," *Nomodeiktes: Greek Studies in Honor of Martin Ostwald* (Ann Arbor, MI, 1993), 4. See also the stress on the investigative role of the historian in P.S. Derow, "Historical explanation; Polybius and his predecessors," in S. Hornblower (ed.) *Greek Historiography* (Oxford, 1994), 73–90; R.L. Fowler, "Herodotus and his contemporaries," *JHS* 116 (1996), 69–80.

17 Compare for example Varro *Ling lat.* 5.30; 5.148; 5.157; Tac. *Dial.* 3.4. It is notable that Livy never uses *historia* to designate a work of history, preferring instead to use *annales*. The same is true of Tacitus. Contrast for example Quint. *Orat.* 10.2.7: *nihil in historiis supra pontificum annales haberemus.* Quintilian regularly uses *historia* for historical works, avoiding *annales* except in the case of works specifically entitled *Annales*.

18 See for example Civ. *Div.* 1.21.43 = Fabius Pictor Fr Peter: *quod nimirum in Fabi Pictoris Graecis annalibus eius Modi est*; Livy 25.39.11 = Acilius Fr. 4 Peter: *auctor est Claudius qui annales Acilianos ex Graeco in Latinum sermonem vertit*; Macrob. *Sat.* 3.20.5 = Postumius Fr. 2 Peter: *Postumius Albinus annali primo* (the book was in Greek, and if Macrobius was using a Latin translation

there is no reason to think that it was done by Postumius himself); Plin. *NH* 10.71 = Fabius Pictor Fr. 24 Peter: *tradit et Fabius Pictor in annalibus suis*; Plin. NH 8.11 = Cato Fr. 88 Peter: *certe Cato, cum imperatorum nomina annalibus detraxerit.*

19 In this regard see also the interesting discussion of J. Rüsen, "Historical narration," *History and Theory* 26 (1987), 89, arguing that the three essential features of historical narration are that it is tied to the medium of memory, that it organizes the internal unity of past, present and future with a concept of continuity, and it establishes the identity of its authors as listeners.

20 *FGrH* 1 F 1; Thuc. 1.22.2.

21 P.A. Brunt, "Cicero and historiography," *Studies in Greek History and Thought* (Oxford, 1993), 181–209; J.L. Moles, "Truth and untruth in Herodotus and Thucydides," in C. Gill and T.P. Wiseman, *Lies and Fiction in the Ancient World* (Exeter, 1993), 114–21.

22 See also *De Thuc.* 6 where the same distinction between *mythos* and *diegesis* is used, and for others who drew the distinction between the pleasure offered by poetry and that offered by the discourse of history see G. Avenarius, *Lukians Schrift zur Geschichtsschreibung* (Meisenheim am Glan, 1956), 16–22.

23 For issues of truth and fiction in the formative period of Greek literature see L.H. Pratt, *Lying and Poetry from Homer to Pindar: Falsehood and Description in Archaic Greek Poetry* (Ann Arbor, MI, 1993), 11–53; E.L. Bowie, "Lies, fiction and slander in Early Greek Poetry," in Gill and Wiseman, *Lies and Fiction in the Ancient World*, 1–37.

24 The fundamental discussion of this division remains K. Barwick, "Die Gliederung der Narratio in der rhetorischen Theorie und ihre Bedeutung für die Geschichte des antiken Romans," *Hermes* 63 (1928), 260–87, a superb example of traditional philology at its best. One issue that may not be sufficiently discussed by Barwick is that the parallel discussions in [Cic] *Inv.* 1.27 and [Cic.] *Ad Her.* 1.12, while offering the tripartite division amply attested elsewhere (in addition to the passages discussed in the text here see *Anon. Seg.* 53 fol; *Schol. in Ter.* 167, 33; Hermog 4.16 R; Nicol. 12.17; Mart. Cap 486.16) are not quite the same as elsewhere in that *historia* is described as *gesta res, sed ab aetatis nostrae memoria remota* (events that occurred, but distant from the memory of our age), but this may simply be a result of the fact that the example that Asclepiades gave seems to have concerned Alexander the Great (Sext. Emp *Adv. gramm.* 263–4), which may have inspired the author of [Cic.] *Inv.* 1.27 to illustrate the point with a quotation from Ennius. The scholiast on Dion. Thrax 173.3, who wrote that "he divides comedy from tragedy in that tragedy has narration (*historia*) and exposition (*apaggelia*) of events that have happened, while comedy provides *plasmata* of daily life," is rather more problematic than Barwick's discussion (p. 273) allows.

25 In addition to Barwick's discussion of this passage ("Die Gliederung der Narratio," 269–70), see R. Reitzenstein, *Hellenistiche Wunderzählungen* (Leipzig, 1906), 90–91; F.W. Walbank, "History and Tragedy," *Historia* 9 (1960), 225–30, F.W. Walbank, *Selected Papers: Studies in Greek and Roman History and Historiography* (Cambridge, 1985), 233–37; R. Meijering, *Literary and Rhetorical Studies in Greek Scolia* (Groningen, 1987), 76–90; M.J. Wheeldon,

"True stories': the reception of historiography in antiquity," in A. Cameron, *History as Text* (London, 1989), 60–2.

26 Marincola, *Authority and Tradition*, 128–33 draws a rather closer connection between the stress on character and rhetorical theories of character than I am inclined to, seeing, as I suggest here, a natural development out of the inherent discourse concerning truth. Similarly, moral failure is not stressed in T.P. Wiseman's important discussion of other reasons for lying, "Lying historians: seven types of mendacity," in Gill and Wiseman, *Lies and Fiction in the Ancient World*, 122–46. Also relevant is the notion of the "appropriate" (*to prepon*) in establishing points of fact, discussed below.

27 *Mor.* 856d; compare *Mor.* 51 c–d. See also the excellent discussion in T.J. Luce, "Ancient views on the causes of bias in historical writings," *CPh* 84 (1989), 21–4.

28 F.W. Walbank, *Polybius* (Berkeley, CA, 1972), 53–4. For the role of polemic as a way of establishing authority see Marincola, *Authority and Tradition*, 225–36.

29 See F.R.D. Goodyear, *The Annals of Tacitus* 1 (Cambridge, 1972) *ad loc* and Marincola, *Authority and Tradition*, 15 for the important observation that Tacitus is stressing the correct interpretation of facts that have been misrepresented through prejudice rather than discovery of new ones. See also Wheeldon, " 'True stories' ": the reception of historiography in antiquity" 48, 50–1; Wiseman, "Lying historians," 126–7; Luce, "Ancient views on the causes of bias," 16–21, 25–31.

30 Compare Sal. *Cat.* 4.2; *Hist.* 1.6 Reynolds; Jos. *BJ* 1.1–2; *AJ* 26.154; Sen. *Apoc.* 1.1. See also Marincola, *Authority and Tradition*, 157–8.

31 Pliny, *Ep.* 5.8.12: *intacta et nova? graves offensae, levis gratia*; compare Plin. *Epp.* 9.19.5 (Cluvius Rufus and Verginius Rufus); 9.27 (possibly referring to Tacitus); Tac. *Hist.* 1.1.

32 Compare D.H. Fischer, *Historians' Fallacies* (New York, 1970), 38–9, with whom I am obviously in agreement, save that his sixth axiom essentially repeats his first, and he does not allow for fields of history where establishing the evidence is a viable sub-field in and of itself.

2 Texts

1 See K. Hopkins, "Novel Evidence for Roman Slavery," *Past and Present* 138 (1993), 3–27.

2 This chapter is in no way intended to be a history of literature and editions. The best introduction to the Greek and Latin literature of the Roman world is A. Dihle, *Greek and Latin Literature of the Roman Empire from Augustus to Justinian* tr. M. Malzahn (London, 1994). Dihle's notes also offer an up-to-date overview of editions of authors covered in his book. G.B. Conte, *Latin Literature: A History* tr. J.B. Solodow (Baltimore, 1994), is useful for part of the story.

3 For papyrus records see R. Coles, *Reports of Proceedings in Papyri* (Brussels, 1966), 19.

4 The question of whether or not they were subsequently edited is another matter. Nepos reports that the correspondence between Cicero and Atticus filled eleven *volumina* (XVI, printed in the standard critical edition is an

emendation). He also distinguishes this collection from books "given to the public" (*Att.* 16.3 = *SB* 413.3). J. Carcopino, *Cicero: The Secrets of his Correspondence*, 2 vols, tr. E.O. Lorimer (London, 1951) argued for two collections, the one seen by Nepos, and another subsequently compiled with Augustan oversight. The view has not found general acceptance. See D.R. Shackleton Bailey, *Cicero's Letters to Atticus* 1 (Cambridge, 1965), 59–76, whose position remains persuasive despite excessive stress on the scholarly capacity of Asconius; for which see now B.A. Marshall, *A Historical Commentary on Asconius* (Columbia, SC, 1985), 62–77.

5 *Fam.* 15.20.4; contrast *Fam.* 2.4 distinguishing between letters filled with personal information, letters intended to amuse and letters on serious topics.

6 For the collection of seventy letters, see *Att.* 16.5.5 (SB 410.5) and, possibly, *Fam.* 16.17.1 (SB 126.1); in 53 he mentioned a possible collection of his letters to Quintus, but nothing seems to have come of it, see *Q. fr.* 1.2.8 (SB 2.8). In general see Carcopino, *Cicero: The Secrets of his Correspondence*, 483–8. For the possibility that the collection is the basis of *Fam.* 13 see Shackleton-Bailey, *Letters to Atticus* 1, 59.

7 J. Bidez, *L'empereur Julien: lettres* (Paris, 1924), viii–xiv (for Julian). For letters describing martyrdoms see H. Musurillo, *Acts of the Christian Martyrs* (Oxford, 1972) n. 1 (Polycarp, though there are two versions of this letter in the manuscript tradition); 5 (Lyons).

8 For Marcus, see J. Farquharson, *The Meditations of the Emperor Marcus Aurelius* 1 (Oxford, 1964) 1, xiii–xiv.

9 For the textual history of Pliny's letters, see L.D. Reynolds in L.D. Reynolds (ed.) *Texts and Transmission: A Survey of the Latin Classics* (Oxford, 1983), 316–22.

10 Suet. *Caes.* 73: *Valerium Catullum, a quo sibi uersiculis de Mamurra perpetua stigmata imposita non dissimulauerat* (presumably referring to Cat. 29, the opening lines of which are cited as "*aspera vero et maledicta,*" in Quint. *Inst.* 9.4.141).

11 See now K.M. Coleman, "Fatal charades: Roman executions staged as mythological enactments," *JRS* 80 (1990), 44–73.

12 Autobiographies see e.g. Ovid *Trist.* 4.10; Stat. *Silv.* 5.3.215–38; *Silvae* 3.3 for Claudius Etruscus.

13 *Anth. Pal.* 9.287 = Apoll. 23 (Gow and Page) with G.W. Bowersock, "Augustus and the East: the problem of the succession," in F. Millar and E. Segal, *Caesar Augustus: Seven Aspects* (Oxford, 1983), 181.

14 *Anth. Pal.* 7.391 Bassus 5 (Gow and Page). The connection with the *Phaenomena* is made in Gow and Page's note *ad loc.*

15 *Anth Pal.* 9.283 (Germanicus) = Crinagoras 26 (Gow and Page); *Anth. Pal.* 9.291 = Crinagoras 27 (Gow and Page); *A.Pl.* 61 = Crinagoras 28 (Gow and Page).

16 E. Fantham, *Roman Literary Culture from Cicero to Apuleius* (Baltimore, 1996) for a nuanced treatment that pays attention to both issues.

17 Cic. *Att.* 2.1.3 (SB 21.3). The problem with the publication of the speeches is well discussed in L. Laurand, *Études sur le style des discours de Cicéron avec une esquisse de l'histoire du "cursus"* 2 (Paris, 1925), 1, 1–20; J. Humbert, *Les plaidoyers écrits et les plaidoiries réelles de Cicéron* (Paris, n.d.), 1–21. Cic. *Brut* 91; *Tusc.* 4.55

suggests that published speeches were very much as he delivered them, which is problematic in several cases, see nn. 19–20 below.

18 *Att.* 3.12.2 (SB 57.2); compare Front. *Ad Ver.* 2.9.1: *cupivi equidem abolere orationem, sed iam pervaserat in manus plurium quam ut abolere possem.*

19 For the relationship between the published version and the process of the trial see Humbert, *Les plaidoyers écrits et les plaidoiries réelles*, 204–15. Nepos is supposed to have remarked that the published version represented the substance of what was said, (Jer. *Ep.* 72). The length of the Verrines roused comment in the generation of Tacitus, see *Dial.* 20. Asconius (*In Corn.* 62C) says that Cicero condensed four days of speaking into two speeches; Pliny knew the same speech in one volume (*Ep.* 1.20.8). Caesar appears to have published his attack on Dolabella in more than one book, which may be a parallel (AG, *NA* 4.16.8).

20 Dio 40. 54.3–4; Asc. *In Mil.* 42 C.2–4. For the problem of the two versions of the speech see J.N. Settle, "The Trial of Milo and the other *Pro Milone*," *TAPA* 94 (1963), 268–80; A.W. Lintott, "Cicero and Milo," *JRS* 64 (1974), 74; Marshall, *A Historical Commentary on Asconius*, 190–1. There is no need to believe with Settle that the "other" *Pro Milone* was a forgery, though there was at least one case where a speech got away from Cicero when it was most inconvenient. The one major divergence between the two speeches appears to have been the argument that killing Clodius was good for the state, see Asc. *In Mil.* 41C 10–14 with Cic. *Pro Mil.* 72–83.

21 Quint. *Inst.* 10.7.30; Asc. *In tog. cand.* 87C 11–13.

22 For stenographic recording in the late republic (without a developed system of shorthand) see Cic. *Sull.* 42 (despite Plut. *Cato Min.* 23.3 this is not a reference to shorthand; it is clear from the context that Plutarch does not know what he is talking about). So too Cic. *Att.* 13.32.3 (SB 305.3), often cited as a reference to shorthand, is actually a reference to abbreviation (see Shackleton-Bailey *ad loc.*). Suet. *Caes.* 55. 3 and Asc. *In Mil.* 42C show that efforts were made to record what was said, even if they do not prove that shorthand writers were employed; the same is true of Sen. *Apoc.* 9.2. The first explicit reference occurs in Suet. *Tit.* 3.2: *notis quoque excipere velocissime solitum.* In Egypt, the earliest appearance of shorthand writing occurs in the unpublished *P. Brem.* 82, dated to *c.*120 BC. For a collection of the sources see. H. Boge, *Griechische Tachygraphie und Tironische Noten. Ein Handbuch der Antiken und mitelalterlichen Schnellschrift* (Tübingen, 1981). For papyrus record, see n. 3 above.

23 Cic. *In Cat.* 10: *haec ego omnia vixdum etiam coetu vestro dimisso comperi*; Cic. *Att.*1.14.5 (SB 14.5): *me tantum comperisse omnia criminabatur*; Cic. *Fam.* 5.5.2 (SB 5.2): *nam comperisse me non audeo dicere, ne forte id ipsum verbum ponam quod abs te aiunt falso in me solere conferri.*

24 Cic. *Att.* 13.20.2 (*SB* 328.2). But see *Att.* 12.6a.1 (*SB* 243.1): *mihi quiden gratum, et erit gratius si non modo in tuis libris sed etiam in aliorum per librarios tuos Aristophanem reposueris pro Eupoli.* The text in question is *Orat.* 29. This appears to have been at the stage when copies were being prepared but had not yet been given to the public; see B.A. van Groningen, "EKDOSIS," *Mnemosyne* 16 (1963), 8.

25 For the evolution of Constantine's image, see especially T. Grünewald,

Constantinus Maximus Augustus. Herrschaftspropaganda in der zeitgenössischen Überlieferung (Stuttgart, 1990).

26 Lib. *Ep.* 818 (Foerster) with Lib. *Ep.* 1430 (Foerster) J. Vanderspoel, *Themistius and the Imperial Court* (Ann Arbor, 1995), 128–34.

27 Lib. *Ep.* 770; 610; (Foerster) with Lib. *Or.* 13, and A.F. Norman, *Libanius: Autobiography and Selected Letters* 2 (Loeb), 453–4.

28 Jul. *Ep.* 96; 97 (Bidez) and Lib. *Ep.* 760; 758 with Lib. *Or.* 14. Libanius is using these speeches for other ends as well: he sought the restoration of a friend named Aristophanes, who had been convicted of illicit magical practices in 357. See Bidez, *L'empereur Julien: lettres*, 111–12.

29 At issue here is *BG* 6.13–26; see G. Walser, *Caesar und die Germanen: Studien zur politischen Tendenz römischer Feldzugsberichte*, Historia Einzelschriften 1 (Wiesbaden, 1956), 52–77.

30 Amm. Marc. 15.5.23 (the journey to Cologne); 18.8–19.8 (Amida).

31 For the description of Gaul, compare especially Amm. 15.11.1 and Caes. *BG* 1.1; note also Amm. 15.8.9 with *FGrH* 88 F 2. For the Persian expedition, see J.F. Matthews, *The Roman Empire of Ammianus* (London, 1989), 161–75. His view of the relationship between Ammianus and Eunapius has recently been challenged, but not convincingly, by C.W. Fornara, "Julian's Persian Expedition in Ammianus and Zosimus," *JHS* 111 (1991): 1–15.

32 Cic. *Att.* 13.20.2 (SB 328.2). For other problems see *Att.* 6.2.3 (SB 116.3) (correcting *Rep.* 2.8 from *Phliuntios* to *Phliasios*, without success since the Vatican Palimpsest has *Phliuntios*); *Att.* 12.6a. 1 (SB 243.1) changing Aristophanes for Eupolis at *Orat.* 29 (Aristophanes appears in the manuscripts); *Att.* 13.21a.1 (SB 351.1) concerns multiple versions of the *De finibus* in circulation prior to official "release." For Horace, see Hor. *AP* 389–90 with Brink *ad loc.*

33 Plin. *Ep.* 1.20; 7.20.

34 Suet. *Verg.* 32; Propert. *Carm.* 2.34b 59–80.

35 Diog. Laert. 66; see the important discussion of van Groningen, "EKDOSIS," 8–10.

36 van Groningen, "EKDOSIS," 1–2.

37 All that follows on Galen as a textual critic is owed to A.E. Hanson, "Galen: author and critic," *Aporemata* 2 (1997). I am deeply grateful to Professor Hanson for allowing me to make use of this work prior to publication. See also van Groningen, "EKDOSIS," 2–3 pointing out, as does Hanson, that Galen is somewhat disingenuous.

38 R.J. Starr, "The circulation of literary texts in the Roman world," *CQ* 37 (1987), 213–15.

39 Pliny. *Epp.* 4.7. Pliny affected to despise Regulus. Regulus also had a copy read out by a decurion, and Pliny expressly says that he sent copies to the provinces. Recent commentators have rightly pointed out that Regulus's behavior is not a good guide to the size of editions in antiquity (see J.E.G. Zetzel, *Latin Textual Criticism in Antiquity* (New York, 1980), 233).

40 Lib. *Or.* 1.111 with Lib. *Ep.* 345 (Foerster), dating the event to 358. See in general A.F. Norman, "The book trade in fourth-century Antioch," *JHS* 80 (1960), 122–6.

41 See the excellent discussion by E. Dekkers in the introduction to the text of the Apologeticum in vol. 1 of the Corpus Christianorum edition of Tertullian's works.

42 For Ovid, see *Am. Praef.* with McKeown *ad loc.*

43 See D.S. Potter, *Prophets and Emperors: Human and Divine Authority from Augustus to Theodosius* (Cambridge, MA, 1994), 195 with note 35 for bibliography.

44 S. West, *The Ptolemaic Papyri of Homer*, Papyrologica Coloniensia 3 (Cologne, 1965), 16–17.

45 AG *NA* 2.3. It was sold for 20 *aurei* in a bookshop in the Sigillaria to a friend of his. Other literary marvels seen by Aulus include Cicero's fifth Verrine, produced *Tironiana cura et disciplina* and cited at *NA* 1.7.1 on the text of Cic. *In Verr.* 5.167, quoting a variant not found in the manuscript, and on a point, the reading of *futurum* rather than *futuram*, a solecism that does not appear in the manuscript either. The manuscript in question is also cited at *NA* 13. 21.16 for the text of *In Verr.* 5.169 where he asserts that *fretu* appears instead of *freto*, the reading of extant manuscripts. He also saw an old copy of Claudius Quadrigarius in the library at Tibur (*NA* 9.14.3), a very old copy of the *Jugurtha* (*NA* 9.14.26) and, in the library at Patras in Achaea, an old copy of Livius Andronicus (*NA* 18.9.5). He records an ancient copy of the Latin version of N. Fabius Pictor's *Annales* for sale in a bookshop in the Sigillaria (*NA* 5.4). For the distinction between N. Fabius Pictor's work in Latin and Q. Fabius Pictor's work in Greek see B.W. Frier, *Libri Annales Pontificarum Maximorum: The Origins of the Annalistic Tradition* (Rome, 1979), 247–9 (including suggestions on Indian cuisine). For other autographs, these in the first century see Plin. *NH* 13.83. For deluxe editions of antiquity in the second century AD see also Luc. *Ind.* 2.

46 See the enormously convenient tabulation of literary papyri in O. Montevecchi, *La papirologia* (Milan, 1988), 360–3.

47 P. van Minnen, "House-to-house enquiries: an interdisciplinary approach to Roman Karanis," *ZPE* 100 (1994), 227–51, especially p. 244. I am indebted to Dr. Traianos Gagos for my entire knowledge of this subject. He is not to be blamed for any failures of comprehension on my part.

48 J. Dillery and T. Gagos, "P. Mich. Inv. 4922: Xenophon and an unknown Christian text with an appendix of all Xenophon papyri" *ZPE* 93 (1992), 171–90; see also E.G. Turner, *Greek Papyri* (Oxford, 1980), 7–8 on other papyri with long lives. For reports of antiquarian texts (some of them probably fakes) see n. 45 above.

49 Amm Marc. 28.4.18; for Ammianus's Latin reading list see Matthews, *The Roman Empire of Ammianus*, 482 n. 45.

50 The topos appears to be the logical extension of the Aristotelian notion that oratory developed when tyrants were expelled from Sicily (Cic. *Brut.* 46). Cicero applies it to the situation under Caesar (*Brut.* 333). See also Sen. *Cons. ad Marc.* 1.4; Tac. *Dial.* 36–7; *Ann.* 1.1.2; 4.32.1; [Long.] *Subl.* 44.

51 For Tacitus in the fourth century, see K.C. Schellhase, *Tacitus in Renaissance Political Thought* (Chicago, 1976), 3–4. For the *Historia Augusta* see pp. 145–7 below.

52 J. Marincola, *Authority and Tradition in Ancient Historiography* (Cambridge, 1997), 281–2.

53 W.V. Harris, *Ancient Literacy* (Cambridge, MA, 1989), 233–48.

54 R. Kaster, *Guardians of Language: The Grammarian and Society in Late Antiquity* (Berkeley, CA, 1988), 24–5.

55 Cic. *Att.* 12.32.2 (SB 271.2).

56 Cic. *Fam.* 9.16.7 (SB 190.7). His literary career seems to have begun a year later with an attack upon Cato that he asked Atticus to distribute, see Cic. *Att.* 12.40.1; 12.41.4; 12.44.1; 12.48.1; 12.45.2 (SB 281.1; 283.4; 285.1; 289.1; 290.2).

57 J.E.G. Zetzel, *Latin Textual Criticism in Antiquity* (New York, 1980) for a valuable general study.

58 Pfeiffer, *History of Classical Scholarship* 1 (Oxford, 1968), 110 suggests that this was a fiction of the Alexandrian period. The story is treated more indulgently in recent scholarship, and the argument that the tradition is attached to such an odd figure (Hipparchus) that it may not be a complete fantasy is compelling; see S. West in A. Heubeck, S. West and J.B. Hainsworth, *A Commentary on Homer's Odyssey* 1 (Oxford, 1987), 36–7. For an excellent survey of the evolution of the text of the Homeric poems, see now M. Haslam, "Homeric papyri and transmission of the text," in I. Morris and B. Powell, *A New Companion to Homer* (Leiden, 1997), 54–100, especially 63–4 and 69–71 on city texts and 82–4 on the "Athenian recension."

59 Pfeiffer, *History of Classical Scholarship*, 95 on the intellectual isolation of Antimachus of Colophon, the only named pre-Hellenistic editor of Homer. For the influence of Aristotle, both directly and indirectly, on Zenodotus and his successors, see K. Nikau, *Untersuchungen zur textkritischen Methode des Zenodotos von Ephesos* (Berlin, 1977), 134–9; N.J. Richardson, "Aristotle and Hellenistic scholarship," in F. Montanari (ed.) *La philologie grecque à l'époque hellénistique et romaine*, Entrentiens Foundation Hardt 60 (Geneva, 1994), 7–27.

60 Pfeiffer, *History of Classical Scholarship* 1, 105–19; for the role of Aristarchus, see Haslam, "Homeric papyri and transmission of the text," 84–7.

61 For more on autograph texts see p. 112 below.

62 For full discussion of this passage, see R. Kaster, *Suetonius: De Grammaticis et Rhetoribus* (Oxford, 1995) *ad loc.*

63 See n. 45 above for some examples of old books for sale. Starr, "Circulation of literary texts," 219–23 argues, convincingly, that booksellers supplemented rather than competed with private distribution. People who fell outside ordinary circles of distribution could use them, and they were a source for books by individuals who lacked ready access to the highest levels of literary society.

64 Quint. *Inst. Orat.* 9.4.39; 74.

65 *De libr. prop.* prooemium with Hanson, "Galen: author and critic." The *philologos* here preforms the task that Lucian describes in *Ind.* 2.

66 A.H.M. Jones, "Notes on the genuineness of the Constantinian documents in Eusebius's Life of Constantine," *JEH* 5 (1954), 196–200, repr. in *The Roman Economy: Studies in Ancient Economic and Administrative History* ed. P.A. Brunt (Oxford, 1974), 257–62.

67 *ILS* 705 with J. Gascou, "Le rescript d'Hispellum," *MEFR* 79 (1967), 617–23; *ILS* 6090: *quod omnes ibidem sectatores sanctissimae religionis habitare*

dicantur, with A. Chastagnol, "L'inscription constantinienne d' Orcistus," *MEFR* 93 (1981), 409–10.

68 Eus. *V. Const.* 2.69 with A. Adam, *Texte zu manichäismus*(Berlin, 1969) n. 56.

69 See B. Sirks, "The sources of the code," in J. Harries and I. Wood, *The Theodosian Code* (Ithaca, NY, 1993), 45–67.

70 Tac. *Ann.* 2.83. For the *Tabula Siarensis* and the *Tabula Hebana*, see now M.H. Crawford (ed.) *Roman Statutes*, 2 vols (London, 1996), n. 37–38.

71 W. Eck, A. Caballos and F. Fernández, *Das senatus consultum de Cn. Pisone patre* (Munich, 1996).

72 ibid., 293–6, see also p. 93 below.

73 A. Adam, *Texte zu manichäismus*, n. 56 with Potter, *Prophets and Emperors*, 209–10.

74 J. Evans-Grubb, "Abduction-marriage in antiquity: a law of Constantine (CTh IX.24.1) and its social context," *JRS* 79 (1989), 59–83.

75 P. Veyne, "The Roman Empire," in P. Veyne (ed.) *A History of Private Life from Pagan Rome to Byzantium*, tr. A. Goldhammer (Cambridge, 1987), 34–5.

76 See, for instance S. Treggiari, *Roman Marriage: Iusti Coniuges* From the Time of Cicero to the Time of Ulpian (Oxford, 1991), 243–9.

77 For these issues see P.A. Brunt, "Philosophy and religion in the Late Republic," in M. Griffin and J. Barnes, *Philosophia Togata: Essays on Philosophy and Roman Society* (Oxford, 1989), 174–98.

78 For the abuse of the religious system in Republican politics, see L.R. Taylor *Party Politics in the Age of Caesar* (Berkeley, CA, and Los Angeles, 1971), 76–97; but see now M. Beard "Religion," in J.A. Crook, A. Lintott and E. Rawson *The Cambridge Ancient History*, 2nd edn (Cambridge, 1994), 739–42; T.P. Wiseman "Lucretius, Catiline and the survival of prophecy," *Ostraka* 1.2 (1992), 7–18.

79 D.S. Potter, *Prophecy and History in the Crisis of the Roman Empire: A Historical Commentary on the Thirteenth Sibylline Oracle* (Oxford, 1990), 111; D.S. Potter *Prophets and Emperors*, 100.

80 J. Richardson, "The ownership of Roman land: Tiberius Gracchus and the Italians," *JRS* 70 (1980), 8–9.

81 Tac. *Ann.* 4.35.5; Sen. *Cons. ad Marc.* 2.5

82 Suet. *Cal.* 16.1, though Seneca says that it was his daughter Marcia who kept copies and restored them *in publica monumenta* (Sen. *Cons. ad Marc.* 1.3); for Cordus and Sejanus, see especially Sen. *Cons. ad Marc.* 1.2; Dio 57.24 (also crediting Marcia for the reappearance of the books). For another comment reflecting the symbolic nature of book burning at Rome, see Sen. Maior *Contr.* Praef. 8.

83 See G. Iggers, *Historiography in the Twentieth Century: From Scientific Objectivity to the Postmodern Challenge* (Middletown, CN, 1997), 78–94 for an excellent short survey of the European tradition.

84 R. Cobb, *The Police and the People: French Popular Protest 1789–1820* (Oxford, 1970); G. Lefebvre, *The Great Fear of 1789: Rural Panic in Revolutionary France*, tr. J. White (Princeton, 1973).

85 E.P. Thompson, "An open letter to Leszek Kolakowski," *The Poverty of Theory and Other Essays* (London, 1978) especially 322–35 on different traditions of Marxism.

86 E. Hobsbawm, "What do historians owe to Karl Marx," *Marx and Contemporary Scientific Thought/Marx et la pensée scientifique contemporaine* (The Hague and Paris, 1969), 197–211, repr. in E. Hobsbawm, *On History* (New York, 1997), 141–56 (the list given here is derived from pp. 145–6). For a defense of Marxism against postmodernism, see also Ely, G. and Nield, K., "Starting over: the present, the postmodern and the moment of social history" *Social History* 20 (1995), repr. in Jenkins, *The Postmodern History Reader*, 366–79.

87 P. Novick, *That Noble Dream: The "Objectivity Question" and the American Historical Profession* (Cambridge, 1988), 398–9; 408.

88 Novick, *That Noble Dream*, 440–3; 640–64.

89 E. Fox-Genovese and E. Genovese, "The political crisis of social history: a Marxian perspective," *Journal of Social History* 10 (1976), 205–20 (high marks for polemic); G. Ely and K. Nield, "Why does social history ignore politics" *Social History* 5 (1980), 249–71 (social history, especially labor history from a British perspective compared with German). E.P. Thompson, "History and anthropology," in E.P. Thompson (ed.) *Making History: Writings on History and Culture* (New York, 1994), 200–25, stresses that historians and anthropologists do not necessarily have the same interests.

90 For a lucid and valuable account see P. Burke, *The French Historical Revolution: The* Annales *School 1929–89* (Stanford, CA, 1990), 16–31; J. Revel, "Introduction," tr. A. Goldhammer, in J. Revel and L. Hunt (eds) *Histories: French Constructions of the Past* (New York, 1995), 1–63. Revel is particularly valuable in situating the work of Bloch and Febvre in the context of developments in French historiography during the late nineteenth century (pp. 5–9). Considerably less lucid, but with more detail on the history of French historiographic practice in the context of the *Annales* school, is T. Stoianovich, *French Historical Method: the Annales Paradigm* (Ithaca, NY, 1976).

91 Burke, *The French Historical Revolution*, 32–53.

92 Burke, *The French Historical Revolution*, 51–53.

93 Iggers, *Historiography in the Twentieth Century*, 51; Revel, "Introduction," 17–40, stressing the importance of Labrousse as a teacher.

94 P. Burke, *History and Social Theory* (Ithaca, NY, 1993), 1–21; J. Appleby, L. Hunt and M. Jacob, *Telling the Truth about History* (New York, 1994), 52–90; E. Hobsbawm, "British history and the annales: a note," *Review* 1 (1978), 157–62= E. Hobsbawn, *On History* (New York, 1997), 178–85; Revel, "Introduction," 28–50.

95 Novick, *That Noble dream*, 577–92; on the rise of subdisciplines, Iggers, *Historiography in the Twentieth Century*, 118–33 in the context of postmodernism. A recent example of vitriol is offered by K. Windschuttle, *The Killing of History: How Literary Critics and Social Theorists are Murdering our Past* (New York, 1997), 253–56 (on Sahlins) and passim for others.

96 L. Stone, "History and the social sciences," in C. Delzell (ed.) *The Future of History* (Nashville, 1976), repr. in L. Stone, *The Past and the Present Revisited* (London, 1987), 16–19.

97 See, for instance, S.R.F. Price, *Rituals and Power: The Roman Imperial Cult in Asia Minor* (Cambridge, 1984); J. Rives, *Religion and Authority in Roman Carthage from Augustus to Constantine* (Oxford, 1995).

98   R.S. Bagnall and B.W. Frier, *The Demography of Roman Egypt* (Cambridge, 1994).

99   S.P. Oakley, *A Commentary on Livy Books VI–X* 1 (Oxford, 1997), 22–72.

100 G.E.M. de Ste. Croix, *The Class Struggle in the Ancient Greek World* (London, 1983).

101 L. Robert, *A travers l'Asie Mineure: poètes et prosateurs, monnaies grecques, voyageurs et géographie* (Paris, 1980) 393–422, L. Robert, "Catalogue agonistique des Romaia de Xanthos," *Rev. Arch.* (1978), 277–90 = *Opera Minora Selecta* 7 (Amsterdam, 1990), 681–94. This selection is manifestly *exempli gratia*.

102 W.R. Johnson, *Darkness Visible: A Study of Vergil's Aeneid* (Berkeley, 1976), 8–16.

103 For an excellent survey of these issues see D.C. Earl, *The Political Thought of Sallust* (Cambridge, 1961), 41–59.

104 H. Butterfield, *The Whig Interpretation of History* (Cambridge, 1931); see also O. Handlin, *Truth in History* (Cambridge, MA, 1979), 85–110 for the prevalence of other "progressive" schools of thought.

105 Dio 51.1; for Dio's view of Augustus, see now A.M. Gowing, *The Triumviral Narratives of Appian and Cassius Dio* (Ann Arbor, MI, 1992), 90–2.

106 Potter, *Prophets and Emperors*, 101–4.

107 Tac. *Ann.* 1.1; 3.24 with R. Syme, *Tacitus*, 2 vols (Oxford, 1958), 369–70.

108 P. Zanker, *The Power of Images in the Age of Augustus* tr. A. Shapiro (Ann Arbor, MI, 1988) especially 79–100.

109 R. Syme, *History in Ovid* (Oxford, 1979), 72–93.

110 The content of *Tristia* 2 is underplayed in the otherwise superior discussion of the problem with interpreting the career of Ovid offered in F. Millar, "Ovid and the domus Augusta: Rome seen from Tomoi," *JRS* 83 (1993), 1–17.

111 Millar, "Ovid and the domus Augusta," 10.

112 For a very different view, see most recently M. Leigh, *Lucan: Spectacle and Engagement* (Oxford, 1997), 5. See also, along these lines, F. Ahl, *Lucan: an Introduction* (Ithaca, NY, 1976). Both books contain numerous interesting readings of the text, even though, as is clear, full agreement with all their propositions may not be forthcoming.

113 P. Bourdieu, *Language and Symbolic Power*, tr. G. Raymond and M. Adamson (Cambridge, MA, 1991), 137–59.

114 Eck, Caballos and Fernández, *Das senatus consultum de Cn. Pisone patre*, 167–8.

115 Fantham, *Roman Literary Culture*, 102–25, though Fantham suggests rather more strongly than is suggested here that more attention needs to be given to changes in Augustus's own conduct.

116 For Cato, see especially Cic. *Pro Mur.* 74; Sall. *Cat.* 53–4; Plut. *Cato min.* 9; 17; 24–5; for Caesar, see especially Suet. *Caes.* 45.3; 50, and in general, the sensitive treatment in C. Meier, *Caesar* trans. D. McLintock (New York, 1996), 56–72.

117 G.B. Conte, *Genres and Readers* (Baltimore, 1994) 35–65 in general.

118 M.W. Gleason, *Making Men: Sophists and Self-Presentation in Ancient Rome* (Princeton, NJ, 1995), 159–60.

119 Gleason, *Making Men*, 3–20.

120 For the language and techniques of Latin invective, see R.G.M. Nisbet, *Cicero: In Pisonem* (Oxford, 1961), 192–7.

121 Cic. *Verr.* 2.5.31; 86; 137 (seaside debauchery in purple cloak), *Phil.* 2.63 (public vomiting); 77–8 (visit to his wife); 104–5 (general drunkenness); Gleason, *Making Men*, 86–7 with n. 30.

122 See, in general, J. Lendon, *Empire of Honour: the Art of Government in the Roman World* (Oxford, 1997), 50–1.

123 Cic. *Fam.* 5.2; Suet. *Caes.* 73 with n. 10 above and 49; 80.2 (Nicomedes). He also disliked comments on his hair loss (Suet. *Caes.* 45.2).

124 See especially F. Cairns, *Generic Composition in Greek and Latin Poetry* (Edinburgh, 1972), 9–15.

125 K.S. Myers, "The poet and the procuress: the lena in Latin love elegy," *JRS* 86 (1996), 1–21.

126 See the discussion in B.M. Levick, "The *senatus consultum* from Larinum," *JRS* 73 (1983), 88–115.

127 See especially A. Kuttner, *Dynasty and Empire in the Age of Augustus: The Case of the Boscoreale Cups* (Berkeley, CA, 1995) 56–68; 71–83; R. Gurval, *Actium and Augustus: The Politics and Emotions of Civil War* (Ann Arbor, MI, 1995), 19–85.

128 For an extensive recent discussion see G. Nugent, "*Tristia* 2: Ovid and Augustus," in K. Raaflaub and M. Toher (eds) *Between Republic and Empire* (Berkeley, CA, 1990), 239–57.

129 Tac. *Hist.* 4.8. The line is given to Eprius Marcellus, anything but a sympathetic character in Tacitus's works.

130 The most eloquent statement of this theme appears in E.L. Bowie, "Greeks and their past in the Second Sophistic," *Past and Present* 46 (1970), 1–41 reprinted in M.I. Finley, (ed.) *Studies in Ancient Society* (London, 1974), 166–209. The contrary position adopted here is founded upon G.W. Bowersock, *Greek Sophists in the Roman Empire* (Oxford, 1969); A.D. Momigliano, *Alien Wisdom* (Cambridge, MA, 1975) and the work of Louis Robert, esp. his "Une épigramme d'Automédon et Athènes au début de l'empire," *REG* (1981), 348–61. Further discussion of the problem of "hellenized" non-Greek easterners may be found in Potter, *Prophets and Emperors*, 183–5.

131 S. Swain, *Hellenism and Empire: Language, Classicism and Power in the Greek World AD 50–250* (Oxford, 1996), 18–64, for an extensive exposition of the opposite view to the one taken here. For a rather different approach, denying the relevance of treating the period as a whole, and suggesting that the "second sophistic" is essentially an invention of Philostratus see P.A. Brunt, "The Bubble of the Second Sophistic," *BICS* 39 (1994), 25–52.

132 See Burke, *History and Social Theory*, 84–8, for a lucid summary of work in this area.

133 P. Brown, *Power and Persuasion in Late Antiquity: Towards a Christian Empire* (Madison, WI, 1992), 35–70; R. Kaster, *The Guardians of Language*, 11–31; Gleason, *Making Men*, 162–6.

134 C.P. Jones, *Culture and Society in Lucian* (Cambridge, MA, 1986) 149–59.

135 C. Habicht, *Pausanias's Guide to Ancient Greece* (Berkeley, CA, 1985) 117–40.

136 R.J. Hoffman, *Celsus On the True Doctrine: A Discourse against the Christians* (New York, 1987), 29–44 for Celsus. For a suggestive discussion on the context see now G.W. Bowersock, *Fiction as History* (Berkeley, CA, 1994), 1–27.

137   F.W. Walbank, *Polybius* (Berkeley, CA, 1972), especially 157–183, pointing
out that while Rome is the focus of the history, the interpretation becomes
increasingly personal. See also J. Davidson, "The gaze in Polybius's
history," *JRS* 81 (1991), 10–24 for the way that Polybius interprets history
through the perceptions of those about whom he writes.

138   S. Mitchell, *Anatolia: Land Men and Gods in Asia Minor* 2 (Oxford, 1993), 147.

139   See especially K. Hopkins, "Rules of evidence," *JRS* 68 (1978), 181, 185,
although not contemptuous and to the point.

140   As asserted by F. Millar, *The Emperor in the Roman World* (London, 1977), 3.

141   H.L. Strack and G. Stremberger, *Introduction to the Talmud and Midrash*, tr. M.
Bockmuehl (Minneapolis, MN, 1992) is an invaluable introduction to this
literature.

142   Verg. *Aen.* 5. 144–7; Ovid *Ars* 1.136–62.

143   S. Lieberman, "Roman legal institutions in early rabbinics and in the acta
martyrum," *JQR* 35 (1944–5) 17–19. The redaction of the *Bereshit Rabbah*,
also known as the *Genesis Rabbah*, is datable to the mid-fourth through early
fifth century, although it contains earlier material; see Strack and
Stremberger, *Introduction to the Talmud and the Midrash*, 304. Parallels in
earlier texts suggest that the behavior illustrated in this passage is datable to
the high empire.

144   See H. Strasburger, "Umblick im Trümmerfeld der griechischen
Geschichtsschreibung," *Historiographia Antiqua* 14–15, repr. in *Studien zur
Alten Geschichte* 3 (New York, 1990), 180–1.

145   S.C. Humphries, "Fragments, fetishes and philosophies: towards a history
of Greek historiography after Thucydides," in G. Most (ed.) *Collecting
Fragments – Fragmente sammeln* (Göttingen, 1997), 211. Her stress on fragment as fetish is evocative of E.H. Carr, *What is History?* (New York, 1961),
15.

146   For the Parian Marble see *FGrH* 239; for the *Chronicon Romanum* see *IG*
14.1297; *FGrH* 252.

147   *FGrH* 257; 257a.

148   The dependence of Diodorus upon Ephorus has been challenged by
K. Sacks, *Diodorus Siculus and the First Century* (Princeton, NJ, 1990), but is
reasserted by P.J. Stylianou in his review of Sacks in *BMCR* 2.6 (1991), the
crucial issue being confusions in Diodorus that stem from his use of
Ephoran prefaces, see A. Andrewes, "Diodorus and Ephorus: one source of
misunderstanding," in J.W. Eadie and J. Ober (eds) *The Craft of the Ancient
Historian: Essays in Honor of Chester G. Starr* (Lanham, MD, 1985), 189. The
case for Hieronymus is argued in J. Hornblower, *Hieronymus of Cardia*
(Oxford, 1991).

149   Tac. *Ann.* 11.23–24; *ILS* 212; M.T. Griffin, "The Lyons tablet and Tacitean
hindsight," *CQ* 32 (1982), 404–18.

150   G. Rotondi, *Leges publicae populi Romani* (Milan, 1912); M.H. Crawford,
Roman Statutes.

151   See especially G.W. Bowersock, "Jacoby's fragments and two Greek historians of Pre-Islamic Arabia," in G. Most (ed.) *Collecting Fragments – Fragmente
sammeln* (Göttingen, 1997), 173–85.

152   R. Syme, "Missing senators," *Historia* 4 (1955), 53, repr. in *Roman Papers* 1
(1979), 272.

153 Peter, *HRF* v–vi. For discussion of the problems with his arrangement, see B.W. Frier, *Libri annales Pontificum Maximorum: The Origins of the Annalistic Tradition* (Rome, 1979) 15–17.

154 R.C. Blockley, *The Fragmentary Classicizing Historians of the Later Roman Empire*, 2 vols (Liverpool, 1981, 1983) for Eunapius, Olympiodorus, Priscus and Malchus; R.C. Blockley, *The History of Menander the Guardsman* (Liverpool, 1985).

155 The first volume, edited by C.W Fornara, appeared in 1994 with commentary on numbers 608a–608.

156 Jacoby's thinking emerges most clearly in an article that was published in 1909, "Über die Entwicklung der griechischen Historiographie und der Plan einer neuen Sammlung der griechischen Historikerfragmente," *Klio* 9 (1909), 1–44. For discussion of the continuing importance of Jacoby's discussion on the subject see the lucid analysis in C.W. Fornara, *The Nature of History in Ancient Greece and Rome* (Berkeley, CA, 1983), 1–46 and R.L. Fowler, "Herodotus and his contemporaries," *JHS* 116 (1996), 62–9. For an updated version of the stemmatic approach, see S. Hornblower, "Introduction," in S. Hornblower (ed.) *Greek Historiography* (Oxford, 1994), 1–54.

157 Jacoby, "Über die Entwicklung der griechischen Historiographie," 20.

158 ibid., 4.

159 ibid.

160 ibid., 20–4.

161 ibid., 6.

162 ibid., 30–2

163 The issue of tragic history, as understood by Jacoby and others (deriving from Aristotelian theory) has been shown to be problematic see F.W. Walbank, "History and Tragedy," *Historia* 9 (1960), 216–34, F.W. Walbank, (ed.) *Selected Papers. Studies in Greek and Roman History and Historigraphy* (Cambridge, 1985), 224–41, showing that it is a feature of negative critical discourse; see also Fornara, *The Nature of History in Ancient Greece and Rome*, 25–34.

164 Dion Hal. *De Thuc.* 5; for the connection with Theophrastus see D.L. Toye, "Dionysius on the first Greek historians," *AJP* 116 (1995), 280–1.

165 See especially F. Jacoby, *Atthis: The Chronicles of Ancient Athens* (Oxford, 1949), 178 n. 13; Fornara, *The Nature of History in Ancient Greece and Rome*, 16–23, supports Jacoby's view of a late rather than mid-fifth century development but points, quite reasonably, to a connection with the spirit of scientific enquiry as a key feature rather than nostalgia for the past.

166 See now Fowler, "Herodotus and his contemporaries," 62–9.

167 Jacoby, "Über die Entwicklung der griechischen Historiographie," 24–5 n. 1.

168 The particular problem here is that Xanthus was said by Ephorus to have given Herodotus his *aphormê*, or starting point *FGrH* 70 F 180; 765 F 5. The statement is somewhat problematic, see R. Drews, *Greek Accounts of Eastern History* (Princeton, NJ, 1973), 102.

169 Jacoby, "Über die Entwicklung der griechischen Historiographie," 9 n. 3.

170 ibid., 30–40.

171 ibid., 43.

172 G. Schepens, "Jacoby's *FGrHist*: problems, methods, prospects," in G. Most (ed.) *Collecting Fragments – Fragmente sammeln* (Göttingen, 1997), 148–54.

173 A.D. Momigliano, *The Development of Greek Biography*, revised edn (Cambridge, 1993), 23–42; 108–11.

174 J. Geiger, *Cornelius Nepos and Ancient Political Biography* (Stuttgart, 1985), 9–29.

175 Cic. *De orat.* 2.53.

176 P.S. Derow, "Historical explanation: Polybius and his predecessors," in S. Hornblower, *Greek Historiography* (Oxford, 1994), 72–81; Fowler, "Herodotus and his contemporaries," 69–76.

177 See especially Stoianovich, *French Historical Method*, 165–6, on Michelet as well as Braudel's statement in his introduction to this book that the "preliminary period corresponds to the agony of positivism in France at the close of the nineteenth century" (pp. 10–11).

178 See most recently, M. Elefante, *Velleius Paterculus: ad M. Vinicium consulem libri duo* (Hildesheim, 1997), 2–13.

179 R.J. Tarrant, "Tacitus" in L. Reynolds (ed.) *Texts and Transmissions* (Oxford, 1983), 406–9.

180 See, for instance *Ann.* 1.13 (the demise of those judged to be *capax imperii*) *Ann.* 4.31 (the carer of Suillius under Claudius); *Ann.* 4.71 (the fate of those who had assisted Sejanus in his attack on Agrippina); *Ann.* 11.11 (the secular games under Domitian); *Ann.* 15.72.2 (Nymphidius Sabinus); *Ann.* 15.73 (the revolt of Vindex); *Ann.* 1.35 (the murder of Caligula, foreshadowing the event rather than the treatment).

181 Jer. *Comm. in Zach.* 3.14: *Cornelius Tacitus, qui post Augustum usque ad mortem Domitiani vitas Caesarum triginta voluminibus exaravit.*

182 See now the excellent edition of M.-P. Arnaud-Lindet, *Orose: Histoires (Contre les Païens)* (Paris, 1990–4).

183 For the transmission of the *Periochae* see M.D. Reeve, "The Transmission of Florus and the Periochae again," *CQ* 41 (1991), 453–83.

184 For a basic account see K. Krumbacher, *Geschichte der byzantinischer Literatur von Justinian bis zum Ende des oströmischen Reiches²* (Munich, 1896), 258–60.

185 U.P. Boissevain, *Cassii Dionis Cocceiani: Historiarum Romanarum quae Supersunt* 1 (Berlin, 1897), xxvi.

186 W. Treagold, *The nature of the Bibliotheca of Photius*, Dumbarton Oaks Studies 18 (Locust Valley, 1980), 4; 27.

187 ibid., 81–2.

188 For basic information see Krumbacher, *Geschichte*, 563–8.

189 Krumbacher, *Geschichte*, 563 describes it as "in the modern sense" a universal dictionary.

190 P.A. Brunt, "On Historical Fragments and Epitomes," *CQ* n.s. 30 (1980), 494.

191 For a useful and intelligible summary see F. Millar, *A Study of Cassius Dio* (Oxford, 1964), 1–4.

192 For Xiphilinus see Krumbacher, *Geschichte*, 370.

193 Boissevain, *Cassii Dionis Cocceiani: Historiarum Romanarum quae Supersunt* 1, lv n. 2.

194 Gowing, *The Triumviral Narratives of Appian and Cassius Dio*, 90.

195 M. Reinhold and P.M. Swan, "Cassius Dio's Assessment of Augustus," in K. Raaflaub and M. Toher (eds) *Between Republic and Empire: Interpretations of Augustus and his Principate* (Berkeley, CA, 1990), 156.
196 Boissevain, *Cassii Dionis Cocceiani: Historiarum Romanarum quae Supersunt* 3 (Berlin, 1900), xi.
197 Boissevain's text gives this as number 48.
198 Boissevain's text gives this as number 49.
199 Boissevain prints a composite version of the story, combining elements from both accounts.
200 Boissevain's text gives this as number 50.
201 The text in the *Excerpta* is very short and not printed separately.

3 Scholarship

1 Pol. 4.2.3–4, the notion also appears to have been present in Ephorus, whose views on the subject Polybius quotes with approval at 12.7.7 (*FGrH* 70 Fr. 110).
2 Pol. 3.33.17–18 with F.W. Walbank, *A Historical Commentary on Polybius* 1 (Oxford, 1957) *ad loc.*
3 Pol. 3.26 with R.E.A. Palmer, *Rome and Carthage at Peace*, Historia Einzelschriften 113 (Stuttgart 1997), 15–21.
4 See also Pol. 12.25e.1; 5 and, in general, F.W. Walbank, *Polybius* (Berkeley, CA, 1972), 71–4.
5 *HA V. Aurel.* 1.5–7; *HA V. Tacitus* 8.1 for another remarkable document allegedly in the library (with shelf reference, no less). See also Diod. 1. 4.2 on the abundance of materials for writing history at Rome; for the evolution of libraries, public and private in the city see A.J. Marshall, "Library resources and creative writing at Rome," *Phoenix* 30 (1976), 252–64. There were no public libraries until the reign of Augustus, so if Diodorus is suggesting that he had access to libraries, he is implicitly suggesting that he had good connections with important people.
6 See, for instance, Tac. *Ann.* 1.81.1; 2.63. 3; 3.3; 12.24.2; 15. 74. Not all references to *senatus consulta* and imperial *orationes* need come directly from the *acta* into the text of Tacitus, but the cases listed here should, however be sufficient to illustrate the point that Tacitus himself claims to have used them directly. See, in general, R. Syme, *Tacitus* (Oxford, 1958) 1, 280–6. Direct use of the *acta* has been denied, but, with the discovery of the *SCPP*, the completely sceptical position would now appear to be untenable; see A.J. Woodman and R.H. Martin, *The Annals of Tacitus Book 3* (Cambridge, 1996), 114–16, though raising the possibility that Tacitus knew it from a public monument rather than inspection in the *aerarium*. The passages quoted above suggest that consultation of documents from the *aerarium* was part of Tacitus's research. In this, Tacitus's conduct may be compared with Pliny's search for the decrees in honor of Claudius's freedman, Pallas, after he had seen the public monument (*Ep.* 7.29; 8.6; esp. 8.6.1–2: *adnotasse me nuper monumentum Pallantis sub hac inscriptione....Postea mihi uisum est pretium operae ipsum senatus consultum quaerere. Inueni tam copiosum et effusum, ut ille superbissimus titulus modicus atque etiam demissus uideretur*). There is nothing in the context to suggest that Pliny's conduct was to be regarded as

unusual. If a senator could search for a decree of the Senate simply to satisfy curiosity, it is would be perverse to suggest that a senator who was writing history would not do likewise.

7 Suet. *Aug.* 57: *omitto senatus consulta, quia possunt uideri uel necessitate expressa uel uerecundia. equites R. natalem eius sponte atque consensu biduo semper celebrarunt.*

8 See for example Plin. *Ep.* 10. 31; 10.49–50 (missing record); 10.56; 10. 58; 10. 65–6; and C. Williamson, "Monuments of bronze: Roman legal documents on bronze tablets," *CA* (1987) 160–81, on the nature of archives.

9 D.S. Potter, *Prophets and Emperors: Human and Divine Authority from Augustus to Theodosius* (Cambridge, MA, 1994), 118–20.

10 H. Musurillo, *Acts of the Pagan Martyrs* (Oxford, 1972) remains the basic treatment. For some difficulties with Musurillo's understanding of the *acta*, which should not, in my view, be treated as single corpus, see D.S. Potter, "Performance, power and justice in the high empire," in W.J. Slater (ed.) *Roman Theater and Society* (Ann Arbor, MI, 1996), 146.

11 See now P. Maraval, *La passion inédite de S. Athénogène de Pédachthoé en Cappadoce* (Brussels, 1990), 7–8.

12 See, for instances *Ann.* 1.10; 1.11; 1.13; 1.52; 1. 77; 1. 81; 2.36; 2.63; 2.87; 3.12; 3. 31; 3. 57; 4.4; 4.8; 4.17; 4.34; 4.37; 5.6; 6.9; 11.23–5; 12.6; 12.11; 12.25; 12.52; 13.3; 13.11; 13.43; 14.11; 15.35; 15.73; 16,7; 16. 27 (orations); *Ann.* 2.66; 2.79; 2.88; 3.35; 3.47; 3.52; 3.56; 3.59; 4.70; 5.2; 6.4–6; 6.12; 6.24; 6.27; 6.36; 6.47; 11.20; 12.19; 14.10; 14.22; 14.59; 15. 8; 15.16; 15.30 (letters). This list is illustrative rather than exhaustive.

13 See J. Ginsburg, "*In maiores certamina*: past and present in the *Annals*," in T.J. Luce and A.J. Woodman, *Tacitus and the Tacitean Tradition* (Princeton, NJ, 1993), 86–103 for a valuable discussion of debates in the senate, for which documentary record would have been available. Tacitus uses the material to make points about senatorial competence that were clearly unintended by the original speakers. That was the historian's job.

14 D.S. Potter, "Emperors, their borders and their neighbors: the scope of imperial *mandata*," in D.L. Kennedy, *The Roman Army in the East*, Journal of Roman Archaeology Supplementary Series 18 (Ann Arbor, MI, 1996), 55.

15 Dio 74.7–8; 75.6–7.

16 Dio 79.27.3. Contrast Herod. 4.15 with Whittaker's note *ad loc.*

17 Dio 76.3.1, 4, with E. Hohl, "Kaiser Pertinax und die Thronbesteigung seines Nachfolgers im Lichte der Herodiankritik," *SDAW* (1956), 2,58; Millar, *A Study of Cassius Dio* (Oxford, 1964), 145–6.

18 T.D. Barnes, "Ultimus Antoninorum," *BHAC 1968/9* (Bonn, 1970), 60. It is also interesting that Dio seems to have known very little indeed about the God Elagabal, not even that he took the form of a conical black stone or that the emperor had tried to arrange a marriage between him and Athena; Herod. 5.6.3; *HA V. Elag.* 6.8–9; G.W. Bowersock, "Herodian and Elagabalus," *YCS* 24 (1975), 234–5; Barnes, "Ultimus Antoninorum," 68.

19 D. Braund, "River frontiers in the environmental psychology of the Roman Empire," in D.L. Kennedy, *The Roman Army in the East*, 43–7.

20 See Her. 7.2.1–9 with Whittaker's notes *ad loc.* The picture of Maximinus's conduct here may also be compared with Josephus's description of Titus at Tarachaeae; see Jos. *BJ* 3.485–91.

21 The view taken here is the traditional one. For a radically different approach, see T.D. Barnes, "The editions of Eusebius's *Ecclesiastical History*," *GRBS* 21 (1980), 191–201, arguing for three editions, the first comprising books 1–7 dating to the late third century. For the problems here, see R.J. Lane Fox, *Pagans and Christians* (London, 1987), 607–8. For an excellent discussion of the contents of the work (independent of the dating issue), see T.D. Barnes, *Constantine and Eusebius* (Cambridge, MA, 1981), 126–47.

22 For distinctions between what Eusebius wrote, the tradition that he established, and pagan historiography, see A.D. Momigliano, "Pagan and Christian historiography in the fourth century A.D.," in A.D. Momigliano (ed.) *The Conflict Between Paganism and Christianity in the Fourth Century A.D.* (Oxford, 1963), 73–99; R. Markus, "Church history and early Church historians," *Studies in Church History* 11 (1975), 1–17; T. Urbainczyk, *Socrates of Constantinople: Historian of Church and State* (Ann Arbor, MI, 1997), 82–105. Greater connection to the classical tradition is suggested by R. Mortley, "The Hellenistic foundations of ecclesiastical historiography," in G. Clarke (ed.) *Reading the Past in Late Antiquity* (Rushcutters Bay, 1990), 225–50; R. Mortley, *The Idea of Universal History from Hellenistic Philosophy to Early Christian Historiography* (Lewiston, MA, 1996), 31–61.

23 T. Rajak, *Josephus* (London, 1983), 225.

24 See for example *Contra Ap.* 1.3–4; 15; 24–5; 44–6; 53–6; 58; 223; 229; 251; 293–5; 312–20.

25 *Contra. Ap.* 1.19–23; contrast the Phoenicians at *Contra Ap.* 1.106–9; 112. For a Phoenician version of their own story, see Philo of Byblos's *Phoenician History* (*FGrH* 790). For the assertion of a documentary basis of the "Phoenician History" of "Sanchuniathon of Beirut," an alleged contemporary of Semiramis and the Trojan War (if not earlier), see *FGrH* 790 F.1 20–1 (the alleged book of Hierombalos) and the statement that he worked from city records and records stored in temples. For a good treatment of the fragments, see A.I. Baumgarten, *The Phoenician History of Philo of Byblos* (Leiden, 1981). Baumgarten (p. 51) tends to date Sanchuniathon to the Hellenistic period, not an unreasonable view in light of the fact that he writes under his own name and is familiar with the canons of Hellenistic historical research.

26 For the date and circumstances, see now the introduction to the excellent edition of M. Labrousse, Optat de Milève, *Traité contre les donatistes* (Paris, 1995), 12–18; and Urbainczyk, *Socrates of Constantinople*, 57, for the authority that accrued to documents in Christian circles by being copied.

27 See the lucid discussion in A. Grafton, *The Footnote* (Cambridge, MA, 1997), 57–61.

28 E. Schwartz, "Cassius Dio," *RE* 3 1716–17; P. Fabia, *Les Sources de Tacite dans les Histoires et les Annales* (Paris, 1893), a volume that contains many useful observations in individual passages even if its conclusions are no longer accepted, thanks to R. Syme, *Tacitus* (Oxford, 1958), 272–3; 688–92.

29 G.B. Townend, "The sources of Greek in Suetonius," *Hermes* 88 (1960), 98–120; G.B. Townend, "Traces in Dio Cassius of Cluvius, Aufidius and

Pliny," *Hermes* 89 (1961), 227–48 retain value as studies of the non-Tacitean tradition.

30 J.F. Matthews, *The Roman Empire of Ammianus* (London, 1989), 8–32. For the importance of the time lag, see now the penetrating study of R. Smith, *Julian's Gods: Religion and Philosophy in the Thought and Action of Julian the Apostate* (London, 1995), 1–22.

31 Amm. 16.7.5 with Matthews, *The Roman Empire of Ammianus*, 25; 101; 268; 378.

32 Matthews, *The Roman Empire of Ammianus*, 94.

33 For Zosimus's use of Eunapius, see Eun. T 2 (Blockley); for the relationship between Eunapius and Oribasius, see Eun. F 15 (Blockley). R.C. Blockley, *The Fragmentary Classicising Historians of the Later Roman Empire* 1 (Liverpool, 1981), 1–26 remains a valuable introduction.

34 For the Persian expedition see Zos. 312–29 with Amm. 23.2–25.3 with Matthews, *The Roman Empire of Ammianus*, 161–79; for Paris see Potter, *Prophets and Emperors*, 179 n. 71.

35 Amm 28.1 (an enormous chapter). For discussion see Matthews, *The Roman Empire of Ammianus*, 209–17.

36 W. Eck, A Caballos and F. Fernández, *Das senatus consultum de Cn. Pisone patre* (Munich, 1996), for the text with a superior commentary.

37 Eck, Caballos and Fernández, *Das senatus consultum de Cn. Pisone patre*, 265–6.

38 Eck, Caballos and Fernández, *Das senatus consultum de Cn. Pisone patre*, 1–6 for details of the finds and p. 279–87 for the role of the governor, Vibius Serenus, in seeing to the publication of both this dossier and that connected with the honors for Germanicus. For some questions with regard to the number of copies, see D.S. Potter, review of Eck, Caballos and Fernández, *Das senatus consultum de Cn. Pisone patre*, *JRA* 11 (1998) 439–41.

39 *Ann.* 3.12.1 with *SCPP* 29–31; 3.12.4 with *SCPP* 45–8; 3.13.2 with *SCPP* 59–61; 52–7; 3.17.4 with *SCPP* 93–8 in each case; see also A.J. Woodman and R.H. Martin, *The Annals of Tacitus Book 3* (Cambridge, 1996) *ad loc.*

40 *SCCP* 37–45 (Piso and Vonones); 49–56 (brutality and donatives); 120–23 (Visellius Karus and Sempronius Bassus). There will remain much debate as to the date of the trial; Eck, Caballos and Fernández, *Das senatus consultum de Cn. Pisone patre*, argue for close proximity to the date of the decree (10 December) which would suggest that Tacitus has distorted the chronology of the year 20 well beyond what would be normal. Their solution has been adopted by Woodman and Martin, *The Annals of Tacitus Book 3*, 71–9. For another view see M.T. Griffin, "The Senate's story," *JRS* 87 (1997), 258–9, and Potter, review of Eck, Caballos and Fernández, *Das senatus consultum de Cn. Pisone patre* 452–4.

41 J. Ginsburg, *Tradition and Theme in the Annals of Tacitus* (New York, 1981), 53–79.

42 H. Timpe, *Der Triumph des Germanicus* (Bonn, 1968), 43–6 followed by Ginsburg, *Tradition and Theme in the Annals of Tacitus*, 18, 67–72, though noting the objection raised by R. Syme, *History in Ovid* (Oxford, 1978), 59–61 on p. 107 n. 13. The crucial issue is, however, the counting of imperatorial salutations for Augusts and Tiberius. See R. Syme, "Some imperatorial

salutations," *Phoenix* 33 (1979), 322, repr. in R.Syme, *Roman Papers* 3, ed. A.R. Birley (Oxford, 1984), 1211–12.

43 See the valuable discussion of rumor and innuendo as motivating forces in Tacitus by H.Y. McCulloch, *Narrative Cause in the Annals of Tacitus* (Koenigstein, 1984).

44 See especially M. Sahlins, *Islands of History* (Chicago, 1985), challenged with great force by G. Obeyesekere, *The Apotheosis of Captain Cook: European Mythmaking in the Pacific* (Princeton, NJ, 1992) and defended in M. Sahlins, *How Natives Think* (Chicago, 1995). The methodological issues raised here are of importance for any area of historical study.

45 R. Lane Fox, *The Unauthorized Version: Truth and Fiction in the Bible* (London, 1991), 161–74 offers a valuable discussion of the distinction between Greek and Jewish traditions.

46 J. van Seters, *In Search of History: Historiography in the Ancient World and the Origins of Biblical History* (New Haven, CN, 1983), 209–48 on various forms of the earlier tradition; Lane Fox, *The Unauthorized Version*, 172 on the character of the compiler. For a detailed defense of the Deutornomist as a critical historian, see B. Halpern, *The First Historians: The Hebrew Bible and History* (New York, 1988), 1–35 (history of the question); 275–78 (on the character of the historian).

47 For contradictions see, for instance, 1 Sam.16:14–22, where David enters Saul's service as a harpist; 1 Sam. 17:58, where Saul asks to meet David after the killing of Goliath, as he did not know who he was. For repetition (with variants in detail), see for instance the leaders of David's kingdom (2 Sam. 8:15–18; 2 Sam. 20:23–6), repetition with the same information see 2 Sam. 5:4–5 and 1 Kings 2:10. For an overview of traditional source criticism of the "Old Prophets," see O. Eissfeldt, *The Old Testament: An Introduction* tr. P. Ackroyd (Oxford, 1965), 241–301.

48 Very different is the view in Halpern, *The First Historians*, 207–40. For the view adopted here see van Seters, *In Search of History*, 358–62.

49 See now the valuable summary of scholarship in J.J. Collins, *Seers, Sibyls & Sages in Hellenistic-Roman Judaism* (Leiden, 1997), 1–21.

50 A.K. Grayson, "Histories and historians of the Ancient Near East: Assyria and Babylonia," *Orientalia* 49 (1980), 140–94 is a fundamental survey of the subject. For a rather broader definition of historical consciousness, see J.J. Finkelstein, "Mesopotamian Historiography," *PAPS* 107 (1963), 461–72.

51 E. Reiner, *Your Thwarts in Pieces, Your Moorin' Rope Cut, Poetry from Babylonia and Assyria* (Ann Arbor, MI, 1985), 3.

52 A.K. Grayson, *Assyrian and Babylonian Chronicles*, (Locust Valley, NY, 1975), 51–6 for discussion of the sources and content.

53 Grayson, *Assyrian and Babylonian Chronicles*, 56–9.

54 *FGrH* 688 T 8; F 1–8.

55 J.W. Swain, "The Theory of the Four Monarchies," *CPh* 35 (1940): 1–5; Potter, *Prophets and Emperors*, 187–8. For Velleius, see also D.S. Potter, review of M. Elefante (ed.) *Velleius Paterculus, Ad M. Vinicium consulem libri duo, BMCR* (1997).

56 Dion. Hal. *Ant. Rom.* 1.2.2–4 with E. Gabba, *Dionysius and the History of Archaic Rome* (Berkeley, CA, 1991), 193 n. 7; for Trogus, see Swain, "The Theory of the Four Empires," 16–17.

57 App. *Praef.* 9, with Swain, "The Theory of the Four Empires," 14.

58 Tac. *Ann* 6. 31. It is worth noting that there was still a significant Greek cultural presence at Seleucia on the Tigris in this period.

59 Dio 80.4; Herod. 6.4.4–5. For Sapor's stated aims, contra Dio and Herodian, see D.S. Potter, *Prophecy and History in the Crisis of the Roman Empire: A Historical Commentary on the Thirteenth Sibylline Oracle* (Oxford, 1990), 370–8. For Sapor II, see Amm. Marc. 17.5.5 with Matthews, *The Roman Empire of Ammianus* (London, 1989), 485 n. 12.

60 D.S. Potter, "Gaining information on Rome's neighbours," *JRA* 9 (1996), 528–31.

61 L. Robert, "Deux concours grecs à Rome," *CRAI* (1970), 6–27, repr. in *Opera Minora Selecta* 5, 647–68 remains fundamental on this point, though see now the excellent discussion in A.J. Spawforth, "Symbol of Unity? The Persian-wars tradition in the Roman Empire," in S. Hornblower ed., *Greek Historiography* (Oxford, 1994), 233–47.

62 For a basic survey of forms of Egyptian Historiography see the valuable summary in van Seters, *In Search of History*, 127–87.

63 For Manetho see now the useful discussion in G.P. Verbrugghe and J.M. Wickersham, *Berossus and Manetho* (Ann Arbor, 1996), 95–120.

64 For this tendency, as manifested in lists of cities founded by Alexander the Great see P.M. Fraser, *Cities of Alexander the Great* (Oxford, 1996), 44–5.

65 Potter, *Prophets and Emperors*, 192–203.

66 L. Ranke, *Geschichten der romanischen und germanischen Völker von 1494 bis 1514*, ed. W. Andreas (Wiesbaden, 1957), 4. Interestingly, Ranke omitted the preface from the 1874 edition. For von Humbolt, see W. von Humbolt, "Über die Aufgabe des Geschichtschreibers," in *Wilhelm von Humbolts Gesammelte Schriften* (Berlin, 1903), 4, 35–56; see especially p. 35, "Die Aufgabedes Geschichtschreibers ist die Darstellung des Geschehenen" (the mission of the historian is the representation of what happened). An English translation appears as W. von Humbolt, "On the Historian's Task," *History and Theory* 6 (1967), 57–71. The translation is somewhat tendentious in that the passage quoted above is rendered "the historian's task is to present what *actually* happened." Otherwise, it is possible that the phrase is an allusion to a sixteenth-century historiographic topos; see P. Burke, "Ranke the Reactionary," *Syracuse Scholar* 9 (1988), 25 (I am indebted to Dr. J. Marvil lending me his copy of this issue, devoted to studies of Ranke). For a demolition of the suggestion that Ranke was actually thinking of Thuc. 2.48.3, see R. Stroud, "'wie es eigentlich gewesen' " and Thucydides 2.48.3," *Hermes* 115 (1987), 379–82.

For the fate of the pure objectivist position as it was established from the 1950s to the 1970s in the American historical profession, see the account in P. Novick, *That Noble Dream: The Objectivity Question and the American Historical Profession* (Cambridge, 1988), 415–68 and pp. 126–30 below.

67 On Ranke's view of history in terms of contemporary German thought, showing that there was a great deal more to what Ranke's was saying than is suggested by a single quotation dragged out of context, see T. Nipperdey, "Zum Problem der Objectivität bei Ranke," in W.J. Mommsen (ed.) *Leopold von Ranke und die moderne Geschichtswissenschaft* (Stuttgart, 1988), 215–22.

68 D.M. Schenkenveld, "Scholarship and grammar," in F. Montanari (ed.) *La philologie grecque à l'époque hellénistique et romaine* Entrentiens Foundation Hardt 60 (Geneva, 1994), 269–81.

69 Schenkenveld, "Scholarship and grammar," 281–92.

70 See here the discussion in A.D. Momigliano, "History between medicine and rhetoric," *ASNP* ser. 3 n. 15 (1985), 767–80, especially 767–70; repr. in A.D. Momigliano, *Ottavo contributo alla storia degli studi classici e del mondo antico* (Rome, 1987), 13–25 especially 13–15.

71 οὕτω καὶ φυλάττοντας, ὡς γέγραπαι, βραχείαις τέ τισιν ἢ προσθέσ-εσιν, ἢ ὑπαλλάξεσι διαλύεσθαι τὰς ἀπορίας; for the meaning of ὑπάλλαξις (change) in Galen's critical vocabulary see *In Hipp. de vict acutorum* iv [Kühn p.15 424]: ὅταν τὴν ὑπόθε″ιν ἔχον τὴν αὐτὴν καὶ τὰ″ πλεί″τα″ τῶν ῥή″εων τὰ″ αὐτὰ″ τινὰ μὲν ἀφηρημένα τῶν ἐκ τοῦ προτέρου ″υγγράμματο″ ἔχῃ, τινὰ δὲ προ″κείμενα τινὰ δ᾿ ὑπηλλαγμένα. See also, Hanson, "Galen: author and critic" *Aporemata* 2 (1997).

72 See the discussion in Nikau, *Untersuchungen zur textkritischen Methode*, 35–6.

73 Ar. *Poet.* 1460b 6–22; for the importance of Aristotle's criteria see Richardson, "Aristotle and Hellenistic scholarship," 17–18; for Zenodotus see Nikau, *Untersuchungen zur textkritischen Methode*, 185–6. See also M. Haslam, "Homeric papyri and transmission of the text," in I. Morris and B. Powell, *A New Companion to Homer* (Leiden, 1997), 73–4.

74 Nikau, *Untersuchungen zur textkritischen Methode*, 187–93.

75 Dio 42.2; 50.12; 54.35; 57.3; 58.11; 63.22; 67.15; 68.27 (especially revealing as he says that he knows what he has seen and what he has heard). For contemporary events see 71.33.3; 71.33.4; 72.7; 72.18; 75.4; 78.7; 78.2 (all personal informants or the result of being present himself). See also G. Avenarius, *Lukians Schrift zur Geschichtsschreibung* (Meisenheim am Glan, 1956), 71–85.

76 R. Syme, "The year 33 in Tacitus and Dio," *Athenaeum* 61 (1983), 8, repr. in R. Syme, *Roman Papers* 4, ed. A.R. Birley (Oxford, 1988), 229. What follows is heavily derivative from R.J. Starr, "Lectores and Roman reading," *CJ* 88 (1991), 337–43; N. Horsfall, "Rome without spectacles," *G&R* 42 (1995), 49–55.

77 Suet. *Aug.* 78.2; and in general, Starr, "Lectores and Roman reading," 339.

78 Cic. *Ad Quint. fr.* 7.1 with Starr, "Lectores and Roman reading," 340.

79 Ennius, *Scipio* fr 2 with E. McCartney, "A note on reading and praying audibly," *CPh* 43 (1948), 186–7.

80 Optatus 7.1 (*CSEL* 26.165) with McCartney, "Reading and praying audibly," 185.

81 W.P. Clark, "Ancient reading," *CJ* (1931), 698–9; for a misreading of Augustine on Ambrose, see B.M.W. Knox, "Silent reading," *GRBS* 9 (1968), 422, though correctly interpreting *Conf.* 8.12.

82 See Horsfall, "Rome without spectacles," 51.

83 Knox, "Silent reading," 422.

84 Dio 72.23.5 with Millar, *Cassius Dio*, 28–33.

85 C.B.R. Pelling, "Plutarch's method of work in the Roman lives," *JRS* 99 (1979), 74–96; C.B.R. Pelling, "Plutarch's adaptation of his source material," *JHS* 100 (1980), 127–40.

86 See also G. Avenarius, *Lukians Schrift zur Geschichtsschreibung* (Meisenheim am Glan, 1956), 85–104.

87 *Att.* 2.1 = SB 21; for bilingualism see E. Fantham, *Roman Literary Culture: From Cicero to Apuleius* (Baltimore, 1996), 4–5.

88 E. Fisher, "Greek Translations of Latin Literature," *YCS* 27 (1982), 183–9. For a summary of the subject in general, see V. Reichmann, *Römische Literatur in griechischer Übersetzung, Philologus* suppl. 34.3 (1943).

89 P.G. Walsh, "The negligent historian: howlers in Livy," *G&R* 5 (1958), 84–5.

90 Livy 33.13.7 with Pol. 18.38 (Phthiotic Thebes); compare Livy 28.7.12; 32. 33.16; 33.5.1; 33.13.7; 33.34.7 contra Walsh, "The negligent historian: howlers in Livy," 86–7; 38.3 with Pol. 21.26 (the siege of Ambracia); Livy 33.35 with Pol. 18.48.5 (Thermum versus Thermopylae). For an explanation of the error with regard to Thermopylae, see J.-A. de Foucault, "Tite-Live traducteur de Polybe," *Revue des études latines* 46 (1968), 209.

91 de Foucault, "Tite-Live traducteur de Polybe," 221.

92 Plin *NH* 13.83 (autographs of the Gracchi, Cicero, Augustus and Vergil). Not all may have been genuine of course, see p. 176 n. 45 above, but Suetonius does at least confirm the possibility of seeing an autograph of Augustus. Quintilian also mentions autographs of Cicero and Vergil (*Inst.* 1.7.20). For autographs in general, see T. Dorandi, "Den Autoren über die Schulter geschaut Arbeitsweise Autographie bei die antiken Schriftstellern," *ZPE* 87 (1991), 11–33.

93 Plin. *NH* 7. 91 for Caesar's compositional habits. For letters presumably in his own hand, see Suet. *Caes.* 56.6.

94 Hirt. *BG* 8 praef. 6: *ceteri enim quam bene atque emendate, nos etiam quam facile atque celeriter eos perfecerit scimus*; 8: *quae bella quamquam et parte nobis Caesaris sermone sunt nota.*

95 Petron. *Sat.* 115.2; Horace *Sat.* 1.10.70–73; Pers. *Sat.* 1.106; Mart. *Ep.* 7.11; 17, Dorandi, "Den Autoren über die Schulter geschaut Arbeitsweise Autographie bei die antiken Schriftstellern," 21–4.

96 Dorandi, "Den Autoren über die Schulter geschaut Arbeitsweise Autographie bei die antiken Schriftstellern," 16–17.

97 W.K. Prentice, "How Thucydides wrote his history," *CPh* 25 (1930), 117–27.His conclusion, endorsed in A.W. Gomme, A. Andrewes, and K.J. Dover, *A Historical Commentary on Thucydides* 5 (Oxford, 1981), 401, that Thucydides spent time cutting up rolls of papyrus to glue in new sections, would seem to be slightly off the mark, since the completed sections would only have come together at the very last stage.

98 Gomme, Andrewes, and Dover, *A Historical Commentary on Thucydides* 5, 382.

99 See here the excellent discussion in T.J. Luce, *Livy: The Composition of His History* (Princeton, NJ 1977), 3–32.

100 Luce, *Livy: The Composition of his History*, 194–5.

101 For the six "natural" divisions of the surviving account, see Gomme, Andrewes, and Dover, *A Historical Commentary on Thucydides* 5, 389; for an excellent discussion of the problem with 2.1.1, see H. Rawlings, *The Structure of Thucydides's History* (Princeton, NJ, 1981), 25–8.

4 Presentation

1 See for example the manifesto in A.J. Woodman, *Rhetoric in Classical Historiography* (London, 1988) 197–201; for more general discussion, with pointed observations on the situation in ancient historiography, see N.F. Partner, "Historicity in an age of reality-fictions," in F. Ankersmit and H. Kellner (eds) *A New Philosophy of History* (Chicago, 1995), 26–31; for White's position in the postmodernist hierarchy as a whole, see, for instance, G. Eley, "Is all the world a text? From social history to the history of society two decades later," in T. McDonald (ed.) *The Historic Turn in the Human Sciences* (Ann Arbor, MI, 1996), 207; K. Jenkins, *On "What is History?" From Carr and Elton to Rorty and White* (London, 1995), 1–42; 133–79.

2 See especially D. La Capra, *History and Criticism* (Ithaca, NY, 1985), 15–44.

3 See especially E.H. Carr, *What is History?* (London, 1961); G.R. Elton, *The Practice of History* (London, 1967). It is revealing that Carr refers to C.L. Becker, a noted historian of American foreign relations, as a philosopher (*What is History?*, 22). For an interesting review of Elton's book from the perspective of the debate at the time within the American profession, see P.L. Ward, review of G.R. Elton, *The Practice of History*, *History and Theory* 8 (1969), 112–19, especially 114, noting that Elton likewise seems unaware of either Beard or Becker, whose work did not overlap with his own. Likewise Jenkins, *On "What is History?" From Carr and Elton to Rorty and White*, takes White out of an American context altogether. For an interesting discussion of initial resistance to White's *Metahistory* in the American community see R.T. Vann, "Turning linguistic: history and theory and *History and Theory*, 1960–1975" in F. Ankersmit and H. Kellner, *A New Philosophy of History* (Chicago, 1995), 69.

  For Braudel, see especially F. Braudel, "Ma formation d'historien," in F. Braudel (ed.) *Écrits sur l'histoire* 2 (Paris, 1990), 9–29. Of Anglophone historians, it was Toynbee who seems to have interested him the most; see the sympathetic treatment in "L'histoire des civilizations: le passé explique le présent" in F. Braudel, *Écrits sur l'histoire* 1 (Paris, 1969), 273–84, repr. as "The history of civilizations: the past explains the present," in F. Braudel, *On History*, tr. S. Matthews (Chicago, 1980), 189–97; J. Revel, "Introduction," tr. A. Goldhammer, in J. Revel and L. Hunt (eds) *Histories: French Constructions of the Past* (New York, 1995), 1–20.

4 H.B. Adams, "Leopold von Ranke," *Papers of the American Historical Association* 3 (1888), 104–5. To be fair to Adams, the burst of rhetoric quoted in the text is based on a deceptive passage of Ranke's autobiography. Adams gets much closer to Ranke's thought (without realizing that he is contradicting himself) on p. 118.

5 G. Iggers, "The image of Ranke in American and German historical thought," *History and Theory* 2 (1962), 17–24, is of great importance for the reception of Ranke's thought in the United States and the almost total divergence from what he actually stood for. Iggers may, however, place too much emphasis on the first generation of professional university historians, many of whom had connections with the non-academic tradition of historiography. The "hard" view of Ranke the positivist appears most prominently in the next generation; see the important study of D. Ross,

"On the misunderstanding of Ranke and the origins of the historical profession in America," *Syracuse Scholar* 9 (1988), 31–41.

6   tr. R. Wines, *Leopold von Ranke: The Secret of World History. Selected Writings on the Art and Science of History* (New York, 1981), 258. For similar sentiments, in his preface to his history of England see L. Ranke, *Englische Geschichte* ed. W. Andreas (Wiesbaden, 1957): "die am besten geschriebene Geschichte wird für die beste gelten".

7   The influence of Ranke on the French system was primarily through his promotion of the seminar as a means of pedagogy; see G. Monod, "Du progrès des études historiques en france depuis le XVI siècle," *Revue historique* 1 (1876), 28–9. Ranke's own model was that of the seminar on classical philology run by Gottfried Hermann at Frankfurt, where he was trained. The response to Ranke in the English community was somewhat muted, as appears for example from his treatment by Lord Acton, J.E.E. Dahlberg-Acton "German schools of history," *Essays in the Study and Writing of History: Selected Writings of Lord Acton* 2, ed. J.R. Fears (Indianapolis, 1985), 325–64; "Leopold von Ranke"*Essays in the Study and Writing of History*, 165–72.

8   See, in an agonistic context, C. Beard, "That noble dream," *AHR* 41 (1935), 79. Beard's own discussion of Ranke's characteristics on pp. 77–8 is first rate. For earlier criticism of Ranke, see the interesting discussion in E.W. Dow, "Features of the new history: apropos of Lamprecht's *Deutsche Geschichte*," *AHR* 3 (1898), 444–6, especially 444: "no matter how high the value ascribed to Ranke, he remains the child of another age." Contrast the attitude in T.C. Smith, "The writing of American history in America, from 1884 to 1934," *AHR* 40 (1935), 445–6.

9   Now lost. See L. von Ranke, *Frühe Schriften*, ed. W.P. Fuchs (Munich, 1973), 330.

10   T.H. von Laue, *Leopold Ranke: The Formative Years* (Princeton, NJ, 1950), 9–10. Ranke's notes for courses on Greek and Roman history and literature in 1818–19, including translations of classical texts, are printed in Ranke, *Frühe Schriften*, 505–75. He later wrote histories of both Greece and Rome as parts of his universal history.

11   Von Laue, *Leopold Ranke: The Formative Years*, 38.

12   Wines, *Leopold von Ranke*, 57. The passage here is from the preface to the *Histories of the Roman and Germanic Peoples, 1494–1514* (1824). The German text is reprinted in Andreas's edition of the *Geschichten der romanischen und germanischen Völker von 1494–1535* (Wiesbaden, 1957) 3–5 [p. 4 for the passage in question]; it was omitted from the second edition, published under Ranke's direction in 1874, and from the two English translations of the work.

13   F. Gilbert, *History: Choice and Commitment* (Cambridge, MA, 1977), 42–3.

14   C.L. Becker, "Mr. Wells and the New History," repr. in *Everyman His Own Historian* (New York, 1935), 171; C.L. Becker, "Everyman his own historian," repr. in *Everyman His Own Historian*, 250–1; P. Novick, *That Noble Dream* (Cambridge, 1988), 21–46.

15   F. Gilbert, *History: Politics or Culture* (Princeton, NJ, 1990), 26–9.

16   L. Ranke, "A dialogue on politics," tr. T.H. von Laue in *Leopold Ranke: The Formative Years*, 161, 162.

17 L. Ranke, "The Great Powers," tr. T.H. von Laue in *Leopold Ranke: The Formative Years*, 217, with R. Wines, *Leopold von Ranke*, 11; 15–23. Note especially Wines's observation that Ranke's private papers contain the highly emotive language instanced in the passage here that he sought to keep out of his major works. A particularly purple passage follows upon the one quoted in the text, that was omitted by Ranke in the edition of his collected works (see von Laue, *Leopold Ranke: The Formative Years*, 217).

18 Wines, *Leopold von Ranke*, 243.

19 Wines, *Leopold von Ranke*, 258.

20 L. Ranke, tr. Wines in *Leopold von Ranke*, 39.

21 L. von Ranke, *Das Briefwerk* ed. W.P. Fuchs (Hamburg, 1949), 69–70; well discussed by A. Grafton, *The Footnote* (Cambridge, MA, 1997), 86–7. The debt to Niebuhr is evident in a paper on Martin Luther written while he was still a student; see the discussion by Fuchs in Ranke, *Frühe Schriften*, 329–32.

22 Grafton, *The Footnote*, 67–72. The appreciation of Ranke's style is not helped by the fact that Andreas does not print his notes or appendices in his edition of the major histories.

23 Grafton, *The Footnote*, 94–121.

24 F. Parkman, *The Oregon Trail; The Conspiracy of Pontiac* Library of America edition (New York, 1991), 347.

25 See also J.E.E. Dahlberg-Acton, "Ranke," *Essays in the Study and Writing of History*, 166 for an interesting statement by a contemporary as to the effect of Ranke's printing of documents (and some less complimentary remarks on his thoroughness).

26 Gilbert, *History: Politics or Culture*, 22–5. See also Adams, "Leopold von Ranke," 110–12 for a very interesting discussion of Ranke's teaching and his impact on the staffing of universities in Germany.

27 C.A. Beard, "Written history as an act of faith," *AHR* 39 (1934), 221.

28 F. Parkman, *The Conspiracy of Pontiac*, 772. See also Becker, "Labeling the historians," repr. in *Everyman His Own Historian*, 135: "if Parkman had written badly, no one could question his scientific standing." On the other side of the debate, note the implicitly disparaging remarks in T.C. Smith, "The writing of American history," 440, 443 (also inaccurate).

29 H. Thomas, *Conquest: Montezuma, Cortés, and the Fall of Mexico* (New York, 1993), xiv–xv.

30 Novick, *That Noble Dream*, 253–78.

31 L. Stone, "Prosopography," *Daedalus* (1971), repr. in L. Stone, *The Past and the Present Revisited* (London, 1981), 48–9.

32 Beard, "Written history as an act of faith," 219.

33 Beard, "Written history as an act of faith," 226–7.

34 Becker, "Everyman his own historian," 232, repr. in *Everyman His Own Historian*, 249.

35 Becker, "Everyman his own historian," 231, repr. in *Everyman His Own Historian*, 248.

36 Beard, "Written history as an act of faith," 225; see M. Mandlebaum, *The Problem of Historical Knowledge: An Answer to Relativism* (New York, 1938), 90–2 on Beard. See also Novick, *That Noble Dream*, 262–4, pointing out that the

reception of this and other works was more significant after the Second
World War than before.

37 T.C. Smith, "The writing of American history," 449.
38 C.H. McIlwain, "The historian's part in a changing world," *AHR* 42
    (1937), 207–24.
39 Novick, *That Noble Dream*, 281–319; 603.
40 For the 1960s, see Novick, *That Noble Dream*, 415–68. A notable response to
    the atmosphere at the AHA in 1970 appears in O. Handlin, "A discipline
    in crisis," *The American Scholar* 40 (1971), repr. in O. Handlin, *Truth in History*
    (Cambridge, MA, 1979), 3–24.
41 H. White, *Metahistory: The Historical Imagination in Nineteenth-Century Europe*
    (Baltimore, 1973), 29. The modes of emplotment are borrowed from S.C.
    Pepper, *World Hypothoses: a Study in Evidence* (Berkeley, CA, 1942); the modes
    of argument from N. Frye, *Anatomy of Criticism* (Princeton, 1957); the forms
    of ideological implication derive from K. Mannheim, *Ideology and Utopia*
    trans. L. Wirth and E. Shils (New York, 1936). See White, *Metahistory*, 426
    and J.S. Nelson, review of White, *Metahistory*, *History and Theory* 14 (1975),
    77.
42 White, *Metahistory*, 38.
43 White, *Metahistory* 433, with the critique in Nelson, review of White,
    Metahistory 78–9.
44 White, *Metahistory*, 141.
45 White, *Metahistory*, 42.
46 A.D. Momigliano, "The rhetoric of history and the history of rhetoric: on
    Hayden White's tropes," in E.S. Shaffer (ed.) *Comparative Criticism: A Year
    Book* (Cambridge, 1981), 259–68, repr. in A.D. Momigliano, *Settimo contributo
    alla storia degli studi classici e del mondo antico* (Rome, 1984), 49–59.
47 Partner, "Historicity in an age of reality-fictions," 31.
48 *De Thuc.* 2, presumably a rhetorical assertion in light of the preference
    given to Herodotus in his *Ep. ad Pomp.* 3.
49 See F.W. Walbank, "Speeches in Greek historians," *Myers Memorial Lecture*
    (Oxford, 1965), repr. in F.W. Walbank, *Selected Papers: Studies in Greek and
    Roman History and Historiography* (Cambridge, 1985), 248–9; C.W. Fornara,
    The Nature of History in Ancient Greece and Rome (Berkeley, CA, 1983), 143–58.
    Both Fornara and Walbank offer good discussions of the evolution of
    speeches in Greek historiography in the fourth–third centuries BC.
50 Avenarius, *Lukians Schrift zur Geschichtsschreibung*, 130–40; Fornara, *The Nature
    of History in Ancient Greece and Rome*, 120–34.
51 C.P. Jones, *Culture and Society in Lucian* (Cambridge, MA), 59–60.
52 Avenarius, *Lukians Schrift zur Geschichtsschreibung*, 13–16.
53 F.W. Walbank, *A Historical Commentary on Polybius* 2 (Oxford, 1967) *ad loc.*
54 Compare Pol. 3.4.13; 12.25 f.3; 12.25 g.1–2; 12.25h. 5; 12.27. 7;
    12.28. 6 with Walbank, *A Historical Commentary on Polybius* 2 *ad loc.* and
    Jos. *Contra Ap.* 1.55; *BJ* 1.3.See also Avenarius, *Lukians Schrift zur
    Geschichtsschreibung*, 30–40.
55 Cic. *De Orat.* 2.62–4: *Nam quis nescit primam esse historiae legem, ne quid falsi
    dicere audeat? Deinde ne quid veri non audeat? Ne quae suspicio gratiae sit in scribendo?
    Ne quae simultatis? Haec scilicet fundamenta nota sunt omnibus, ipsa autem exaedifi-
    catio posita est in rebus et verbis: rerum ratio ordinem temporum desiderat, regionum*

descriptionem; vult etiam, quoniam in rebus magnis memoriaque dignis consilia primum,
deinde acta, postea eventus exspectentur, et de consiliis significari quid scriptor probet et in
rebus gestis declarari non solum quid actum aut dictum sit, sed etiam quo modo, et cum
de eventu dicatur, ut causae explicentur omnes vel casus vel sapientiae vel temeritatis
hominumque ipsorum non solum res gestae, sed etiam, qui fama ac nomine excellant, de
cuiusque vita atque natura; verborum autem ratio et genus orationis fusum atque tractum
et cum lenitate quadam aequabiliter profluens sine hac iudiciali asperitate et sine
sententiarum forensibus aculeis persequendum est. The translation of 2.6.3 offered
in the text differs significantly from that offered in Woodman, *Rhetoric in*
Classical Historiography, 80. The subject of the sentence is *ratio*, which
Woodman's rather more eloquent rendition obscures. The point is important since Cicero is explicitly contrasting two different *rationes*.

56 Cic. *Leg.* 1.5–6. The view expressed here, that a well-trained orator is the
    best historian, because he commands the proper style is also expressed at
    De Orat. 2.36. Compare also Cic. *Brut.* 101; 228. The conversation here
    mirrors an actual discussion, Atticus having advised Cicero to write history
    as a solace during the period of Antony's supremacy in 44 BC see *Att.*
    14.14.5 (April); 16.13.2 (November).

57 *Att.* 2.1.1–2 (SB 21.1.1–2) for the history with Peter *HRR* 2, 4 (four frag-
    ments), for the poem, see E. Courtney, *The Fragmentary Latin Poets* (Oxford,
    1993), "Cicero" Fr. 4a–13; for Cicero's poem on his exile, see *Att.* 4.8a. 3
    (SB 82.3); *Fam.* 1.9.23 (SB 20.23); *Quint* 2.14.2; 2.16.2 with Courtney, *The*
    Fragmentary Latin Poets, 173–4.

58 Cic. *Leg.* 1.4–5; especially 1.5.1: *alias in historia leges obseruandas putare, alias in*
    poemate, Att. 1.19.10 (=SB 19.10): *quamquam non ἐγκωμιαστικὰ sunt haec sed*
    ἱστορικὰ quae scribimus.

59 The point is argued with considerable force in Woodman, *Rhetoric in*
    Classical Historiography, 85–90.

60 Avenarius, *Lukians Schrift zur Geschichtsschreibung*, 118–27.

61 P.A. Brunt, "Cicero and Historiography," *Studies in Greek History and Thought*
    (Oxford,1993) passim; T.P. Wiseman, "Lying historians: seven types of
    mendacity," in C. Gill and T.P. Wiseman, *Lies and Fiction in the Ancient World*
    (Exeter, 1993), 126–46.

62 The distinction between direct quotation for "one liners" and summary for
    longer speeches can be seen clearly in Tacitus, for direct quotations see
    Tac. *Ann* 1.11;. 3.65; . 6.5; 6.20; 6.46; 11.21; 11.37;. 12. 21; 14. 59; 15.67;
    Hist. 1.35; 3.39. Contrast *Ann.* 1.58; 2.38: 4. 37; 6.8; 12.36; 15.25; *Hist.*
    4.58.

63 For the early history of this tradition see R. Helm, *Eusebius's Chronik und ihre*
    Tabellenform: Abhandlungen der preussischen Akademie der Wissenschaften
    philosophisch-historische Klasse 1923, 4 (Berlin, 1924), 5–18; F. Jacoby, *Atthis:*
    The Local Chronicles of Ancient Athens (Oxford, 1949), 179–85; A.A.
    Mosshammer, *The Chronicle of Eusebius and Greek Chronographic Tradition*
    (Lewisburg, 1979), 84–105.

64 Pol. 5.33.5 for the habit of inscribing chronicles on stone, see Helm,
    Eusebius's Chronik und ihre Tabellenform, 7; Jacoby, *Atthis*, 179–80; 357 n. 26;
    and the invaluable collection of such texts with excellent discussion by
    A. Chaniotis, *Historie und Historiker in der griechischen Inschriften. Epigraphische*
    Beiträge zur griechischen Historiographie (Stuttgart, 1988), 141–85.

65 New fragments in *SEG* 23, 802, see further Chaniotis, *Historie und Historiker in der griechischen Inschriften*, 231–2, the chronicle is connected with *tabula Iliaca*.

66 For Apollodorus and his precedessors see Mosshammer, *The Chronicle of Eusebius and Greek Chronographic Tradition*, 113–27; W. Burkert, "Lydia between East and West or how to date the Trojan war: a study in Herodotus," in S. Morris (ed.) *The Ages of Homer: A Tribute to Emily Townsend Vermeule* (Austin, 1995), 139–48.

67 *FGrH* 250 F 1 and F 2. The lists as preserved in the Armenian translation of Eusebius's *Chronicle* offer a synchronism between Egialeus of Sicyon and Ninos of Assyria, but an entry under Egialeus states that his first year was the fifteenth of Ninus. The regnal years on the list suggest that this is a later interpolation.

68 Helm, *Eusebius's Chronik und ihre Tabellenform*, 16–18.

69 A. Harnack, *Geschichte der altchristlichen Litteratur bis Eusebius* 1 (Leipzig, 1893), 507. He suggests a date of completion under Gordian III. The fact that the chronicle ended with the first year of Severus Alexander suggests that it was completed in his reign, the failure to go beyond 221 being indicative of the fact that the emperor who ascended in that year was still on the throne and that a complete record of his reign was not possible.

70 For the theory of the sabbatical millennium see D. Potter, *Prophets and Emperors: Human and Divine Authority from Augustus to Theodosius* (Cambridge, MA, 1994), 107 n. 16.

71 For the connection between Apologetic and Chronography, see Helm, *Eusebius's Chronik und ihre Tabellenform*, 1–2; see in general, W. Adler, *Time Immemorial: Archaic History and its Sources in Christian Chronography from Julius Africanus to George Syncellus*, Dumbarton Oaks Studies 26 (Washington, 1989), 19–20.

72 The extent of the debt is open to question. For the traditional view that Africanus was the main source for the Canons see H.Gelzer, *Sextus Julius Africanus und die byzantinische Chronographie* 2.1 (Leipzig, 1885), 23; for the suggestion of greater originality see Mosshammer, *The Chronicle of Eusebius and Greek Chronographic Tradition*, 166–8; T.D. Barnes, *Constantine and Eusebius* (Cambridge, MA, 1981), 116–24 (supporting Mosshammer).

73 The basic edition is J. Karst, *Eusebius's Werke 5: Die Chronik aus dem Armenischen übersetzt mit textkritische Kommentar* (Leipzig, 1911). For an excellent account of the construction of the text see Mosshammer, *The Chronicle of Eusebius and Greek Chronographic Tradition*, 29–67, see also his plate 5 for a reconstruction of the Eusebian page.

74 Mosshammer, *The Chronicle of Eusebius and Greek Chronographic Tradition*, 71–2.

75 Barnes, *Constantine and Eusebius*, 120.

76 S. Jellicoe, *The Septuagint and Modern Study* (Oxford, 1968), 100–18.

77 See the important study of F. Millar, "Reflections on the trial of Jesus," in P.R. Davies and R.T. White, *A Tribute to Geza Vermes: Essays on Jewish and Christian Literature* (1990), 356–81. For a good general discussion of the problem of the gospels from the perspective of an historian of the Roman empire see also R.J. Lane Fox, *The Unauthorized Version* (London, 1989) 114–125; 283–310. For a standard introduction to the problems of the

composition of the gospels see Kümmel, *Introduction to the New Testament*
trans. H.C. Kee (London, 1975), 35–151; 188–247.

78 H. Dessau, "Über Zeit und Persönlichkeit der S.H.A.," *Hermes* 24 (1889),
337; H. Dessau, "Über die S.H.A.," *Hermes* 27 (1892), 561, responding to
T. Mommsen, "Die Scriptores Historiae Augustae," *Hermes* 25 (1890),
228–92, repr. in T. Mommsen, *Gesammelte Schriften* 7 (Berlin, 1909), 302–74.
Since then the critical work defending and refining the late fourth century
date is R. Syme, *Ammianus and the Historia Augusta* (Oxford, 1968), 72–9, and
R. Syme, *Emperors and Biography: Studies in the Historia Augusta* (Oxford, 1971),
1–16. A.R. Birley, "Further echoes of Ammianus in the *Historia Augusta*," in
G. Bonamente and N. Duval (eds) *Historiae Augustae Colloquium Parisinum: Atti
dei Convegni sulla Historia Augusta* n.s. 1 (Macerata, 1991), 53–8, shows that
the author was aware of the later books of Ammianus. The alleged multiplicity of authorship gave rise to the old title of this work *Scriptores Historiae
Augustae* (whence the old abbreviation *SHA*, which should be avoided unless
one wants to believe in the hexaplicity of authorship).

79 R. Syme, "Controversy abating and credulity curbed," *London Review of
Books* (1–17 Sept 1980), repr. in R.Syme, *Historia Augusta Papers* (Oxford,
1983), 221.

80 For Marius Maximus, see especially R. Syme, "Not Marius Maximus,"
Hermes 96 (1968), 494–502, repr. in *Roman Papers* 2, ed. E. Badian (Oxford,
1979), 650–8; R. Syme, "Marius Maximus once again," *BHAC* (1970)
(Bonn, 1972), repr. in Syme, *Historia Augusta Papers*, 30–45; T.D. Barnes, *The
Sources of the Historia Augusta* (Brussels, 1978), 98–107. Syme proposed that
the author used a second, "good" biographer, *Ignotus*, in addition to Marius
Maximus (a position vigorously reasserted by Barnes on various occasions).
The case against is well put by A. Cameron, "Review of Syme, *Ammianus
and the Historia Augusta*," *JRS* 61 (1971), 262–7; A.R. Birley, *Septimius Severus*
(London, 1971), 308–26; A.R. Birley, "Indirect means of tracing Marius
Maximus," in G. Bonamente and N. Duval (eds) *Historiae Augustae
Colloquium Parisinum: Atti dei Convegni sulla Historia Augusta* n.s. 1 (Macerata,
1991), 57–74. Ignotus reappears in R. Turcan (ed.) *Histoire Auguste: vies de
Macrine, Diaduménien, Héliogabale* (Paris, 1993), 1–15 (vol. 3.1 of the ongoing
Budé edition). For yet another statement in Ignotus's favor, with additional
vituperation, see T.D. Barnes, "The sources of the *Historia Augusta*," in
G. Bonamente and N. Duval (eds) *Historiae Augustae Colloquium Parisinum:
Atti dei Convegni sulla Historia Augusta* n.s. 1 (Macerata, 1991), 1–28. Despite
the vituperation, I am inclined to favor the position against Ignotus set
forward by Birley. See n. 82 below.

81 A. Enmann, "Eine verlorene Geschichte der römischen Kaiser," *Philologus
suppl.* 4 (1884), 337–501.

82 D. Potter, *Prophecy and History in the Crisis of the Roman Empire: A Historical
Commentary on the Thirteenth Sibylline Oracle* (Oxford, 1990), 363–9. The view
expressed here (and there) concerning the use of Herodian and Dio through
an intermediary is based upon places where the author is ostensibly quoting
Herodian and suddenly changes details. The points of connection are so
close that it is hard to see why the author would have changed the details
himself. In addition to the cases discussed in *Prophecy and History*, see also
V. Macr. 2 where the author has included the name Symiamiria, an error for

Soaemias, but still a name unknown to Herodian. Likewise, it is not at all clear that the author of the *HA* is quoting Herodian directly for the place of the death of Macrinus (*V. Macr.* 10.3; 15.1) since he does give Chalcedon as the relevant spot, as it is specified by Herodian (Dio 79.40.1–2 shows that this detail is wrong, but that is beside the point). Barnes ("The sources of the *Historia Augusta*," 1–28, though he properly notes that I did not acknowledge – not having read it – that similar conclusions had been reached by L. Homo in 1919) does not address points of detail such as this, resorting simply to assertion and quotation of authors who agree with him (including those whose works precede the discussion in question). I should add that it is not illogical to favor an otherwise unattested source in one place, and to disbelieve in Ignotus; it is rather a question of looking at an author's compositional practice and seeing if the author appears to combine multiple sources in individual passages. In my view, the pattern established for use of the *KG* is different from that established for Ignotus and for the hypothetical Latin author whose used Herodian and Dexippus. F. Paschoud, "L'histoire Auguste et Dexippe," in G. Bonamente and N. Duval (eds) *Historiae Augustae Colloquium Parisinum: Atti dei Convegni sulla Historia Augusta* n.s. 1 (Macerata, 1991), 217–69, while not questioning direct dependence on Dexippus, nonetheless shows that there are a number of errors in places where Dexippus may be the source.

83 A. Wallace-Hadrill, *Suetonius: The Scholar and his Caesars* (London, 1983), 50–72.

84 *HA Quad. Tyr.* 2.1 (Firmus); *HA Aurel.* 2.1 (criticism of "Trebellius Pollio" by "Flavius Vopiscus"); *HA Carus, Carinus, Numerian* 13.4–5 (soldiers in comedy).

85 *HA Tacitus* 3–7; *HA Comm.* 18 (with Barnes, *The Sources of the Historia Augusta*, 102); Suet. *Aug.* 57 (ch. 3, n. 87 above).

86 See for example *HA Val.* 1–3 (letters of eastern kings to Sapor asking mercy for Valerian); *HA Val.* 5.4–6 (testimonial in favor of Valerian by Decius in the senate); *HA Claud.* 14–15 (two letters of Valerian concerning Claudius); *HA Claud.* 16 (letter of Decius on Claudius); *HA Aurel.* 8–9; 12 (three letters of Valerian on Aurelian); *HA Aurel.* 11 (Valerian to Aurelian); *HA Aurel.* 13 (speech of Valerian about and to Aurelian); *HA Aurel.* 17 (letter of Claudius to Aurelian).

87 H. Delehaye, *Les légendes hagiographiques* (Brussels, 1905), 101. See also H. Delehaye, *Les Passions des martyrs et les genres littéraires* (Brussels, 1921), 9, describing three broader categories, "historical passions," "panegyrics concerning a martyr," and "epic passions."

88 The only modern edition is P.F. de' Cavalieri, *Il Martyrii di S. Theodoto e di S. Ariadne con un'appendice sul testo originale del martirio di S. Eleuterio Studi e Testi* 6 (Rome, 1901), 9–84 (text pp. 61–84) references in the text are to de' Cavalieri's divisions. The value of the text has been the subject of debate. De' Cavalieri felt that it was substantially historical, Delehaye that it was essentially fiction (H. Delehaye, "La passion de S. Théodote d'Ancyre," *Analecta Bollandiana* 22 (1903), 320–8). H. Grégoire and P. Orgels, "La passion de S. Théodote, oeuvre du Pseudo-Nil, et son noyau montaniste," *ByZ* 44 (1951), 165–84, showed that there were a number of important points upon which it was accurate. For more recent discoveries,

connected with the later cult but also demonstrating the essential verisimilitude of the text, see S. Mitchell, "The Life of Saint Theodotus of Ancyra" *AS* 32 (1982), 93–113. There is an excellent discussion of the confessional elements in S. Elm, *Virgins of God: the Making of Asceticism in Late Antiquity* (Oxford, 1994), 51–59; and C. Trevett, *Montanism: Gender, Authority and the New Prophecy* (Cambridge, 1996).

89 *PLRE* p. 908.
90 Grégoire and Orgels, "La passion de S. Théodote," 170–5.
91 Grégoire and Orgels, "La passion de S. Théodote," 175–8.
92 R. Syme, "How Gibbon came to history" in P. Ducrey, *Gibbon et Rome à la lumière de l'historiographie moderne. Dix exposés suivis de discussions* (1977), 54, repr. in *Roman Papers* 3, ed. A.R. Birley (Oxford, 1984), 976.

Epilogue

1 If the ideal historian had these qualities it was just possible that the ideal historian might even be a woman. See A. Chaniotis, *Historie und Historiker in der griechischen Inschriften. Epigraphische Beiträge zur griechischen Historiographie* (Stuttgart, 1988), 338–40 (number E. 56). Aristodema, daughter of Amyntas of Smyrna, evidently recited a mythographic poem at Delphi in 218/17 BC that would arguably qualify as a form of historiographic discourse.

2 *Dig.* 40.11.2; 40.11.4; 40.11.5, 40.11.6 (*natalium restitutio*); *CJ* 8.21.1; *Dig.* 40.10.2; 40.10.4; 40.10.5; 40.10.6 on the right to wear the equestrian ring. Money could even make a woman into a gymnasiarch, see *IGR* 3. 373; *SEG* 31 (1981) n. 958, with R. Van Berman, "Women and Wealth," A. Cameron and A. Kuhrt (eds), *Images of Women in Antiquity* (Detroit, 1983), 233–42; R. MacMullen, "Women in Public," *Historia* 29 (1980), 208–18, repr. in R. MacMullen, *Changes in the Roman Empire* (Princeton, NJ, 1990), 162–8.

3 For the invention of traditions as a form of social structuring see E. Hobsbawm, "Introduction: inventing traditions," in E. Hobsbawm and T. Ranger, *The Invention of Tradition* (Cambridge, 1983), 13. For the impact of Hobsbawm's work here, see P. Burke, *History and Social Theory* (Ithaca, NY 1993), 2; 57. N. Dirks, "Is vice versa? Historical anthropologies and anthropological histories," in T. McDonald (ed.) *The Historic Turn in the Human Sciences* (Ann Arbor, MI, 1996), 17–41. For the distinction between the nationalism of governments and that of the "people," see E. Hobsbawm, *Nations and Nationalism since 1780* (Cambridge, 1990) 46–100.

4 For an alternative historiography of the plebs, not based on traditional historiographic forms, see the engaging proposition in T.P. Wiseman, *Remus: A Roman Myth* (Cambridge, 1995), 103–44.

5 For Pictor's work see B.W. Frier, *Libri Annales Pontificorum Maximorum: The Origins of the Annalistic Tradition* (Rome, 1979), 246–53; for Cato, see A. Astin, *Cato the Censor* (Oxford, 1978), 211–39.

6 T.P. Wiseman, *Clio's Cosmetics: Three Studies in Greco-Roman Literature* (Leicester, 1979), 8–26; E. Badian, "The early historians," in T.A. Dorey (ed.) *Latin Historians* (London, 1966), 1–38; T.J. Cornell, "The formation of the historical tradition in early Rome," in I.S. Moxon, J.D. Smart and A.J.

Woodman, *Past Perspectives: Studies in Greek and Roman Historical Writing* (Cambridge, 1986) 67–87, for the evolution of the annalistic tradition.

7   S.P. Oakley, *A Commentary on Livy Books VI–X* 1 (Oxford, 1997), 25–6.

8   Livy 8.40.4–5; Cic. *Brutus* 62 for complaints, for a sensible discussion of what is meant by these passages see Oakley, *A Commentary on Livy Books VI–X* 1, 30–3. For a discussion of the extant remains, see H. Flower, *Ancestor Masks and Aristocratic Power in Roman Culture* (Oxford, 1996), 128–50.

9   T.P. Wiseman, "Monuments and the Roman annalists," in I.S. Moxon, J.D. Smart and A.J. Woodman, *Past Perspectives: Studies in Greek and Roman Historical Writing* (Cambridge, 1986), 87–100; Oakley, *A Commentary on Livy Books VI–X* 1, 36–7.

10 Oakley, *A Commentary on Livy Books VI–X* 1, 39–40; for errors that might be recorded in pontifical records, or the records of other colleges see D.S. Potter, "Roman religion: ideas and actions," in D.S. Potter and D.J. Mattingly (eds) *Life, Death and Entertainment in the Roman Empire* (Ann Arbor, MI, 1998), 147. For the religious explanations of Roman disasters, see N.S. Rosenstein, *Imperatores Victi: Military Defeat and Aristocratic Competition in the Middle and Late Republic* (Berkeley, CA, and Los Angeles, 1990), 54–91.

11 *Dig.* 1.2.2.7. The work in question is Flavius's work, allegedly stolen from his patron Appius Claudius, on actions in civil law. The speech of the same Appius Claudius, against peace with Pyrrhus, may also have survived; see Cic. *Brut.* 61. I am indebted to John Muccigrosso for calling this material to my attention. For the influence of drama on Roman historical consciousness, see especially T.P. Wiseman (ed.) *Historiography and Imagination* (Exeter, 1994), 1–22. He raises the possibility that drama may have influenced depictions of events in later periods as well. See also the intriguing suggestions in T.P. Wiseman, "The tragedy of Gaius Gracchus" and "Crossing the Rubicon," in T.P. Wiseman, *Roman Drama and Roman History* (Exeter, 1998), 52–59, 60–63.

12 D.S. Potter, *Prophets and Emperors: Human and Divine Authority from Augustus to Theodosius* (Cambridge, MA, 1994), 98–145.

Select Bibliography

Issues in modern historiography

Ankersmit, F. and Kellner, H., *A New Philosophy of History* (Chicago, 1995).

Appleby, J., Hunt, L. and Jacob, M., *Telling the Truth about History* (New York, 1994).

Barthes, R, "The Discourse of History," in R. Howard (ed.) *The Rustle of Language* (Berkeley, CA, 1989), 127–40.

Beard, C., "Written History as an Act of Faith," *AHR* 39 (1934), 219–231.

—— "That Noble Dream," *AHR* 41 (1935), 74–87.

Becker, C.L., "Everyman his own Historian. Essays on History and Politics (New York, 1935)," *AHR* 37 (1932), 221–36, repr. in Everyman His Own Historian, 233–55.

Bourdieu, P., *Language and Symbolic Power* tr. G. Raymond and M. Adamson (Cambridge, MA, 1991).

Braudel, F., *On History* tr. S. Matthews (Chicago, 1980).

—— "L'Histoire des civilizations: le passé explique le présent," in F. Braudel, *Écrits sur l'histoire* 1 (Paris, 1969), 273–84.

—— "Ma formation d'historien," in F. Braudel (ed.) *Écrits sur l'histoire* 2 (Paris, 1990), 9–29.

Burke, P., *The French Historical Revolution: The Annales School 1929-89* (Stanford, 1990).

—— *History and Social Theory* (Ithaca, NY, 1993).

—— "Ranke the Reactionary," *Syracuse Scholar* 9 (1988), 25–32.

Butterfield, H., *The Whig Interpretation of History* (Cambridge, 1931).

Cahoone, L., *From Modernism to Postmodernism: An Anthology* (Oxford, 1996).

Carr, E.H., *What is History?* (New York, 1961).

Dirks, N., "Is vice versa? Historical anthropologies and anthropological histories," in T. McDonald (ed.) *The Historic Turn in the Human Sciences* (Ann Arbor, MI, 1996), 17–41.

Eley, G., "Is all the world a text? From social history to the history of society two decades later," in T. McDonald (ed.) *The Historic Turn in the Human Sciences* (Ann Arbor, MI, 1996), 193–244.

Ely, G. and Nield, K., "Why does social history ignore politics" *Social History* 5 (1980), 249–71.

Elton, G.R., *The Practice of History* (London, 1967).

Fischer, D.H., *Historians' Fallacies* (New York, 1970).

Fox-Genovese, E. and Genovese, E., "The Political Crisis of Social History: a Marxian Perspective," *Journal of Social History* 10 (1976), 205–20.

Geertz, C. *Local Knowledge: Further Essays in Interpretive Anthropology* (New York, 1983).

—— "Commonsense as a cultural system," in C. Geertz, *Local Knowledge*, 73–93.

Gilbert, F., *History: Politics or Culture* (Princeton, NJ, 1990).

Grafton, A. *The Footnote* (Cambridge, MA, 1997).

Hobsbawm, E., *Nations and Nationalism since 1780* (Cambridge, 1990).

—— *On History* (New York, 1997)

—— "What do Historians Owe to Karl Marx," *Marx and Contemporary Scientific Thought / Marx et la pensée scientifique contemporaine* (The Hague and Paris, 1969), 197–211, repr. in E. Hobsbawn, *On History*, 141–56.

—— "British history and the Annales: a note," *Review* 1 (1978), 157–62, repr. E. Hobsbawn, *On History*, 178–85.

—— "Introduction: inventing traditions," in E. Hobsbawm and T. Ranger, *The Invention of Tradition* (Cambridge, 1983), 1–14.

Iggers, G., *Historiography in the Twentieth Century: From Scientific Objectivity to the Postmodern Challenge* (Middletown, 1997).

—— "The image of Ranke in American and German historical thought," *History and Theory* 2 (1962), 17–40.

Jenkins, K., *The Postmodern History Reader* (London, 1997).

Laue, T.H. von, *Leopold Ranke: The Formative Years* (Princeton, NJ, 1950).

Lyotard, J.-F. *The Postmodern Condition: A Report on Knowledge* tr. G. Bennington and B. Massumi (Minneapolis, 1984).

McDonald T., (ed.) *The Historic Turn in the Human Sciences* (Ann Arbor, MI, 1996).

Nipperdey, T., "Zum Problem der Objectivität bei Ranke," in W.J. Mommsen (ed.) *Leopold von Ranke und die moderne Geschichtswissenschaft* (Stuttgart, 1988), 215–22.

Novick, P., *That Noble Dream: The "Objectivity Question" and the American Historical Profession* (Cambridge, 1988).

Partner, N.F., "Historicity in an age of reality-fictions," in F. Ankersmit and H. Kellner (ed.) *A New Philosophy of History* (Chicago, 1995), 21–39.

Poster, M., *Cultural History and Postmodernity: Disciplinary Readings and Challenges* (New York, 1997).

Ranke, L., *Geschichten der romanischen und germanischen Völker von 1494–1535*, ed. W. Andreas (Wiesbaden, 1957).

Revel, J. "Introduction," tr. A. Goldhammer, in J. Revel and L. Hunt (eds), *Histories: French Constructions of the Past* (New York, 1955).

Ross, D., "On the misunderstanding of Ranke and the origins of the historical profession in America," *Syracuse Scholar* 9 (1988), 31–41.

Sarup, M., *An Introductory Guide to Post-Structuralism and Postmodernism*, 2nd edn (Athens, GA, 1993).

Spiegel, G.M., "History, historicism, and the social logic of the text in the Middle Ages," *Speculum* 65 (1990), 59–87, repr. Jenkins, *The Postmodern History Reader*, 180–203.

Stone, L., "Prosopography," *Daedalus* (1971), repr. Stone, L., *The Past and the Present Revisited* (London, 1981), 45–73.

—— "History and the Social Sciences," in C. Delzell (ed.) *The Future of History* (Nashville, 1977), 3–42 repr. in Stone, L., *The Past and the Present Revisisted* (London, 1987), 3–44.

Thompson, E.P., "An open letter to Leszek Kolakowski," *The Poverty of Theory and other Essays* (London, 1978), 303–404.

—— "History and anthropology," in E.P. Thompson (ed.) *Making History*, New York, 1994), 200–25.

Vann, R.T., "Turning linguistic: history and theory and *History and Theory*, 1960–1975" in F. Ankersmit and H. Kellner, *A New Philosophy of History* (Chicago, 1995), 40–69.

White, H., *Metahistory: The Historical Imagination in Nineteenth-Century Europe* (Baltimore, 1973).

Windschuttle, K., *The Killing of History: How Literary Critics and Social Theorists are Murdering Our Past* (New York, 1997).

Wines, R., *Leopold von Ranke: The Secret of World History. Selected Writings on the Art and Science of History* (New York, 1981).

Ancient history and historiography

Adler, W., *Time Immemorial: Archaic History and its Sources in Christian Chronography from Julius Africanus to George Syncellus*, Dumbarton Oaks Studies 26 (Washington, DC, 1989).

Avenarius, G., *Lukians Schrift zur Geschichtsschreibung* (Meisenheim am Glan, 1956).

Badian, E., "The early historians," in T.A. Dorey (ed.) *Latin Historians* (London, 1966), 1–38.

Barnes, T.D., *The Sources of the Historia Augusta* (Brussels, 1978).

—— *Constantine and Eusebius* (Cambridge, MA, 1981).

—— "Ultimus Antoninorum," *BHAC 1968/9* (Bonn, 1970), 53-74.

—— "The editions of Eusebius" *Ecclesiastical History*," *GRBS* 21 (1980), 191–201.

Barwick, K., "Die Gliederung der Narratio in der rhetorischen Theorie und ihre Bedeutung für die Geschichte des antiken Romans," *Hermes* 63 (1928), 260–87.

Blockley, R.C., *The Fragmentary Classicizing Historians of the Later Roman Empire*, 2 vols (Liverpool, 1981, 1983).

Boge, H., *Griechische Tachygraphie und Tironische Noten: ein Handbuch der Antiken und mittelalterlichen Schnellschrift* (Tübingen, 1981).

Bowersock, G.W., *Greek Sophists in the Roman Empire* (Oxford, 1969).

—— *Fiction as History* (Berkeley, CA, 1994).

—— "Herodian and Elagabalus," *YCS* 24 (1975), 229–36.

—— "Jacoby's fragments and two Greek historians of Pre-Islamic Arabia," in G. Most (ed.) *Collecting Fragments – Fragmente sammeln* (Göttingen, 1997), 173–85.

Bowie, E.L., "Greeks and their past in the Second Sophistic," *Past and Present* 46 (1970), 1–41, repr. in M.I. Finley (ed.) *Studies in Ancient Society* (London, 1974), 166–209.

Brunt, P.A., "Cicero and historiography," *Studies in Greek History and Thought* (Oxford, 1993), 181–209.

—— "On historical fragments and epitomes," *CQ* n.s. 30 (1980), 477–94.

—— "The bubble of the Second Sophistic," *BICS* 39 (1994), 25–52.

Burkert, W., "Lydia between East and West or how to date the Trojan War: a study in Herodotus," in S. Morris (ed.) *The Ages of Homer: A Tribute to Emily Townsend Vermeule* (Austin, 1995), 139–48.

de' Cavalieri, F., *I Martyrii di S. Theodoto e di S. Ariadne con un'appendice sul testo originale del martirio di S. Eleuterio: Studi e Testi 6* (Rome, 1901), 9–84.

Chaniotis, A., *Historie und Historiker in der griechischen Inschriften. Epigraphische Beiträge zur griechischen Historiographie* (Stuttgart, 1988).

Coles, R., *Reports of Proceedings in Papyri* (Brussels, 1966).

Collins, J.J., *Seers, Sibyls & Sages in Hellenistic-Roman Judaism* (Leiden, 1997).

Connor, W.R., "The *Histor* in History," *Nomodeiktes: Greek Studies in Honor of Martin Ostwald* (Ann Arbor, MI, 1993), 3–15.

Davidson, J., "The gaze in Polybius' history," *JRS* 81 (1991), 10–24.

Delehaye, H., *Les légendes hagiographiques* (Brussels, 1905).

—— *Les Passions des martyrs et les genres littéraires* (Brussels, 1921).

Derow, P.S. "Historical explanation; Polybius and his predecessors," in S. Hornblower (ed.) *Greek Historiography* (Oxford, 1994), 73–90.

Dillery J., and Gagos, T., "P. Mich. Inv. 4922: Xenophon and an unknown Christian Text with an appendix of all Xenophon papyri" *ZPE* 93 (1992), 171–90.

Dorandi, T., "Den Autoren über die Schulter geschaut: Arbeitsweise Autographie bei die antiken Schriftstellern," *ZPE* 87 (1991), 11–33.

Drews, R., *Greek Accounts of Eastern History* (Princeton, NJ, 1973).

Earl, D.C., *The Political Thought of Sallust* (Cambridge, 1961).

Eck, W, Caballos, A., Fernández, F., *Das senatus consultum de Cn. Pisone patre* (Munich, 1996).

Eissfeldt, O., *The Old Testament: An Introduction*, tr. P. Ackroyd (Oxford, 1965).

Fantham, E., *Roman Literary Culture from Cicero to Apuleius* (Baltimore, 1996).

Finkelstein, J.J., "Mesopotamian historiography," *PAPS* 107 (1963), 461–72.

Fisher, E., "Greek translations of Latin literature," *YCS* 27 (1982), 173–215.

Flower, H., *Ancestor Masks and Aristocratic Power in Roman Culture* (Oxford, 1996).

Fornara, C.W., *The Nature of History in Ancient Greece and Rome* (Berkeley CA, 1983).

—— "Julian's Persian Expedition in Ammianus and Zosimus," *JHS* 111 (1991): 1–15

Foucault, J.-A. de, "Tite-Live traducteur de Polybe," *Revue des études latines* 46 (1968), 208–21.

Fowler, R.L., "Herodotus and his contemporaries," *JHS* 116 (1996), 69–80.

Frier, B.W., *Libri Annales Pontificarum Maximorum: The Origins of the Annalistic Tradition* (Rome, 1979).

Gabba, E., *Dionysius and the History of Archaic Rome* (Berkeley, CA, 1991).

Geiger, J., *Cornelius Nepos and Ancient Political Biography* (Stuttgart, 1985).

Ginsburg, J., *Tradition and Theme in the Annals of Tacitus* (New York, 1981).

—— "*In maiores certamina*: past and present in the Annals," in T.J. Luce and A.J. Woodman, *Tacitus and the Tacitean Tradition* (Princeton, NJ, 1993), 86–103.

Gleason, M.W., *Making Men: Sophists and Self-presentation in Ancient Rome* (Princeton, NJ, 1995).

Gomme, A.W., Andrewes, A. and Dover, K.J., *A Historical Commentary on Thucydides* 5 (Oxford, 1981).

Gowing, A.M., *The Triumviral Narratives of Appian and Cassius Dio* (Ann Arbor, MI, 1992).

Grayson, A.K., *Assyrian and Babylonian Chronicles*, (Locust Valley, 1975).

—— "Histories and historians of the Ancient Near East: Assyria and Babylonia," *Orientalia* 49 (1980), 140–94.

Grégoire H., and Orgels, P., "La passion de S. Théodote, oeuvre du Pseudo-Nil, et son noye au montaniste," *ByZ* 44 (1951), 165–84.

Griffin, M.T., "The Lyons tablet and Tacitean hindsight," *CQ* 32 (1982), 404–18.

Gurval, R., *Actium and Augustus: The Politics and Emotions of Civil War* (Ann Arbor, MI, 1995).

Habicht, C., *Pausanias's Guide to Ancient Greece* (Berkeley, CA, 1985).

Halpern, B., *The First Historians: The Hebrew Bible and History* (New York, 1988).

Hanson, A.E., "Galen: Author and Critic," *Aporemata* 2 (1997).

Harnack, A., *Geschichte der altchristlischen Litteratur bis Eusebius* 1 (Leipzig, 1893).

Harris, W.V., *Ancient Literacy* (Cambridge, MA, 1989).

Helm, R., *Eusebius's Chronik und ihre Tabellenform 1923 Abhandlungen der preussischen Akademie der Wissenschaften philosophisch-historische Klasse*, 4 (Berlin, 1924).

Hopkins, K., "Rules of Evidence," *JRS* 68 (1978), 178–86.

—— "Novel evidence for Roman slavery," *Past and Present* 138 (1993), 3–27.

Hornblower, J., *Hieronymous of Cardia* (Oxford, 1991).

Hornblower, S., "Introduction," in S. Hornblower (ed.) *Greek Historiography* (Oxford, 1994), 1–54.

Horsfall, N., "Rome without spectacles," *G&R* 42 (1995), 49–55.

Humbert, J., *Les plaidoyers écrits et les plaidoiries réelles de Cicéron* (Paris, n.d.).

Jacoby, F., *Atthis: The Chronicles of Ancient Athens* (Oxford, 1949).
—— "Über die Entwicklung der griechischen Historiographie und der Plan einer neuen Sammlung der grieschischen Historikerfragmente," *Klio* 9 (1909), 1–44.
Jones, A.H.M., "Notes on the Genuineness of the Constantinian Documents in Eusebius's Life of Constantine," *JEH* 5 (1954), 196–200, repr. in A.H.M. Jones, *The Roman Economy: Studies in Ancient Economic and Administrative History*, ed. P.A. Brunt (Oxford, 1974), 257–62.
Jones, C.P., *Culture and Society in Lucian* (Cambridge, MA, 1986).
Kaster, R., *Guardians of Language: The Grammarian and Society in Late Antiquity* (Berkeley, CA, 1988).
—— *Suetonius: De Grammaticis et Rhetoribus* (Oxford, 1995).
Knox, B.M.W., "Silent reading," *GRBS* 9 (1968), 421–35.
Kuttner, A., *Dynasty and Empire in the Age of Augustus: The Case of the Boscoreale Cups* (Berkeley, 1995).
Lane Fox, R.J., *Pagans and Christians* (London, 1987).
—— *The Unauthorized Version: Truth and Fiction in the Bible* (London, 1991).
Lendon, J., *Empire of Honour: The Art of Government in the Roman World* (Oxford, 1997).
Luce, T.J., *Livy: The Composition of His History* (Princeton, NJ, 1977).
Maraval, P., *La passion inédite de S. Athénogène de Pédachthoé en Cappadoce* (Brussels, 1990).
Marincola, J., *Authority and Tradition in Ancient Historiography* (Cambridge, 1997).
Markus, R. "Church history and early Church historians," *Studies in Church History* 11 (1975), 1–17.
Marshall, A.J., "Library resources and creative writing at Rome," *Phoenix* 30 (1976), 252–64.
Matthews, J.F., *The Roman Empire of Ammianus* (London, 1989).
McCartney, E., "A note on reading and praying audibly," *CPh* 43 (1948), 184–7.
McCulloch, H.Y., *Narrative Cause in the Annals of Tacitus* (Koenigstein, 1984).
Millar, F., *A Study of Cassius Dio* (Oxford, 1964).
—— "Reflections on the trial of Jesus," in P.R. Davies and R.T. White, *A Tribute to Geza Vermes: Essays on Jewish and Christian Literature* (1990), 356–81.
—— "Ovid and the Domus Augusta: Rome seen from Tomoi," *JRS* 83 (1993), 1–17.
Mitchell, S., "The Life of Saint Theodotus of Ancyra" *AS* 32 (1982), 93–113.
Momigliano, A.D., "Pagan and Christian historiography in the fourth century A.D.," in A.D. Momigliano (ed.) *The Conflict Between Paganism and Christianity in the Fourth Century A.D.* (Oxford, 1963), 79–99.
—— *Alien Wisdom* (Cambridge, MA, 1975).
—— *The Development of Greek Biography* revised edn, (Cambridge, 1993).
Montevecchi, O., *La papirologia* (Milan, 1988).
Mosshammer, A.A., *The Chronicle of Eusebius and Greek Chronographic Tradition* (Lewisburg, PA, 1979).

Myers, K.S., "The poet and the procuress: the *lena* in Latin love elegy," *JRS* 86 (1996), 1–21.

Nikau, K., *Untersuchungen zur textkritischen Methode des Zenodotos von Ephesos* (Berlin, 1977).

Norman, A.F., "The book trade in fourth-century Antioch," *JHS* 80 (1960), 122–6.

Nugent, G., "Tristia 2: Ovid and Augustus," in K. Raaflaub and M. Toher (eds), *Between Republic and Empire* (Berkeley, CA, 1990), 239–57.

Oakley, S.P., *A Commentary on Livy Books VI–X 1* (Oxford, 1997).

Pelling, C.B.R., "Plutarch's method of work in the Roman lives," *JRS* 99 (1979), 74–96.

—— Plutarch's adaptation of his source-material," *JHS* 100 (1980), 127–40.

Pfeiffer, R., *History of Classical Scholarship* 1 (Oxford, 1968).

Potter, D.S., *Prophecy and History in the Crisis of the Roman Empire: A Historical Commentary on the Thirteenth Sibylline Oracle* (Oxford, 1990).

—— *Prophets and Emperors: Human and Divine Authority from Augustus to Theodosius* (Cambridge, MA, 1994).

—— "Performance, power and justice in the high empire," in W.J. Slater (ed.) *Roman Theater and Society* (Ann Arbor, MI, 1996), 129–59.

Pratt, L.H., *Lying and Poetry from Homer to Pindar: Falsehood and Description in Archaic Greek Poetry* (Ann Arbor, MI, 1993).

Prentice, W.K., "How Thucydides wrote his history," *CPh* 25 (1930), 117–27.

Reichmann, V., *Römische Literatur in griechischer Übersetzung, Philologus* suppl. 34.3 (1943).

Richardson, N.J., "Aristotle and Hellenistic scholarship," in F. Montanari (ed.) *La philologie grecque à l'époque hellénistique et romaine*, Entrentiens Foundation Hardt 60 (Geneva, 1994), 7–27.

Robert, L. *A travers l'Asie Mineure: poètes et prosateurs, monnaies grecques, voyageurs et géographie* (Paris, 1980).

—— "Deux concours grecs à Rome," *CRAI* (1970), 6–27, repr. in *Opera Minora Selecta* 5, 647–68.

—— "Une épigramme d'Automédon et Athènes au début de l'empire," *REG* (1981), 348–61.

—— "Catalogue agonistique des Romaia de Xanthos," *Rev. Arch.* (1978), 277–90, repr. in *Opera Minora Selecta* 7(Amsterdam, 1990), 681–94.

Sacks, K., *Diodorus Siculus and the First Century* (Princeton, NJ, 1990).

de Ste. Croix, G.E.M., *The Class Struggle in the Ancient Greek World* (London, 1983).

Schenkenveld, D.M., "Scholarship and Grammar," in F. Montanari (ed.) *La philologie grecque à l'époque hellénistique et romaine*, Entrentiens Foundation Hardt 60 (Geneva, 1994), 269–81.

Schepens, G., "Jacoby's *FGrHist*: problems, methods, prospects," in G. Most (ed.) *Collecting Fragments – Fragmente sammeln* (Göttingen, 1997), 148–54.

Schellhase, K.C., *Tacitus in Renaissance Political Thought* (Chicago, 1976).

Sirks, B., "The sources of the code," in J. Harries and I. Wood, *The Theodosian Code* (Ithaca, NY, 1993), 45–67.

Smith, R., *Julian's Gods: Religion and Philosophy in the Thought and Action of Julian the Apostate* (London, 1995).

Spawforth, A.J., "Symbol of unity? The Persian Wars tradition in the Roman Empire," in S. Hornblower (ed.) *Greek Historiography* (Oxford, 1994), 233–47.

Starr, R.J. "The circulation of literary texts in the Roman world," *CQ* 37 (1987), 213–23.

—— "Lectores and Roman reading," *CJ* 88 (1991), 337–43.

Strack, H.L. and Stremberger, G., *Introduction to the Talmud and Midrash* tr. M. Bockmuehl (Minneapolis, MN, 1992).

Strasburger, H. "Umblick im Trümmerfeld der griechischen Geschichtsschreibung," in W. Peremans *et al.* (eds) *Historiographia Antiqua* (Leuven, 1977), 3–52, repr. in *Studien zur Alten Geschichte* 3 (New York, 1990), 169–218.

Stylianou, P.J., review of Sacks, *Diodorus Siculus and the First Century*, in *BMCR* 2.6 (1991).

Swain, J.W., "The theory of the four monarchies," *CPh* 35 (1940), 1–21.

Swain, S., *Hellenism and Empire: Language, Classicism and Power in the Greek World AD 50–250* (Oxford, 1996).

Syme, R., *Tacitus*, 2 vols (Oxford, 1958).

—— *Ammianus and the Historia Augusta* (Oxford, 1968).

—— *Emperors and Biography: Studies in the Historia Augusta* (Oxford, 1971).

—— *History in Ovid* (Oxford, 1979).

—— "How Gibbon came to history," in P. Ducrey, *Gibbon et Rome à la lumière de l'historiographie moderne. Dix exposés suivis de discussions* (1977), 47–56, repr. in R. Syme, *Roman Papers* 3, ed. A.R. Birley (Oxford, 1984), 969–76.

—— "Some imperatorial salutations," *Phoenix* 33 (1979), 308–29, repr. in R. Syme, *Roman Papers* 3, ed. A.R. Birley (Oxford, 1984), 1198–1219.

—— "Controversy abating and credulity curbed," *London Review of Books* (1–17 Sept 1980), repr. in R. Syme, *Historia Augusta Papers* (Oxford, 1983), 209–23.

—— "The year 33 in Tacitus and Dio," *Athenaeum* 61 (1983), 3–23, repr. in R. Syme, *Roman Papers* 4, ed. A.R. Birley (Oxford, 1988), 233–44.

Townend, G.B., "The sources of Greek in Suetonius," *Hermes* 88 (1960), 98–120.

—— "Traces in Dio Cassius of Cluvius, Aufidius and Pliny," *Hermes* 89 (1961), 227–48.

Toye, D.L., "Dionysius on the First Greek Historians," *AJP* 116 (1995), 280–81.

Treagold, W., *The Nature of the Bibliotheca of Photius*, Dumbarton Oaks Studies 18 (Locust Valley, 1980).

Urbainczyk, T., *Socrates of Constantinople: Historian of Church and State* (Ann Arbor, MI, 1997).

van Groningen, B.A., "EKDOSIS," *Mnemosyne* 16 (1963), 1–17.

van Minnen, P., "House-to-house enquiries: an interdisciplinary approach to Roman Karanis," *ZPE* 100 (1994), 227–51.

van Seters, J., *In search of history: historiography in the ancient world and the origins of Biblical history* (New Haven, CN, 1983).

Verbrugghe, G.P. and Wickersham, J.M., *Berossus and Manetho* (Ann Arbor, MI, 1996).

Walbank, F.W. *Polybius* (Berkeley, CA, 1972).

—— *Selected Papers: Studies in Greek and Roman History and Historiography* (Cambridge, 1985).

—— "Speeches in Greek Historians," *Myers Memorial Lecture* (Oxford, 1965), repr. in F.W. Walbank, *Selected Papers*.

—— "History and tragedy," *Historia* 9 (1960), 216–34, repr. in F.W. Walbank, *Selected Papers* 224–41.

Wallace-Hadrill, A., *Suetonius: The Scholar and his Caesars* (London, 1983).

Wiseman, T.P., *Clio's Cosmetics: Three Studies in Greco-Roman Literature*, (Leicester, 1979).

—— "Monuments and the Roman annalists," in I.S. Moxon, I.D. Smart, and A.J. Woodman, *Past Perspectives: Studies in Greek and Roman Historical Writing* (Cambridge, 1986), 87–100.

—— "Lying historians: seven types of mendacity," in C. Gill and T.P. Wiseman, *Lies and Fiction in the Ancient World* (Exeter, 1993), 122–46.

—— (ed.) *Historiography and Imagination* (Exeter, 1994).

—— *Remus: A Roman Myth* (Cambridge, 1995).

—— *Roman Drama and Roman History* (Exeter, 1998).

Woodman, A.J., *Rhetoric in Classical Historiography* (London, 1988).

Zanker, P., *The Power of Images in the Age of Augustus*, tr. A. Shapiro (Ann Arbor, MI, 1988).

Zetzel, J.E.G., *Latin Textual Criticism in Antiquity* (New York, 1980).

Index